Invitation to Linguistics

MARIO PEI is Professor of Romance Philology at Columbia University. Born in Rome, Italy, in 1901, he came to the United States in 1908. He received his A.B. from City College in New York and his Ph.D. from Columbia University. During World War II he created a 37-language course in "War Linguistics" (now called "The World's Chief Languages") at Columbia University. His broadcasting activities for Radio Free Europe, OWI, and Voice of America have included lectures and discussions in French, Italian, German, Dutch, Czech, and Rumanian. He has been a lecturer and visiting professor at various universities throughout the world, including the Universities of Lisbon and Coimbra, Portugal, and the University of Pittsburgh, and Linguistic Consultant and Lecturer at the U. S. Army Language School at Monterey, California. (The present volume is largely based upon the series of lectures he delivered to the School's instructional staff.) Among his books are *The Story of Language, All About Language, The Story of English, The World's Chief Languages,* and *The Families of Words.* He is co-editor of *College Subjects Self-Taught* and has also published numerous articles in leading periodicals and journals.

Invitation to Linguistics

A BASIC INTRODUCTION TO
THE SCIENCE OF LANGUAGE

by Mario Pei, 1901 -

DOUBLEDAY & COMPANY, INC.
GARDEN CITY, NEW YORK

Library of Congress Catalog Card Number 64–22315
Copyright © 1965 by Mario Pei
All Rights Reserved
Printed in the United States of America

Preface

Linguistics, which is the scientific study of language and languages, has recently become a vogue, not only in colleges and universities, but also in government circles and among educated laymen. It is felt, confusedly perhaps, that in the expanded and internationally minded world of today a knowledge of individual languages no longer suffices, particularly in connection with certain callings and occupations. What is wanted is a broader, more organic knowledge of the way all language functions, what makes it operative, what can and cannot be done with it in the way of establishing communications. To supply this knowledge is the task of the descriptive linguist.

People also want to know about the relationship of the various languages to one another, the way they group themselves into families and subfamilies, their historical evolution out of earlier stages into their present-day forms. Here the historical linguist supplies the knowledge.

Lastly, there is justified curiosity about the present-day status of the world's many languages—how many and what sort of people speak them, where they are spoken, of what practical and cultural use they are, both individually and in groups. Here it is the specialist in the youngest branch of the science, geolinguistics, who takes over.

None of these three branches of the science of linguistics, it will be noted, deals specifically with the teaching or learning of any one individual language. This is the task traditionally reserved for the language teacher, who deals with his own particular tongue and is a specialist in the methods of imparting it. But the language teacher, like the layman, can profit by the general language information that the linguists of the three varieties enumerated above have to offer. This may be expected to occur in any or all of three ways: by putting his specific language into the focus of the general principles that underlie and govern all language; by clarifying its historical development so that he can answer questions of the "How?," "When?" and "Why?" variety; by placing it in the proper world perspective and indicating precisely what practical purposes it may serve.

It is therefore not surprising that there is a growing interest in the subject of linguistics among the professionals of language teaching, and that courses in linguistics are being offered at an ever increasing rate in our universities, colleges, and even high schools. Neither is it surprising that what goes on in the field of linguistics should be of great interest to numerous agencies of both government and business, now forced to operate on a world-wide scale in a world where distances are constantly shrinking, and that more and more such agencies should call for the services of men and women who not only know foreign languages but have some knowledge of the general principles of linguistics. Lastly, it is not surprising that this interest should be spreading to the vast world of educated and cultured laymen, whose attention is arrested by the fact that language and languages are more and more in the news and seem destined to play an ever increasing role in the world of tomorrow, a world of expanding communications and international diplomatic and business relations.

* * *

It is the purpose of this relatively brief work to set forth the basic facts of linguistics in a language that all can understand. The basic facts are those which can be easily demonstrated, and on which substantial agreement reigns among the linguists. These constitute the only part of the vast domain to which the beginner can properly be introduced. The minutiae and most of the controversial points can be acquired later, from more advanced works.

Additional information of a more specialized nature will be found in the Appendices. These may be consulted by those readers who wish to explore a few of the more intricate aspects of linguistics or who seek specific items of information concerning some of these aspects. For more complete coverage, the reader is referred to the Selective Bibliography, which is designed to represent various and often conflicting shades of opinion.

Controversy in a scientific field is not only natural and normal; it is to be welcomed. The objective truth may be one, but it has many facets and is subject to various interpretations. The criticisms of linguistic schools and methodologies that appear in the Appendices represent a personal and subjective but sincere point of view, based on long experience in the field. They are meant to be constructive, not destructive. Above all, they are not to be interpreted as invalidating those basic principles, set forth in the main body of the work, which are accepted by the majority of linguists.

Contents

Invitation to Linguistics

PART I

Basic Subject Matter

1. LINGUISTICS AND PHILOLOGY

Philology deals not only with languages but also with the culture and history of languages, the traditions behind languages, and the literary output of languages. **Linguistics** concentrates on language itself, with only occasional reference to cultural or literary values. The problems of linguistics concern mainly the spoken language, though written language forms are also considered.

Linguistics is the study of language, and the etymological meaning of language is "that which pertains to the human tongue." There is a broader interpretation of language as "that which carries a meaning," "everything that is meaningful," "everything that transmits a meaning from one human mind to another." In this broader definition, language includes not only spoken forms and their written counterparts but also gestures, facial expressions, signs and symbols of all sorts, such as traffic lights and arrows, even pictures and paintings, as well as the tomtoms of the African jungle and the smoke signals of the American Indians. All these forms of meaningful transfer are of interest to the semanticist, who is concerned with all meaningful symbols, of whatever source and nature, and their interpretation. But they concern the linguist only to a limited degree.

Present-day linguistics has so far had two main subdivisions, the descriptive and the historical. **Descriptive linguistics**, as the name implies, describes language and investigates its phenomena and manifestations (e.g., the sounds or structure of a given language at a given historical stage). **Historical linguistics** traces the development and evolution of language in the course of time (e.g., the evolution of Latin into the Romance languages, or of Anglo-Saxon into modern English). A term often used as a synonym for historical linguistics is **diachronic linguistics** (*dia*, "across"; *chronos*, "time"). **Synchronic linguistics** (*syn*, "with"; *chronos*, "time"; the study of language as it appears at a given point of time) is often used as a synonym for descriptive linguistics.

There is also **comparative linguistics**. This is the comparison of the structures of two or more languages (e.g., English, German, Dutch, and Swedish), often for the purpose of determining their common ancestry. This means that comparative linguistics is more often of the historical variety; one may, however, also compare two modern languages, without any reference to their historical evolution or ancestry, for the purpose of determining the similarities and differences in their present-day structures.

The term **structural linguistics** is frequently used as a synonym for descriptive linguistics, since the main task of the structural linguist is to describe the structure of a language. Structural linguistics may also, however, be taken in a narrower sense to refer to the work of a particular school of descriptive linguistics which holds that language changes occur not in an individual or haphazard fashion but throughout the entire pattern or system of the language, with a definite interrelation linking the changes to one another.

Geolinguistics is a relatively recent concept, which is making headway by reason of its vast practical relevance. Its function is to describe, scientifically and objectively, the distribution of languages in the various regions of the earth, to point out their political, economic, sociological, strategic, and cultural importance, to study the ways in which they interact upon one another and the ways in which the linguistic factor influences the development of national cultures and points of view. As a single example, one might cite the distribution of Slavic and non-Slavic languages in the U.S.S.R., their relative importance, and the role of Russian as the nation's predominant or "binding" tongue.

Geolinguistics deals with the present-day product and outcome of historical factors and events and is therefore linked with historical linguistics. Its present-day aspects, however, are largely descriptive, geographical, and sociological. A particular language has a given number of speakers, large or small, a certain pattern of distribution, extensive or narrow, over the regions of the world. It is used in connection with the production and distribution of goods and the creation of cultural values, and it holds political and military sway in certain areas. These factors set that language's practical value as a widespread subject of study. Subsidiary items are the use of the language for liturgical or other religious purposes, its dominance over colonial or former colonial areas, the possibility of its use as a substitute for other languages current in the area.

It is true that all these factors are shifting and temporary, not everlasting. But language itself is a shifting and temporary phenomenon, subject to the laws of change and evolution. Geolinguistics may therefore be described as the practical present-day application of linguistic science, in the same sense that engineering is a practical application of the laws of physics, and medicine and surgery the practical applications of physiology and anatomy.

While descriptive and historical linguistics are of immediate interest only to their specialists, geolinguistics is of interest to everybody who has any occasion whatsoever to travel abroad, establish foreign contacts, or be concerned with the state of the world.

2. LANGUAGE, WRITING, GESTURES, SIGNALS, SYMBOLS

If we accept the narrower etymological definition of language as "that which has to do with the human tongue," we must still circumscribe our definition. The human vocal organs (the tongue is only the chief one among them) are capable of producing sounds or noises that are no more language than the noises produced by a machine in operation. To be language in the generally accepted sense, the noises produced by the vocal organs must be meaningful and carry a definite, specific message from one human mind to another. One might even go further and say that the message must be of such a kind that it can cover non-immediate situations. A dog's bark may warn you of an immediate danger; but when I use the noises of my vocal organs to warn you of a danger that lies out of sight over the next hill, or that will not arise until tomorrow, I am using human language to its fullest extent and setting it apart from the noises that an animal might make in response to an immediate stimulus.

No one knows when, where, or in what fashion man first learned to speak, though unproved theories abound.[1]

[1] Some of these are highly imaginative, if nothing else. The so-called "bow-wow" theory, for instance, holds that language first arose in imitation of sounds heard in nature (the barking of a dog, imitated as "bow-wow"; the falling of a tree, imitated as "crash"). The "pooh-pooh" theory holds that language originated from exclamations or ejaculations of surprise, pain, pleasure, fear, and other sudden emotions; this would account for "ouch" but does not explain why speakers of other languages prefer "ay" or "au" when pain strikes suddenly. The "yo-he-ho" theory is to the effect that language started as a series of grunts and wheezes of physical exertion (the *ey ukhnem* of the Volga boatmen, for instance). The "singsong" theory claims that speech first arose out of primitive, inarticulate chants, as when a small child mouths a tune he has himself composed. There are plenty of other such theories.

We do know that there is no human group on earth, no matter how backward or uncivilized, that does not possess language as a meaningful transfer of ideas.

Speech can operate while you are doing something else with your hands. Speech can operate in the dark, and you don't need a light to see by while you are conversing. It is likely that these factors led our remote ancestors to prefer the spoken form of communication over the gestural, which probably antedated speech, and over the pictorial, which probably came later, and eventually led to writing.

Until very recently the written form of language enjoyed two distinct advantages over the spoken. It was enduring, which the spoken form was not, and it could be transmitted across great distances. Today recordings, tapes, and other forms of "canned" speech permit the spoken tongue to enjoy the same advantages of permanence in time and transmission in space, so that some people wonder whether the day may not come when writing disappears and speech alone remains. This, however, shows no sign of happening as yet, and literacy is reaching out more and more to backward populations, while the uses of the written language multiply.

But the fact remains that the primary and by far the most important and widespread means of human communication is speech. The average human being speaks far more than he writes, gesticulates, or makes signals. It is therefore legitimate for the linguist, as distinguished from the philologist, to be primarily concerned with speech, secondarily with writing (as a more or less faithful reflection of speech), and little if at all with other systems of communication.

3. CHARACTERISTICS OF SPOKEN LANGUAGE

Spoken language extends to all branches of the human race, without exception or distinction. All men communicate basically through the sounds of speech. This means that language is all-pervasive, that it guides and accompanies every activity of man in which two or more individuals take part.

Being a system of meaningful transfer and involving two or more individuals (even when you speak to yourself you are splitting your personality, with one part of you playing the role of speaker, the other the role of hearer), language depends upon a convention, a common agreement among members of the speaking community to the effect that the language sounds will convey certain pre-established meanings. Objectively speaking, a language that you do not understand is still a language; subjectively (and for practical purposes), it is no language at all, but only a series of jumbled sounds. It is only when this language—these sounds, grammatical forms, words and sentences—is accepted as common currency by at least two people that you have language in the subjective and utilitarian sense of the word.

Despite their vast number and variety, all languages hold certain characteristics in common. First and foremost, language consists of sounds produced by the human vocal apparatus. These sounds, to be meaningful, must be arranged in certain definite sequences, forming words or word groups. The words or word groups must be accepted by all members of the speaking community as having approximately the same symbolical value to represent ideas.

It is fairly obvious that the symbolical value is altogether arbitrary and that there is no inherent link between the thought-concept and the spoken word or word group that symbolizes it. If there were such an inherent link, all people would speak the same language. Instead, the animal that is "dog" to the American is *chien* to the Frenchman, *perro* to the Spaniard, *inu* to the Japanese. Spoken language, therefore, depends on human convention and common acceptance by the members of the speaking group, however limited in numbers this may be. This places language definitely within the category of symbols, like the dollar bill that is a symbol of purchasing power and depends for its value upon general acceptance by the community, not upon its intrinsic worth.

The speaking process is therefore both physiological and psychological. The action of speech begins with the psychological link that has been previously established in the speaker's mind between a given concept and the set of sounds used to symbolize it. But almost immediately a physiological process sets in. A nerve impulse sends out the command from the brain to the vocal organs to produce the sound sequence that it is desired to transmit. The vocal organs go into the physiological operation and produce the audible sound sequence, which is transmitted by physical sound waves to the listener's ear. The ear, in turn, transmits the sounds it has received to the hearer's brain, which decodes the message in terms of the hearer's previously established psychological link between the set of sounds serving as a symbol and the thought-concept that is symbolized and that more or less coincides with the thought-concept in the speaker's mind.

The crux of the speaking operation lies in the link established in two minds between a thought-concept and a series of speech sounds that symbolize that concept. The rest of the operation is purely physiological, physical and mechanical. How the link between the thought-concept and the speech sounds was originally established, even in a single human mind, is still a mystery, though, as we have seen, theories abound. Another mystery is how this link was originally extended from one member of the community to another until it became common property, though we can readily see how the process operates today.

4. RAMIFICATIONS OF LANGUAGE,

Language has important links with the physical sciences. Spoken-language sounds have to be produced and received by human bodily organs. The structure and functioning of these organs (lungs, windpipe, mouth, tongue, nose, ears, etc.) is a part of physiology. The transmission of speech sounds in sound waves through the air pertains to the domain of physics, particularly of that branch known as acoustics.

But language has also a definite link with anthropology and sociology, since it is the mode of expression of a social group, the vehicle and expression of their culture, which in the anthropological sense is the sum total of their customs and usages. Serving as the expression of thought makes language a part of psychology. Language enters into all human co-ordinated activities—religion, war, politics, law, amusement. Language serves as the vehicle of exalted thought—oratory, literature, poetry, philosophy, science, all of which have to be expressed in terms of language.

For all these reasons linguistics is a study which cannot be precisely classified as a physical science, a social science, or a branch of the humanities. It has extensive footholds in all three divisions of human knowledge. Language is a tool of paramount importance in human civilization. It is indispensable.

Also, language is the common possession of all classes, from the highest to the lowest. Not all people write, and relatively few indulge in literary pursuits. But all people speak.

This makes linguistics (the conscious study of language) a topic of prime importance. Yet the language process itself is basically unconscious, and in the nature of a reflex action, once language has been thoroughly acquired.

5. COMPARTMENTS OF LANGUAGE

Traditionally the study of language, whether descriptive or historical, has been subdivided into four areas whose boundaries are perhaps not so well defined as we should like them to be:

1. **Phonology**, or the study of language sounds; this includes both **phonetics** and **phonemics**, terms which will shortly be defined.

2. **Morphology**, or the study of language forms, and particularly of those changes in the form of the individual word which modify the meaning of that word, such as **inflectional endings** (e.g., the -s added to *cat* which turns it into the plural *cats*); **prefixes** (e.g., the *re-* prefixed to *tell*, which gives it the meaning of "tell again"); as well as **internal changes** (e.g., the change of vowel in *sang* which marks it as the past of *sing*).

3. **Syntax**, which is the arrangement of words within the sentence or word group (e.g., the arrangement "John hit George," which informs us, by the way the words are arranged, that John did the hitting and George received the blow).

4. **Vocabulary**, which is the study of individual words, their origin, historical evolution, present meaning and usage; comprised in vocabulary are **etymology**, the history of words, and **semantics**, the study of word meanings. **Lexicography**, the art of dictionary making, is basically a combination of etymology and semantics, plus a statement of how words are pronounced, accented, spelled, and used in present-day language.

The boundaries of the four compartments are ill defined in spots because language sounds are often influenced by language forms and vice versa; because both sound and form are often influenced by meaning; and because there is frequent interplay of morphology and syntax, some languages making use of one of these structural devices to the practical exclusion of the other.[2] For this reason morphology and syntax are often combined under a single heading, **grammatical structure**.

From the standpoint of language learning, those who are native to the speaking community normally acquire the sound-pattern and basic grammatical structure of the language at an early age. They thereafter hold these two features in common, with relatively slight variations due to geographical location (local dialects) and to class and educational differences. The same cannot be said of vocabulary, which presents startling differences of range within the same speaking community. At the same time there is a basic vocabulary of use which all the speakers of a language hold in common.

The natural process of language learning is one of repetition and imitation, particularly for what concerns sounds and intonation patterns and basic grammatical structures. The study of language through grammar is best described as a time-saving makeshift, in which the adult mental faculties of generalization and abstraction are brought into play to avoid the endless repetition and imitation which go on when one acquires one's own native language as a child.

[2] In Latin or Russian, for instance, morphological endings are highly important and syntax is secondary. In Chinese, morphology is non-existent and syntax alone gives meaning to the phrase or sentence.

6. PHONOLOGY, PHONETICS, AND PHONEMICS

The number of sounds that can be produced by the human speech organs has never been accurately determined or even estimated. This is because a very small shift in the point of articulation can bring about a different result, perceptible to precision instruments like the spectrograph or the sound-wave frequency recorder, even if not to the ear. Also, many vocal sounds which are not speech sounds to the speakers of one language are definite speech sounds to the speakers of another tongue. The sounds we produce when blowing out a match, kissing, or clucking to a horse form part of the speech-sound equipment of languages like Japanese or Hottentot. Speech sounds are traditionally (and somewhat arbitrarily) classified into vowels, semivowels, and consonants of different classes and orders (plosive, fricative, lateral, nasal; voiced, unvoiced, etc.; see Section 18, Phonetics).

Phonology, previously defined as the study of language sounds, is used by some writers to cover only the changes and transformations occurring in those sounds as language evolves (but this study of historical changes in sounds could also be labeled **historical** or **diachronic phonetics**). By other writers phonology is considered synonymous with **phonetics** in general.

If phonology is accepted as the historical study of language sounds, then **phonetics** may be defined as the science, study, analysis, and classification of speech sounds without reference to their historical evolution, but with reference to their production, transmission, and perception. In the latter sense it is definitely a part of descriptive linguistics and has several subdivisions (articulatory, acoustic, experimental, genemmic, genetic, physiological, etc.) of which only two can be described here. Our terminological choice, therefore, lies between restricting phonology to the historical study of sound changes, and phonetics to the description of sounds at one point in time, on the one hand, and, on the other, using the two terms as synonyms, prefixing to either of them "historical" ("diachronic") or "descriptive" ("synchronic"), as the case may be.

The basic unit, or raw material, of phonetics is the **phone**, which is defined as any rudimentary, simple, objective language sound, as it would be recorded by precision instruments in the laboratory.

Articulatory phonetics bases itself upon the point of articulation and mode of production of speech sounds. It gives us an objective description of such sounds and how they are produced, and establishes a broader or narrower classification among them (for example, how is the English initial *p* of *pit* produced, and how does it differ from the *f* of *fit?*). This classification is reflected in the **International Phonetic Alphabet (IPA)**, which, at least in theory, lists the major possible varieties of speech sounds and arranges them in accordance with the vocal organs used in producing them and the positions those vocal organs assume.

But there is another way of classifying the sounds of a given language, as aside from an objective, mechanical classification of the sounds of all languages. **Acoustic phonetics** deals with the sounds of speech as they are perceived by the ear of the listener. **Phonemics**, a science younger than phonetics, describes and classifies the sounds of a specific language according to the way those sounds are referred to the consciousness of the speakers and interpreted by the speakers as the same sound or as separate sounds. (For instance, what causes the English speaker to accept as one sound the *p* of *pit*, the *p* of *spit*, and the *p* of *sip*, despite their perceptible differences, but to reject the identity of the *p* of *pit* and the *f* of *fit?*)

Here meaning comes into play. Let us examine this contrast more closely.

Objectively, and from the standpoint of articulatory
phonetics, the three so-called *p*-sounds of *pit, spit,* and
sip (the last as usually uttered by American speakers,
with final closure of the lips, in a phrase like "Take a
sip!") are three separate and distinct speech sounds
(phones), even though they are closely related. But it
is difficult to convince the lay American speaker that
they are distinct. For one thing, the three sounds are all
represented in writing by the same symbol, *p.* But, what
is more important, the three sounds never get in one another's way. Above all, they never lend themselves to
erroneous meanings. The strongly uttered *p* of *pit,* followed by a perceptible puff of breath, comes only at the
beginning of a word or breath group. The much gentler,
unaspirated *p* of *spit* occurs regularly after initial *s,* often
in other positions within the word. The imploded *p* of *sip,*
for which the lips are not opened, and which never really
comes out, normally occurs at the end of a word or word
group. These three speech sounds, so far as English is
concerned, are said to be in **complementary distribution**.
They are three **positional variants** of what constitutes in
the English speaker's consciousness a single unit. The
English speaker, though he produces them regularly, is
unaware of the difference among them. But (and this is
the acid test) if one is accidentally used for another (if a
speaker were to feel weak, for instance, and utter *pit*
with less force than normal, so that he actually uses the
p-sound of *spit;* or if he were strongly excited, and said
forcefully, "I'll spit in your eye!" using the strongly aspirated *p* of *pit*) no misunderstanding would result, as
would be the case if a *k*-sound were to be substituted for
p in any one of the three words.

There is therefore, to the American English speaker, a
single *p*-phoneme, with three separate phones as positional variants. The **phoneme** may thus be defined as a

group or variety or class of related sounds (phones) which the speakers accept as a single unit, regardless of positional variants.

The picture would change radically if we were to attempt to use the *p* of *pit* and the *p* of *spit* interchangeably in certain other languages, like Chinese or Hindi. There, the two sounds could occur in precisely the same position or **environment**, and the word would change its meaning if one were used for the other. Consequently, the *p* of *pit* and the *p* of *spit* (along with the occasionally imploded *p* of *sip*) constitute a single phoneme in English, but two different phonemes in Chinese.[3] From the English point of view, the two (or three) sounds of *p* are defined as **allophones** (literally, "other-sounds," or more precisely sounds occurring in other places or other environments) of the same basic phoneme.

To reverse the picture, *leave* and *live* have vowel sounds which, while similar, constitute two different phonemes in English. Everything else in the two words being the same, the distinction between the vowel sound of *leave* and that of *live* makes for a basic difference in the meaning of the two words. A speaker of Spanish, on the other hand, could conceivably use either sound in a word such as *vivo* ("I live"), and the meaning would be unaltered. The first sound might appear in very deliberate, emphatic Spanish speech, the second in hurried, careless diction. Therefore these two objectively different sounds (or phones) constitute two separate phonemes in English, while in Spanish they are two variants (not positional, but free; see p. 56).

The subject matter of phonetics, therefore, is objective language sounds (phones) which are universal realities and are subject to precise measurement by mechanical devices. The subject matter of phonemics is sounds or classes of related sounds which are referred to the con-

[3] E.g., Mandarin *p'u* (with *p* of *pit*) means "shop"; *pu* (with *p* of *spit*) means "part."

sciousness of the speakers of an individual language. The objective test for phonemes is an **opposition**, or difference in meaning, which appears or fails to appear when one sound is substituted for the other in otherwise identical words. Use the *p* of *pit* in *spit,* and the meaning is still the same; but use the *k* of *kit,* and the meaning changes. Therefore the two varieties of *p* are one phoneme; but *p* of *pit* and *k* of *kit* are two different phonemes, so far as English is concerned.

7. PHONETIC AND PHONEMIC TRANSCRIPTIONS

Since linguistic data must often appear in written form, linguists find it convenient to use two systems of transcription of language sounds, both of which attempt to avoid the pitfalls and inconsistencies involved in conventional writing systems. One form of transcription is phonetic, and uses the symbols of the International Phonetic Alphabet (IPA); these are normally enclosed in brackets [ ], and indicate, at least theoretically, the objective reality of speech sounds. They can be used to transcribe the sounds of any language, though some symbols will naturally appear in the transcription of one language and not in that of another.

The second form of transcription is phonemic, and uses, for the most part, the letters of the conventional Roman alphabet, though IPA symbols may also appear where it is expedient to use them. Phonemic symbols are enclosed within slanted bars / /, and each language is given its own individual system of transcription, not applicable to another language.

To illustrate the difference between the two: in presenting spoken French, there is a clear distinction of quality (openness) between the vowel sound often represented in conventional French spelling by *è* and the

sound represented by é. A phonetic transcription, concentrating on the objective reality of the two sounds,
will use for them different symbols, [ε] and [e]. A phonemic transcription bases itself upon the fact that in the
mouths of most French speakers the two sounds occur
in complementary distribution (like the p of pit and the
p of spit, they never get in each other's way, but appear in
different positions or environments), and may represent
both sounds indifferently by /e/. The theory is that [ε]
usually occurs when a consonant sound follows in the
same syllable, [e] when the sound is final in the syllable;
there is still some controversy about this point among
French phoneticians. Thus the two words mère and
parlé will appear in a phonetic transcription as [ˈmɛr]
and [parˈle], but in a phonemic transcription as /mer/
and /parle/. In like manner, a strict phonetic transcription of English pit, spit would call for [p'it], [spit]; but
a phonemic transcription could well dispense with the
extra symbol and use /pit/, /spit/; it would be understood that the two sounds are in **complementary** or **non-
contrastive distribution**, and the principles of that distribution would be known in advance to the transcriber
and his readers.

The phonemic transcription is more economical of
time and symbols. It is applicable to one language only,
however, and requires full knowledge of that language's
phonemic structure. The phonetic transcription is more
cumbersome, but more precise and of universal applicability.

8. GRAMMATICAL STRUCTURE:
MORPHOLOGY AND SYNTAX

"Grammar" is a traditional term used to cover what
might be described as the traffic rules or code of behavior of a language. Etymologically, "grammar" comes

from a Greek root that expresses the idea of writing. Since writing is secondary in linguistics, and speech is primary, the term **structure**, which etymologically has to do with the way something is built up, is preferred by most modern linguists.

While it is true that all languages, without exception, consist basically of speech sounds, and that in most languages these speech sounds regularly arrange themselves into word units (in some languages the distinction between word and word group or sentence is blurred), the words are seldom used in isolation. On the one hand, the words regularly come in groups, and then the order in which they are arranged often becomes significant and even paramount to the meaning ("John hit George" and "George hit John," for example, involve a considerable difference of meaning, though the three words used are the same). On the other hand, the words themselves often undergo certain modifications in form which modify the meaning ("I see the dog"; "I saw the dogs"). The modifications occurring within the word itself (*dog-dogs, see-saw*) form the subject matter of **morphology**, the study of forms. The word arrangement forms the subject matter of **syntax** ("arranging together"). Morphology and syntax combined go to make up a language's grammar, or structure, or traffic rules, which cannot be violated under penalty of getting into a snarl that will impede the proper flow of meaning from one speaker to another, which is after all the basic and indeed the only purpose of language.

In morphology, the proper topic of study is the play of prefixes and suffixes, or the internal changes within the word, which modify that word's basic meaning (*tell, re-tell, foretell; dog, dog's, dogs; walk, walked, walking; see, saw, seen; write, wrote, written*).

Modern descriptive linguistics prefers to such traditional terms as "inflectional endings," "root," and "stem" an all-embracing term, **morpheme**, which is defined as

the smallest unit of meaning. Where the traditional grammar would describe *dogs* as consisting of a root *dog* plus
an inflectional plural ending *-s,* the modern structural
linguist would describe both *dog* and *-s* as two separate
morphemes, or units of meaning, one carrying the basic
meaning of the word, the other the accessory notion of
plurality. However, a distinction would be set up between the two by labeling *dog* as a **free morpheme** (that
is, one that could be used in isolation), and *-s* as a **bound
morpheme** (one that has no separate existence save in
so far as it is attached to another morpheme).

Syntax, the arrangement of words within the word
group or sentence, is sometimes extended by traditional
grammars to cover features which properly belong to
literary style and have little if any connection with basic
spoken-language patterns. In certain languages (Chinese,
for instance) syntax is of paramount importance, since
morphology is non-existent. In others, like Latin, syntax
plays a very secondary role, since the morphological
equipment of inflectional endings takes care of most of
the problems of meaningful transfer. In most modern
Western languages there is a blend of the two devices,
which is sometimes redundant. In the English sentence
"John hit George" it is only the syntactical arrangement
that tells the hearer who does the hitting and who is hit.
In "He hit me," however, we have a double meaning
check. *He* not only comes in the position normally reserved for the doer of the action; it indicates the doer by
its form (*he,* not *him*). At the same time, *me,* coming in
the normal position for the receiver of the action, also
shows by its form (*me,* not *I*) that it is the receiver. By
way of comparison, Chinese could only say "He hit I,"
with no possibility of variation of form for either pronoun,
but only position to indicate who is the doer and who is
the receiver of the action; while Latin would find a word
order such as "Me hit he," or even "Hit he me" or "Hit
me he," quite acceptable, even if nouns were substituted

for the pronouns, as the nouns would have distinctive
endings to indicate the doer or the receiver of the action.

9. VOCABULARY: SEMANTICS AND ETYMOLOGY

Some linguists deny that language is acquired in the
form of individual words or that the speaker is conscious
of individual words as he speaks. They prefer to view
the language process as being built around sentences or
word groups. For this view there seems to be doubtful
justification, but whether or not it is basically correct,
the individual word is generally accepted as one of the
main compartments of linguistics and forms the subject
of the study of **vocabulary**.

As indicated by our comprehensive dictionaries, the
main problems connected with vocabulary are **semantics**
(the meaning of individual words) and **etymology** (their
history, evolution, and development). Both these topics,
especially the second, are of greater interest to the historical than to the descriptive linguist. It is perfectly
possible, however, to study semantics in purely descriptive fashion, concentrating on the meaning or meanings
the word has today (or at any given point of time),
without reference to how that meaning has been historically arrived at.

10. LANGUAGE CLASSIFICATION

So far we have discussed matters which pertain to language in general and which all languages, ancient and
modern, hold in common. This discussion has pertained
to the field of general, descriptive, structural linguistics.
When we come to classifying languages, we discover

that there are two main systems of classification, the genetic and the typological, of which one is predominantly historical, while the other follows the line of descriptive linguistics.

A third, non-scientific classification is the geographical (European languages, African languages, etc.). This is occasionally still used in fields where our information is (or was until recently) insufficient to permit the use of the other bases of classification, so that we still speak of native Australian languages or Papuan languages, for example, putting under one geographical heading what should perhaps be broken up into several distinct genetic or typological classes. The geographical classification may also be legitimately used, however, for geolinguistic purposes.

The **genetic classification**, which inevitably involves the historical factor, links languages in accordance with their known or surmised origin and ancestry. "Romance languages," for instance, is a term used to cover all the tongues that stem from Latin. But Latin itself is a member of a still broader group called Indo-European. The broadest groupings, such as Indo-European, Hamito-Semitic, Dravidian, include languages of which the common origin, though more remote and not always historically attested, is nevertheless fairly obvious or at least probable.

The **typological classification**, which may or may not be based in part on historical factors, goes primarily by the present-day structure of a language and is therefore largely descriptive. Here the main categories are the following:

1. **Inflectional**, indicating grammatical relations by prefixes, suffixes, and internal changes in words; or, to use a more structural terminology, by the combination of separate free and bound morphemes: English *walk, walk-s, walk-ing*. In languages like Latin or Russian the free

morphemes are sharply reduced in number, since nouns, adjectives, and verbs cannot generally be used in their root forms, but only in conjunction with an ending (the Latin root *mūr-*, "wall," cannot appear by itself but only in case forms such as *mūrus, mūrō, mūris*).

2. **Agglutinative**, adding separate suffixes which, unlike the inflectional endings, may enjoy separate existence as free morphemes: Hungarian *ház-ak-ban*, "house-s-in," "in the houses"; but the boundary between the inflectional and the agglutinative type is not always well defined.

3. **Isolating**, using only free morphemes and indicating grammatical relations only by word order: Chinese *wǒ*, which may mean, according to its position in the sentence, "I," "me," "my," "to me."

4. **Polysynthetic** or **Incorporating**, combining within a single utterance numerous bound morphemes, so that the unit is not the word but the word group or sentence: Oneida *g-nagla-sl-i-zak-s*, "I am looking for a village," where *g* carries the meaning of "I"; *nagla* conveys the idea of "living"; *sl* is an element that gives *nagla* the force of a noun, so that the combination conveys the idea of "village"; *i*, a verbal prefix, indicates that *zak* is to carry a verbal idea; *zak* has the general meaning of "look for"; *s* is the sign of continued action; none of these parts would convey any very definite meaning if used by itself.

Languages which genetically are known to belong together often redistribute themselves when typologically classified. Within the Indo-European genetic family, which in origin is highly inflectional, English and Afrikaans, with their widespread dropping of endings and their use of bare roots, often monosyllabic, whose function is indicated only by word order, tend toward the isolating type, while Hindi, replacing the old inflectional endings of Sanskrit with post-positions, tends toward the agglutinative type, and French, in some of its spoken combinations, tends towards polysynthetism.[4]

The distributional or geolinguistic aspect of language is largely descriptive, since it deals with the geography of language. It may, however, contain historical features, if the extent and importance of a language at one point of time is compared with an earlier state of affairs. North America, for instance, was covered exclusively by American Indian and Eskimo languages in the fourteenth century but is today covered by English, Spanish, and French, with the original languages restricted to minor and highly localized groups.

11. COMPARATIVE LINGUISTICS; LINGUISTIC RECONSTRUCTION

Comparative linguistics, in its nineteenth-century acceptance, coincided almost completely with historical linguistics. It consisted primarily of a methodology whereby languages, usually in their earliest attested forms, were laid side by side to determine the relationship among them and to reconstruct from those forms the hypothetical, unrecorded parent language from which they had sprung. It is thanks to this methodology that a truly scientific genetic classification of many languages was achieved. A comparison of the forms of such early languages as Sanskrit, Greek, Latin, Old Irish, Old Slavic, Gothic, proved quite conclusively that they all stemmed from an unwritten parent tongue whose later ramifications extended from northern India to Iceland, covering most of Europe and large sections of southwestern Asia. This led to the name Indo-European for the family. On

[4] A striking example is Albert Guérard's transcription *shtawfûbok* for *Je t'offre un bock*, "I'll treat you to a beer." In slow motion, the words would appear in some such transcription as: *zhuh tawfruh ûh bawk*.

the one hand, this comparative method enabled the linguists to reconstruct, at least tentatively, this parent language; on the other, it enabled them to state with confidence that such modern tongues as English, German, the Scandinavian, Romance, and Slavic languages, Lithuanian, Greek, Albanian, Armenian, Iranian, and most of the languages of present-day northern India and Pakistan are all descended from a single original tongue.

Language comparison, however, can also be carried on descriptively, with present-day spoken tongues, to determine how they coincide and how they differ in their phonemic pattern, in their grammatical structure, and in their word stock. In fact it may be said that comparative linguistics in rudimentary form enters into all learning and teaching of foreign languages, unless such instruction is carried on by an absolutely direct method, with no use of or reference to the learner's own language. (Even here, it is impossible to prevent the learner from making in his own mind suitable comparisons between the forms of the language he knows and speaks and those of the tongue he is trying to acquire.)

The comparative-historical methodology may even be combined with the descriptive by taking the same language at two historical stages, handling each of them descriptively (that is, by setting up a phonemic pattern, a grammatical structure, and a word stock for each of the two stages), then comparing the two to determine the intervening changes in each of the features studied.[5]

[5] An extremely rudimentary and oversimplified sample of this procedure would be the Latin phrase *Pater et filius mortui sunt*, "The father and son died." Carried on to the hypothetical sixth- or seventh-century Vulgar Latin of Gaul, this phrase would change to *Illi pater et illi filius sunt morti*. In the Old French of the twelfth century the phrase would read *Li pedre et li filz sunt mort*. Finally, in twentieth-century French, it would be *Le père et le fils sont morts*. These four progressive samples would then be accompanied by a description of the various phonological, structural, and lexical changes illustrated by each step in the progression.

12. WRITING

The written form of the language, which has been, is, and will be of immense practical importance to the human race in transmitting meanings across time and space (though some of its advantages are dwindling in the face of twentieth-century recordings of actual speech), is, from the standpoint of linguistics, both a help and a hindrance.

It is a help in so far as it gives us partial access to speech forms that have disappeared from the world's scene. It is a hindrance because it does not always faithfully portray such speech forms and often proves misleading. No better example of this state of affairs can be offered than present-day English spelling, which gives only a partial and frequently deceptive clue to present-day English pronunciation.

Writing is of two main varieties: the **pictographic-ideographic** or **logographic** (like the Chinese), where there is no link with the spoken sounds, and the written symbol is directly tied to the thought-concept;[6] and the **syllabic-alphabetic**, where the written form tends to portray the sounds of the spoken language, thereby setting itself up as a symbol of a symbol (the spoken language itself is a series of arbitrary symbols of thought-concepts).[7] The fact that the spoken language changes rapidly, while the written form tends to remain static and traditional,

[6] In Chinese writing the spoken word for "horse" is betokened by a symbol that was originally an actual picture of a horse; this is a *pictogram*. The word for "east" is symbolically denoted by the pictogram for "sun" rising over the pictogram for "tree"; this is an *ideogram*.

[7] In the written system of the Amharic of Ethiopia, each symbol stands for a syllabic combination, usually consonant + vowel (ba, be, bi, bo, bu, etc.); this is a *syllabic* script. In an *alphabetic* system, each symbol stands ideally for a single spoken sound (English b + a = ba; s + o = so).

distorts the ideal relationship of written symbol and spoken sound.

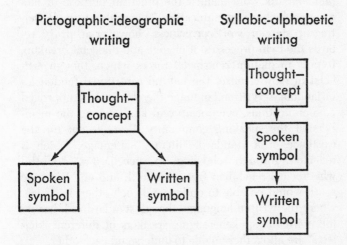

This means that in linguistic research, whether of the descriptive or the historical variety, we must guard against the tendency to accept the written language at its face value or to think of it as paramount and superior to speech. The testimony of written documents must always be carefully weighed. This does not mean that they are to be excluded from our consideration, particularly in historical research, where they are often, despite their shortcomings, the only reasonably trustworthy material at our disposal. In the case of synchronic, descriptive work, the existence of living speakers and their availability for audible recordings tend to supersede the use of written forms.

It should not be forgotten, however, that the existence of a written form of the language, particularly when it is in widespread use, acts as a powerful brake upon the tendency of the spoken tongue to change. Spoken language, left to itself, is subject to inherent **centrifugal** tendencies which resolve themselves into rapid change across time and widespread dialectalization across space.[8] Both these factors work against the practical purpose of language, which is communication. The written form, by setting up standards of "**correctness**," however arbitrary, retards the twin processes of change and dialectal breakup. It puts in motion **centripetal** forces which, though artificial in nature, offset the natural centrifugal tendencies of language. Written language thereby leads to improved communications, even of an oral kind, among the members of the speaking community. Were it not for the existence of a standard, "literary" language, which is reflected, through schooling, in speech, it is doubtful whether a Frenchman from the north and one from the south would be able to understand each other. In China, where the written language, though standardized, has no link with the spoken tongue, speakers of different "dialects" are altogether unable to understand each other.

It is probable that the conservative, standardizing influence which has hitherto been exerted by the written form will in the future be more and more taken over by such powerful and widespread means of oral communication as the radio, TV, and spoken films. For these, in most civilized countries, a fairly standardized form of oral language has been or is being set.

[8] Latin, originally spoken in Rome and the immediate vicinity, changed on its own home soil, turning eventually into the present-day Roman dialect of Italian. After spreading to most of southwestern Europe, it also broke up into Gaulish, Iberian, and other varieties of Vulgar Latin which, as they developed into French, Spanish, Portuguese, etc., also broke up into different dialects. Seventeenth-century English, with its dialectal varieties, not only evolved into differing twentieth-century English dialectal varieties on its own soil; it also gave rise to forms of American English, which in turn broke up into local varieties (Ozarkian, Brooklynese, Bostonese, Charlestonese, etc.).

13. LANGUAGE DISTRIBUTION AND GEOLINGUISTICS

One of the most important practical applications of linguistics is a knowledge of what languages, at least major ones, are spoken throughout the world and in each area, how many and what manner of people speak them, in what fashion these languages may be used, how, if possible, they may be replaced by other and more familiar languages. Beyond this information of a general type, which is geographical as well as linguistic, there is the question of **language identification**. This involves a rudimentary familiarity with the appearance of these languages in written form and their basic sound characteristics in spoken form, so that one may be told apart from another by a process of ready recognition.

Fairly detailed information of this kind forms part of the equipment and training of all linguistic specialists. In addition, the outstanding facts concerning language distribution and the relative importance of the major languages should and can be made known to all intelligent and educated persons, even if unspecialized.

This body of information, of greater practical importance to the non-specialist than either descriptive or historical linguistics, is imparted only superficially and coincidentally by either of the senior disciplines. Descriptive linguistics is primarily concerned with the structural facts that are common to all language and languages. In its demonstration of general language principles, it descends only occasionally, and by way of example, to the individual language; where it describes a language in detail, it normally isolates the language in order to concentrate on the relevant facts about it in juxtaposition with the principles of language in general. Historical linguistics, on the other hand, concentrates on the evolution of language and languages across time. Its normal form of comparison is between two or more stages of the same language, or of two languages that were once the same language, rather than between two or more present-day languages in their modern manifestations.

Geolinguistics covers in detail the current status of the world's languages, comparing them with respect to objective present-day factors: number of speakers, geographical distribution, possibilities of utilization, and commercial, scientific, political, strategic, and cultural importance, in the framework of the world in which we live.

Among its functions are the consideration of such factors as **area languages** and **linguistic spheres of influence**; **indigenous** and **colonial** (or **superimposed**) languages, with the lasting effects of the latter even after colonialism is at an end; **primary** and **secondary languages** in a given area, with attendant **bilingualism** and **multilingualism**; the **substitution** of one language for another; the workings of **languages of immigration** and **naturalization**; the range and extent of **koines** and other types of language of common intercourse (**pidgins**, **creoles**, **modified languages**); the **social and educational stratification** of languages (**official language, national language, literary language, dialect, patois, class language, jargon, slang**); the **literacy coefficient**, which indicates the range and potentialities of the written language; the **nationalistic** and **liturgical coefficients**, which influence the survival of a given language; the problems of **symbiosis** and **languages in contact**. (For a definition of some of these terms, see Section 37, The Function of Geolinguistics.)

14. LOCATION, NUMBER OF SPEAKERS, AND DISTRIBUTION OF PRESENT-DAY LANGUAGES

There are in spoken use throughout the world today nearly three thousand separate languages, exclusive of dialects. Each has its own body of speakers, to whom that language is a normal vehicle of oral communication. In its own area, each of these languages is paramount and must be taken into consideration.

There is wide variation, however, in both number of speakers and extent of area among these languages. The majority of the three thousand or so languages have relatively small bodies of speakers, ranging from below a million to a few hundred, and areas of predominance ranging from a few hundred square miles to a single village.

The total number of languages having one million or more speakers does not go much beyond one hundred. Even among these hundred leading languages in point of numbers, there is wide fluctuation. Only thirteen languages have more than fifty million speakers.[9]

Among the thirteen languages, and even among the hundred, there are wide discrepancies of area and distribution. Some languages are official over vast regions of the earth, others are severely restricted to relatively small areas. Some are widely spoken in non-contiguous parts of the world, others are localized in a single region.

Some languages, like English, French, German, enjoy high coefficients of productivity, trade, and scientific and literary output. Others are used by groups which may be described as backward, whose productivity is low, whose trade is narrowly limited, and whose scientific and intel-

[9] The hundred-odd languages having more than a million speakers, and the thirteen having more than fifty million, are for the most part listed in Appendices II and VI.

lectual achievements are nil, or nearly so. This is the case
with most American Indian languages of the U.S., and
with the native tongues of Australia. Some languages are
the vehicles of expression of groups whose political and
military prestige is at the present time high (Russian,
English), others of groups whose current political and
military import is insignificant (Hawaiian, the Maori of
New Zealand). But some of the latter languages often
appear in areas that have high political and strategic
significance, even though that of their speakers may be
low (Vietnamese, the Swahili of East Africa).

The detailed, scientific, objective study of all these factors constitutes the proper sphere of geolinguistics. In
view of their traditional outlook and present commit-
ments, neither descriptive nor historical linguistics is
properly qualified to handle this field as it should be
handled.

15. AREA LANGUAGES AND THEIR
RELATIVE IMPORTANCE

Some languages, by reason of past historical factors,
have set themselves up as tongues of common intercourse
in areas which outstrip the regions to which they are native, and may be used with reasonable assurance in these
wider areas. Such is the case with German in central Europe, French in North Africa, English in India. The degree of their importance and usefulness in this function
varies widely.

In antiquity, Greek and Latin were used as area languages throughout the entire Mediterranean basin and
western Europe, and the latter ultimately implanted itself as a popular spoken tongue in vast regions whose
inhabitants had originally spoken other languages. In the
Middle Ages, Latin was used as a common tongue of
scholarly and religious intercourse throughout western

Europe. Today, English may be used as a substitute tongue in vast regions, like India and Pakistan, which were once British possessions, and French may be similarly used in nearly half of Africa, while Russian is the tongue of common intercourse throughout the Soviet Union in Asia, to which Russian is not native.

This spreading of some tongues to cover, in one fashion or another, vast areas to which they are not indigenous gives rise to the concept of **area languages**. In some cases it is possible to prophesy, on the basis of present-day factors and phenomena, that a certain language will eventually impose itself in a given area and displace other tongues now current in that area. In other cases it is possible to prophesy, on the same basis, that the area language will recede and eventually disappear from one or more segments of the area where it is now current. Swahili may thus replace English in East Africa, and Dutch is already disappearing from Indonesia.

These linguistic projections, with their far-reaching implications, call for specialized study.

16. LITERARY LANGUAGE, NATIONAL LANGUAGE, DIALECTS, COLLOQUIAL FORMS, SLANG

Both descriptive and historical linguists endeavor to make clear-cut distinctions between languages and dialects, and between the various social and educational strata of a single given language. They seldom, however, take a realistic attitude with reference to these linguistic phenomena, or attempt to interpret them in the light of what is of practical importance either to the social group or to the individual. This is due in the main to a misunderstanding of what constitutes a scientific attitude, and to an inclination to regard facts as "value judgments."

It is not a value judgment to describe one language as
having greater practical importance than another, when
that judgment is based on objective, clearly ascertainable
factors, such as census figures, area, and productivity. It
is not a value judgment to assert that one language is, at
the present moment, culturally superior to another, when
the fruits of culture are plainly ascertainable in terms of
intellectual, literary, and scientific output. Lastly, it is
not a value judgment to state that one form of language,
current throughout an entire nation and used by the
educated classes, is preferable to another, localized as to
area or used by illiterate or semiliterate speakers.

Of course, under special circumstances it may be more
desirable to possess the more restricted or less cultured
type of language. A missionary to the Amazon jungles
will find greater use for an unimportant Indian language
than for the tongue of a hundred million Europeans. A
police officer dealing with gangsters will find their jargon
more useful than the tongue of lawyers, doctors, and
professors. But these are exceptional situations and should
be viewed as such.

The existence of large and powerful national units normally gives rise to **national languages**. In origin these are
artificial phenomena, consisting for the most part either
of a dialect which is selected to fulfill a nationwide function or of a merger or compromise among various local
dialects. The merger of dialects arises out of the necessity for a medium of common intercourse, particularly for
purposes of interregional commerce. The national language is the speech form which enjoys governmental support and is taught, at least in theory, in the nation's
schools.

Often, but not invariably, the national language coincides with the **literary language**, in which most writing
takes place. This is the case with Florentine Tuscan in
Italy, though with significant modifications and contributions from other dialects. Often a dialect has a literary

form and a literary output and may in a sense be described as a literary language. Such was the case with the Picard dialect of medieval France and is the case with modern Neapolitan. However, the emergence of a national language tends to discourage the use of dialects as media for literary expression.

Dialects are local speech forms used over extensive areas. It is possible to group dialects into large units on the basis of common features, but precise research has led to the conclusion that such groupings, though convenient, are largely figments of the imagination. There is, objectively, no such thing in the United States as a "Southern dialect" or a "Midwestern dialect" or a "New England dialect," but rather an infinite series of localisms with features partly held in common, partly diverging from one locality to the next. On a purely factual basis, each city, town, and village has its own dialect. The French have devised for these restricted, unwritten speech forms the term **patois**. To carry analysis further, each individual has his own speech peculiarities, which distinguish him even from members of his own immediate family and permit those who know him to identify him, unseen, by his speech. These individual speech forms are termed **idiolects**.

On the other hand, the boundaries of individual diverging speech forms may be represented by imaginary lines called **isoglosses**. There is, for example, a clearly defined isogloss running from the southwest to the northeast across most of Germany. On one side of this line the speakers say *dat,* on the other side *das.* Often the isoglosses, while not coinciding absolutely, tend to run in bundles, with relatively slight divergences. If one takes a mean or average of the isoglosses, it is possible to trace a single line which separates one major dialect area from another. This is the sole scientific basis for our classification of the major dialects of a given language.

Practically every language has some measure of social

and educational stratification, resulting in what one may term **class languages**. Where the educated people of one community will use one form of speech, the less educated classes will use another, giving rise to such terms as the British "U" and "non-U" language (*lidy, guv'nor, quid, bob,* are forms which British U-speakers would normally avoid). In addition, various professions and callings evolve their own specialized vocabulary or **jargon** (medicalese, pedagese, bureaucratic gobbledegook, legal parlance, etc.). **Colloquialisms** are language forms which may appear in the informal speech of even the more educated classes but are seldom used in official speech or writing ("I've *got* five dollars"). The colloquial language may sink still further into what the older dictionaries label **vulgarisms** ("I ain't seen him"), and even into **slang** ("He packs a gat"), which may be local but is more often nationwide. This social-educational stratification of language is important from the point of view of geolinguistics, as it rounds out the total picture of the language varieties in use throughout the globe.

The class distinctions in language described above are far more operative in large, important, cultural languages than they are in the tongues of small and less advanced groups. Yet on occasion the latter can present what practically amounts to a social stratification through the use of forms which are taboo to a given portion of the speaking population. In certain American Indian tribes, for example, the women speak a language which differs considerably from that of the men.

For a further discussion, from the historical standpoint, of some of the terms defined above, see Section 28, Points of Contact with Descriptive Linguistics and Geolinguistics.

17. THE CHANGING LINGUISTIC PICTURE

The natural tendency of language, particularly in spoken, colloquial form, is **centrifugal**. Language tends to change, both in time and in space, to the extent that it is not restrained by **centripetal**, man-made factors. This universal characteristic of language is important to the historical linguist, since it forms the basis of all language change. It is important to the descriptive linguist because it forms the basis of the dialectal and class differences he finds in the language he is trying to describe and analyze. It is important to the geolinguist, not only because it gives him a more accurate picture of the world's languages and their relative importance, but also because it forms the basis of his projections into the future status of the world's languages.

It is common knowledge that, in the past, certain languages, once important and widespread, utterly disappeared and became extinct, leaving behind them nothing but written records and a few words borrowed by other, more fortunate languages that survived and flourished. Other languages have displayed great power of expansion and absorption, attracting to themselves vast bodies of speakers that they did not possess at the outset. Latin was such a language, absorbing speakers of Etruscan, Oscan, Umbrian, Iberian, Gaulish, and many other tongues that became extinct. Latin lived on and prospered, continuing its existence to the present day in its numerous descendants, the Romance tongues, all of which are nothing but Latin modified in the course of time. In more recent times we have witnessed the phenomenal increase in prestige and number of speakers of English, French, Spanish, and Russian. All of these have acquired speakers by absorption as well as by natural growth. Occasionally we encounter a language, like Chinese, whose numerical in-

crease is due almost exclusively to internal population
growth.

It is among the functions of geolinguistics to study the
factors that lead to the growth and decline of languages
and to project present situations into the future. The
latter task is made difficult by the number and variety of
historical factors that enter the picture. These are of a
military, political, economic, religious, and cultural nature. Latin, for example, expanded as a result of military
conquest, political wisdom, and administrative skill, but
its later survival in vast areas was largely due to a religious factor, since Latin became the official language of
the Western Christian Church. The expansion of Arabic
was the outcome of military conquest coupled with religious expansion. Castilian became the predominant dialect of the Spanish peninsula by reason of the military
role played by its speakers in the reconquest of Spain
from the Moors. The subsequent extension of Castilian
to large areas of the New World was due to the process
of colonization, in which military, religious, and economic
motives were merged. Something similar occurred in the
case of English, with the further factor of the absorption
of vast numbers of immigrants originally speaking other
tongues, and of their descendants. The Francien dialect
of northern France, having triumphed over equally literary medieval French dialects because it happened to be
the local speech form of Paris, where the court was situated, later imposed itself over broad areas of the earth
partly by force of arms and colonization, partly by reason
of its cultural appeal.

Going by the lessons of the past, the geolinguist must
guard against assuming that the present relative status of
world languages is eternal. The geolinguistic picture is
a rapidly changing one, and probably at no historical
period has this been truer than at present. While the
geolinguist should objectively describe the picture of the
world's languages as it appears today, and even make

cautious prognostications for the future, he must also be ready for sudden and startling changes. We have witnessed several such changes in the course of the present century.[10]

[10] Among them are the perhaps only temporary diminution of prestige and importance of German and French at the time of the two world wars, the rise in prestige of Spanish after the First World War, of Russian, Chinese, and Arabic after the Second. One may also mention the rise of brand-new, partly artificial tongues such as Indonesian, which is at present the official language of a state numbering nearly a hundred million inhabitants; of Hindi, Urdu, and Tagalog, which have become the official tongues of India, Pakistan, and the Philippines, respectively, though not without opposition from the speakers of other tongues in those areas.

PART II

Descriptive Linguistics: Basic Terminology

18. PHONETICS

Individual speech sounds (also called **phones**; cf. Section 6, Phonology, Phonetics, and Phonemics) are produced by the human vocal organs. The lungs act as a bellows, to supply the stream of air which is the raw material for speech sounds. This stream comes up through the windpipe and encounters various possible fields of constriction or occlusion. Once past the vocal cords and the larynx, the air stream can be directed into the mouth or nose, which act as resonating chambers. The vocal cords, which can be felt by touching your Adam's apple, can be closed off entirely, vibrated, or held fully open. If they are closed off and then released, the result is the **glottal stop**, or onset of the breath stream, perceptible in such combinations as German *die Eier* (also occasionally in English between the two *o*'s of *co-operate*, or in some dialectal pronunciations of words like *bottle*, where the *t*-sound is replaced by the glottal stop and the result sounds like *bo'le*). If the air stream is directed into the mouth, we have **oral** sounds; if into the nose, **nasal** sounds. Even before the breath stream reaches the mouth or nose, however, there is the possibility of producing a speech sound by contracting the pharynx. **Pharyngeal** speech sounds occur in numerous languages, notably Arabic.

As the air stream enters the mouth or nose the vocal

cords may be vibrated, in which case we get **voiced**, or **sonant**, sounds, such as *b, v, m*. If the vocal cords are simply held open without vibration the sound is **unvoiced**, or **surd**, such as *p, f*. The distinction among the various sounds, both oral and nasal, is caused by duration, sonority, energy of utterance, and, above all, point of articulation. The **point of articulation** refers to the precise spot in the speech organs where a modification is effected. This may be done by creating a complete road block, or **occlusion**, at that point, then lifting the road block and allowing the air to escape suddenly (this occurs, for instance, with *t, d, p, b*). It may also be done by creating a partial road block, through which the air stream issues with audible friction (this happens with *f, v,* and *th,* either voiced, as in *this,* or unvoiced, as in *thing*). The tongue, which is the most movable among the speech organs, usually determines the point of articulation and the nature of the sound. Occasionally only the lips, or lips and teeth, are involved (*p, b, f, v*).

Vowel sounds are produced with a maximum of duration and sonority and a minimum of constriction and friction (note the possibility of indefinite prolongation, the resounding qualities, and the relative openness of the vocal passage in such sounds as *ah, oh*). **Consonant sounds** involve a greater amount of constriction and friction, and, in some cases, a complete road block followed by a sudden release (note the firm closure of the lips and their subsequent release in the utterance of *p*). Vibration of the vocal cords regularly attends the production of vowel sounds; it may or may not attend the production of consonant sounds (place your fingers on the sides of your throat and feel the vibration of the vocal cords as you utter, *ah, b, g,* as against the lack of vibration as you utter *p, t, k*).

The back of the highly mobile tongue coincides with the soft palate, or velum; the middle part of the tongue coincides with the juncture of the hard and soft palate;

the front part of the tongue coincides with the hard palate; the tip of the tongue generally rests against the upper or lower teeth. Second to the tongue in mobility among the speech organs are the lips. There is also the uvula, which can be set into vibration by the breath stream to produce the so-called uvular *r* of French (this has been compared to a gentle clearing of the throat). Teeth, palate, and nasal cavity are immovable.

It is an interesting fact that physiologically the so-called speech organs are not designed to serve the purpose of speech but other, more elemental functions of the human organism, such as breathing and eating.

In producing vowel sounds the oral passage is relatively more open and free from constriction than in producing consonant sounds. There is, however, some constriction exerted by the position of the tongue and the lips. The tongue may be raised in its front, middle, or back part; the lips may be opened to a greater or lesser degree, and they may also be rounded, as in position for a kiss, or spread. This means that a vowel sound may be described as **front**, **middle** (**central** is a synonym for **middle**), or **back**, depending on which section of the tongue is raised (the *i* of *machine*, for example, is front; the *a* of *hat* is middle or central; the *u* of *rule* is back). The vowel sound may also be described as **high**, **mid**, or **low**, depending on how far the tongue is raised; or as **open**, **half open**, or **close**, depending on the degree of aperture of the lips.[1] The vowel sound may, finally, be described as **rounded**, **half rounded**, or **spread**, depending on the position of the lips. The *u* of *rule* is rounded; the *aw* of *awful*, or, better yet, the *eu* of French *peur* is half rounded; the *a* of *hat* unrounded or spread.

---

[1] To a considerable degree, close and high, half open and mid, open and low, may be used as pairs of synonyms in this connection, because the raising of the tongue is almost automatically attended by a closing of the lips, the lowering of the tongue by an opening of the lips. The *i* of *machine* is high (close); the *e* of *met* is mid (half open); the *a* of *father* is low (open).

We could now describe the vowel sound of *machine* as a front, spread, high (close) vowel. The French *u* of *lune* is also front and high (or close), but rounded, not spread. The *u* of English *rule* is back, rounded, and high (or close). The *a* of *father* is middle, spread, and low (or open). It will be noted that some of these combinations of three vowel qualities appear in one language but not in another (English, for example, does not have a front, high, rounded vowel like the *u* of French *lune*). But it will also be noted that the correct sound of an unfamiliar combination can to some extent be directed by an accurate three-word description like the ones given above, to the point where it can be produced by one who is not in the habit of producing it. This is one of the advantages of a precise, scientific terminology.

Phonetically, a vowel consists of a single sound with no change in the position of the vocal organs. If the position of the vocal organs changes while the utterance of the vowel sound is in progress, as happens in English *sigh* or *bone*, the phonetic result is a **diphthong**, a succession of two vowel sounds in sequence, which nevertheless make only one syllable (two vowel sounds pronounced in the amount of time it would take to pronounce one is a less scientific but perhaps more understandable definition). There is even the possibility of **triphthongs**, as in English *way*, *wow*, Spanish *buey*, or Italian *suoi*, where three separate vowel sounds are combined into a single syllable.

In a diphthong or triphthong, one of the two or three vowels has greater prominence, duration, and stress. The others are described as **semivowels**, **semiconsonants**, or **glides**. The sounds indicated by English written *w* and *y*, particularly the former, are generally semivowels. If the more prominent vowel follows the semivowel, we have a **rising diphthong** (as in the *wa* of *was*, or the *ye* of *yes*). If the more prominent vowel precedes the semivowel, we have a **falling diphthong** (as in the *ow* of either *blow* or *now*, the *oy* of *boy*).

Care must be exercised not to confuse the diphthong, which is a unit of speech, with the **digraph**, which is a unit of writing (two letter symbols used to represent a single speech sound, as in English *th* of *this*, *ph* of *Philadelphia*, *sh* of *shut*, or *ea* of *beat*, which is interpreted by some American phoneticians as consisting of the *i* of *it* followed by a *y*-glide, but which others, along with the British, interpret as a pure long vowel). The unsatisfactory, highly traditional, and antiquated spelling of English leads to the representation of many **monophthongs** (single sounds) by digraphs, and, conversely, of many diphthongs by single letters of the alphabet (*bone, fate* are two illustrations; the *o* of *bone* is phonetically *o* plus *w*, and the *a* of *fate* is *e* plus *y*; this fact is recognized by most British phoneticians in their transcriptions but generally ignored by most Americans, who apparently allow themselves to be influenced by the traditional orthography).

A consonant is that which "sounds with" something else (normally, with a vowel, which ordinarily constitutes the **peak of sonority** of the syllable). The consonant involves either downright **occlusion** (stoppage of the breath stream, followed by release) or a greater degree of constriction and friction than normally occurs with a vowel.

In the case of the sounds usually represented in English writing by *p, b, k, g, t, d,* the breath stream is brought to a halt behind a road block which may be formed by the lips (this happens with *p, b*); by the back of the tongue and the soft palate (*k, g*); or by the tip or front of the tongue and the teeth, or the ridges of the upper gums (*t, d;* front of tongue and ridges of the upper gums are normal for English; tip of tongue and back of upper or lower teeth for other languages, including French and Italian). When the road block is lifted the sound comes out explosively. Such consonants may therefore be called

occlusives, **plosives**, or **stops**. They may be **voiced** (accompanied by vibration of the vocal cords, as in the case of *b, g, d*); or **unvoiced** (unattended by such vibration, as for *p, k, t*). Depending on the point of articulation, or formation of the road block, one may describe the consonants as **labial** (road block formed by closure of the two lips, as for *p, b*); **velar** (road block formed by back of tongue and soft palate, or velum; **guttural** is an equivalent term less frequently used today); or **dental** (road block formed by tip of tongue and back of teeth). While true dentals appear in many languages, they are replaced in English by **alveolars** (road block formed by front of tongue and ridge of upper gums, or alveoli). This slight shift in the point of articulation makes for the phonetic difference between a French and an English *t* or *d*.

At this point we begin to get our basis for classification of consonant sounds. The six we have described (*p, b, k, g, t, d*) are all plosives or stops; *p, k, t* are unvoiced (pronounced without vibration of the vocal cords), while *b, g, d* are voiced (accompanied by the vibration). Furthermore, *p* and *b* are labials; *k* and *g* are velars or gutturals; *t* and *d* are dentals, or, in the case of English, alveolars. We can therefore scientifically describe *b* as a voiced labial plosive, and *k* as an unvoiced velar plosive.[2]

The next class of consonants consists of the **fricatives** or **spirants** (**fricative** means that they involve friction, **spirant** that they are breathed out, not exploded). Here we get not a complete road block but a partial one, through which the breath stream can squeeze, without being halted and then released.

In English we can produce the fricative sounds of *f* and *v* (the first is unvoiced, the second voiced) by putting into loose contact the lower lip and the upper teeth. This means that we have not labial but **dento-labial** (or

[2] Note the similarity to the three-word scientific description of a vowel, p. 41).

labio-dental) fricatives. Japanese produces a pure labial unvoiced fricative *f* by blowing the breath through the two barely open lips, as when you blow out a match; Spanish produces a pure labial voiced fricative (whenever written Spanish *b* or *v* are between vowels) in the same fashion, but with vibration of the vocal cords.

The velar fricatives, produced by raising the back of the tongue until it forms loose contact with the soft palate, do not appear in English, but the unvoiced velar fricative appears in the Scottish *loch,* the German *ach,* or the pronunciation of the name of the composer *Bach,* while the voiced velar fricative appears in Spanish whenever *g* is between two vowels the second of which is *a, o,* or *u* (as in *pagar*). The point of articulation for these two sounds is precisely the same as for *k* and *g,* but the road block is incomplete, and the breath stream can squeeze through gradually, instead of being halted and then released.[3]

For the dental fricatives, we have the two sounds represented in writing by the digraph *th* (as in *thing* or *this;* the first is unvoiced, the second voiced, but English spelling takes no account of this difference). Here we place the tip of the tongue in loose contact with the back of the teeth, or between the teeth, and allow the breath stream to escape gradually through the interstices between the teeth.

A fourth pair of fricatives, of the **palatal** variety, is produced by placing the middle or front part of the tongue in loose contact with the hard palate, giving us the sounds represented in English writing by the *sh* (unvoiced) of *shoot* and the *s* (voiced) of *measure.*

Affricates are combination sounds, in which the mode rather than the point of articulation is shifted. If the

[3] It is instructive in this connection to listen to the native pronunciation of the Spanish *pagar* and compare it with the Italian pronunciation of *pagare.* The Spanish sound in this word is fricative, the Italian plosive.

occlusion and release involved in the production of *t* is immediately followed by the continuant, fricative sound of *sh*, the result will be the *ch* of *church*. In like manner, the voiced occlusion and release of *d* followed by the voiced fricative of *s* in *measure* will yield the sound normally represented in English spelling by the *j* of *jet*. Similarly, we may produce the combination sounds *ts* and *dz*, which the orthography of some languages, notably German and Italian, represents by the single letter symbol *z* (often written double in Italian), by combining a dental plosive with a sibilant spirant without shifting the point of articulation. It is of interest that many phoneticians refuse to recognize the composite nature of the sounds indicated in English by *ch* and *j*, and prefer to regard them as the plosive counterparts of the palatal fricatives represented by English *sh* and *s* of *measure*.

The sounds of *s* and *z*, often described as **sibilants** (whistling or hissing sounds) are in reality a variety of fricative, produced by placing the tip of the tongue in very loose contact with the ridge of the gums and letting the breath stream issue through the opening thus created, with the further hurdle of the interstices between the upper teeth. Depending on how far back the tip of the tongue is placed, we can achieve the **apical** *s* of Castilian Spanish or Greek, sounding like a strong hiss, or the alveolar *s* of English, or the dental *s* of French. Vibration of the vocal cords accompanying the production of this sound gives us the sound of English *z*.

If we shape the organs of the mouth as for *p*, *t*, *k*, or *ch* of *church*, but keep the road block intact and allow the breath stream to go up into the nose, we get **nasal** sounds represented by *m*, *n*, *ng*, and the *ny* of *canyon* (or French and Italian *gn*, Spanish *ñ*). These sounds may be described as a labial nasal, a dental or alveolar nasal, a velar or guttural nasal, and a palatal nasal. In all cases there is vibration of the vocal cords, so all nasal sounds are voiced.

L and *r* are often classified together as **liquids**, but in view of their divergence and variety it is perhaps better to describe *l* as a **lateral** (the tongue blocks the front of the mouth but is lowered at the sides, and the breath stream escapes through the openings at the two sides of the tongue and palate). The blocking effect of the tongue can be produced very far forward in the mouth, in which case we get the so-called **liquid** *l* of *million* (Spanish *ll*, Italian *gl*); around the middle of the mouth (*lamb*, *love*); or far back (*milk*), so that we can have a front, middle, or back lateral. All are accompanied by vibration of the vocal cords in English and most other languages (Welsh, however, produces a voiceless *l* which is represented in Welsh spelling by the *ll* of *Llandudno, Llanfair, Lloyd*, etc.).

R is in most languages a trill or flap of the front part of the tongue, accompanied by vibration of the vocal cords. (It is sometimes called a **vibrant**, because its production is always attended by some sort of vibration, of the vocal cords, or tongue, or uvula.) In French the sound represented in writing by *r* is a voiced vibration of the uvula. In American English it is generally produced by cupping the tongue and allowing the breath stream to escape along the rims of the cup. These three widely divergent varieties of sounds which the spelling of various languages indicates by the same letter symbol are a glaring example of the untrustworthiness of written systems to represent spoken-language sounds, as well as of the Berlitz motto that "the eye is the enemy of the ear." An American trying to learn French from the written form of the language will inevitably be tempted to pronounce what he sees as *r* with its American English value.

The sound represented in English by *h* is simply the unvoiced expulsion of the breath stream from the mouth without block or true friction (there is, however, a slight constriction of the glottis, so that it could be described as a **glottal** sound). If vibration of the vocal cords is added, we get the *gh* sound of Arabic.

This brief and elementary description of the production of language sounds is very far from exhausting the possibilities which appear in the IPA chart, itself very far from complete. No individual language utilizes more than sixty, at the most, of the hundreds of possible varieties of language sounds which the human vocal organs are capable of producing. Some languages, like Hawaiian, utilize only about a dozen.

19. PHONEMICS

What we have been discussing so far pertains to the field of **articulatory phonetics**, or of **phonetics** pure and simple (see Section 6, Phonology, Phonetics, and Phonemics). Turning now to the phonemic aspects of language sounds, we may again define **phonemics** as dealing with those features of language sounds which are relevant in the system of a single language from the point of view of the speaker's consciousness. Here we are generally faced with classes of related sounds (**phonemes**). While a phoneme may on occasion consist of a single **phone** (or objective sound), it more often consists of a group of similar phones, or **phonetic variants**, whose use depends primarily on position in the word (initial, medial, final, etc.), and on the nature of the phonetic **environment** (i.e., before a vowel, before a consonant, between vowels, adjacent to a voiced or voiceless sound, etc.). We have seen that the written *p* of *pit, spit,* and *sip* really represents three different, though similar and related, phones. But we have also seen that the differences are produced automatically when a native speaks, so that he is normally unconscious of those differences unless his attention is drawn to them. Despite the fact that the *p* of *pit, spit,* and *sip* represents three different objective sounds or phones, it constitutes a single phoneme in the normal consciousness of the American speaker. The three phones are then described as **allophones**, or **positional variants**, of the same phoneme.

This in turn means that the phoneme cannot be equated to a mere language sound, or phone. It is rather an ideal, theoretical unit, which has no objective existence and can come into being only through one of its allophones. This coming into being of a phoneme through one of its allophones is known in technical parlance as the **actualization** or **realization** of a phoneme. The phoneme, or ideal unit, *p* of American English can have objective existence only through the phones of *p* in *pit, spit,* or *sip*. But these are allophones, not phonemes.

It is fairly obvious that allophones of the same phoneme must share some phonic similarity as to mode of production and point of articulation. It would be highly unlikely, though not altogether inconceivable, that a given language would use the *p* of *pit*, the *t* of *tit*, and the *k* of *kit* as allophones of the same phoneme.[4]

The principle of general phonic similarity of the allophones of the same phoneme normally has some measure of recognition in the orthographic system of a language. In our own, for instance, the three *p*-phones of *pit, spit,*

---

[4] Note, however, that it is possible for one phoneme to invade, so to speak, the area of another. In German, for example, what is historically and orthographically a *d* assumes, in final position, the sound of *t*, in such words as *Bad,* "bath." This phenomenon is called NEUTRALIZATION between two phonemes which are normally distinct. Such neutralization occurs only in a given position. German carefully distinguishes between *d* and *t* initially and medially, merging (or neutralizing) them only in final position. To cover such cases, the term ARCHIPHONEME has been coined. The archiphoneme includes as members two or more phonemes which in certain positions are neutralized, plus all their allophones. Thus, in the specific case mentioned, German may be said to possess an archiphoneme /t-d/, consisting of the two separate phonemes /t/ and /d/, which are normally kept distinct to the point where the use of one for the other would cause semantic confusion, but which are neutralized or merged in final position.

and *sip* are all represented by the same written symbol. But we cannot always rely on this orthographic aid, particularly in languages like English and French.

Whether two given phones are separate phonemes or allophones of a single phoneme depends, as we have seen (p. 14), on the system of the individual language. The test for phonemic individuality or identity is that of **minimal pairs**: in two words in all other respects identical, will the meaning change if one phone is substituted for the other? If so, we have two separate phonemes. If not, we have two allophones of the same phoneme. If I replace the *p* of *pit* with the *b* of *bit*, I have another and conflicting meaning; therefore I have in English two separate *p*- and *b*- phonemes. If I replace the *p* of *pit* with the gentle, unaspirated *p* of *spit*, the word sounds somewhat distorted, but the meaning to the hearer is still the same; so I have two allophones of one phoneme.

But in normal speech that is not used for testing purposes, I will hardly interchange the two phones. I will use each one, automatically, in its proper environment. They are in **complementary distribution** and do not normally trespass on each other's territory. Taken together, the allophones cover all possible positional occurrences, all actualizations, of the phoneme. In the words of R. Fowkes, "The phoneme is the ideal toward which the speaker strives, the allophone is the performance he achieves," under any given circumstances and in any given environment.

Speakers react sharply to phonemic differences, while they may not even be aware of phonetic differences. This is because the phonemic difference changes the meaning of the word and throws the hearer off balance, while the phonetic difference does not. If the Spanish speaker pronounces *pit* with the unaspirated *p* of *spit*, in accordance with his own linguistic habits, no one will take undue notice. But if he uses *live* for *leave*, or vice versa, he runs the chance of being misunderstood.

Save for cases of neutralization, described above, phonemes normally keep out of one another's territory. Were this not true there would be endless confusion of meaning, and language would fail in its primary purpose of communication.

Historically, however, there are numerous cases of merging and redividing of phonemes. Even descriptively and synchronically, certain American speakers tend to merge intervocalic *t* and *d* (*wetting, wedding*) to the point where no distinction appears if the words are heard in isolation. Here normally the context comes to the hearer's rescue and the message is correctly received and interpreted, despite phonic confusion as well as extraneous noise and distortion. This happens in a telephone conversation, where perhaps only fifty per cent of the phonic content is actually heard, but the balance is supplied by the hearer's knowledge of semantic content and his quasi-instinctive interpretation based on previous experience and habit. Note that if an unfamiliar proper noun, such as a family name, comes into play, there is often a pause in the conversation to permit the name to be spelled out or otherwise properly identified.

The hearer, in view of his general knowledge of context and previous information about the topic of conversation, does not need all of the available phonic or phonemic clues contained in the message, but can get along comfortably on perhaps half of them. **Redundancy** is the name given by communications experts to the state of affairs whereby more phonemic clues appear in a message than are actually needed for full comprehension. The redundancy factor decreases sharply if the hearer is only partly familiar with the language he hears or with the situation it describes. Under these circumstances he "strains his ears" to seize every possible clue and quickly realizes that many elude him.

20. SUPRASEGMENTAL PHONEMES: STRESS, INTONATION, JUNCTURE

Features that may be referred to acoustic rather than to articulatory phonetics are **pitch**, **loudness**, and **timbre**. The first is determined by the frequency of the sound waves, the second by their amplitude, the third by the combination of fundamental tone and overtones (it is the timbre that permits us to identify a person's voice).

Vowel and consonant sounds produce **speech segments** and are consequently described as **segmental phonemes**.[5] There are also additional speech features affecting speech sounds or combinations of speech sounds. These are described as **secondary** or **suprasegmental phonemes**. Chief among them are **accent** (or **stress**), **intonation**, and **juncture**.

Accent means that one syllable in a sequence is given greater amplitude or loudness (**stress accent**), or higher or lower frequency (**pitch accent**). **Intonation** is the succession of relative pitches or cadences in a given utterance. **Juncture** is the linking or absence of linking (**pause of silence**) between the syllables of an utterance. These three elements are occasionally as important to the meaning as the segmental vowels and consonants of the speech sequence.

Concerning accent, for instance, it does not matter to the meaning whether one says *políce*, as is normal in New York, or *pólice*, as the word is pronounced by many Midwesterners. But the differences between *présent* and *presént*, *pérmit* and *permít, bláckbird* and *bláck bírd* are basic to the meaning.

There are said to be in English four degrees of accent or stress, named **primary**, **secondary**, **tertiary**, and **weak**.

[5] Speech is a "spoken chain," a continuum or flow, linear in time. Consequently the flow can be "segmented" into separate phonemes or allophones.

Illustrating them by examples, words like *weather, given, merger,* show primary accent on the first syllable and weak accent on the last. *Baseball* and *windfall* illustrate primary accent on the first syllable, tertiary on the last. *Artifact* and *generate* show primary on the first, tertiary on the last, with weak accent or no accent at all on the middle syllable. Secondary accent appears in word combinations such as *red house* and *fine man,* where the primary accent falls on the second word, the secondary accent on the first. In narrow phonemic transcription, they may be indicated by 1, 2, 3, 4, or by ´, ^, `, ˇ.[6]

While accent is for the most part a matter of vocal energy or loudness, pitch is a matter of musical notes. In Chinese the pitch or **tone** is an inherent part of the word and is just as much phonemic as are the vowels and consonants. In this language *kan shu,* uttered with different tones, may mean "read a book" or "chop wood." *Fu,* pronounced in four different tones, may mean "man," "good luck," "prefecture," or "rich." In Swedish there is a single falling tone and a double tone; *anden* with the single fall means "the duck"; with the double fall, "the spirit." It is claimed that the drum signals of the African tomtoms imitate the intonation of spoken words of the local languages.

In English, pitch or intonation is seldom phonemic, and usually applies to the phrase or sentence rather than to the individual word. But, depending on the situation, intonation may make a difference to the meaning that can only be described as phonemic. One startling example favored by linguists is the question "What are we having for dinner, mother?" with the last word pronounced and intoned either as a form of address or as a possible hypothesis as to what the dinner will consist of. Other humor-arousing samples are: "What's coming up the street?" as against "What's coming up—the street?" and

[6] Note the difference between *greénhoùse* and *greên hoúse.*

"What are you reading, Shakespeare?" intoned as though the Bard were being addressed.

There are said to be in English four varieties of pitch, **low**, **mid**, **high**, and **extra high**. Illustrations of pitch levels are somewhat complicated, by reason of the fact that speakers tend to vary in their use of such levels and that even words of one syllable undergo changes of pitch level from their inception to their conclusion. One might use the word *go* in a noncommittal, unemotional statement, such as "I am going to go there tomorrow"; then in an ordinary question of the type of "Go there?" To this may be added the element of incredulity: "Go there!" Lastly, there is the command "Go!" The first *go* might be described as using a normal mid tone throughout its utterance. The second has a high tone throughout. The third starts low and ends high. The last starts high and ends low. But, as we have said, there is much variation among individual speakers and it is unsafe to make too definite pronouncements and classifications. On the other hand, every language has, for groups of words and sentences, intonation patterns that are thoroughly distinctive, on the basis of which one can identify the language that is being spoken even if one hears none of the actual words.

Juncture, also known as **transition**, is that elusive pause between words and syllables in an utterance that is supposed to tell us where one word or syllable ends and another begins. Some writers claim that the difference consists not so much in a pause as in a different value for the consonants and vowels involved and a difference in tone. The **sharp transition** between *night* and *rate* in "night rate" (often called **open juncture**, and indicated in transcription by a plus sign) is opposed to the **muddy transition** between the *t* and the *r* of *nitrate* (also called **close juncture**, and indicated in transcription by a minus sign).

Confusions of juncture have led in the past to such historical changes as *a newt* from an earlier *an ewt,* and *an apron* from *a napron*. Even today it is juncture that permits us to distinguish between *an icebox* and *a nice box*, or *light housekeeper* and *lighthouse keeper*, though intonation and context also help. As in the case of accent and intonation, even where juncture does not play a phonemic role, it nevertheless contributes heavily to the difference between a native and a foreign pronunciation.

A **syllable** is a **peak of sonority**, usually a vowel sound,[7] with other sounds usually, but not invariably, preceding, or following, or both preceding and following the peak. In *ah,* the peak of sonority is obviously *a;* in *it,* the peak of sonority is *i;* in *do,* it is *o;* in *get,* it is *e.*

Syllabic division is intimately connected with juncture, as there is normally an almost imperceptible **pause of silence** between syllables, and this pause could be equated to open juncture (sharp transition).

Languages tend to have specific syllabic patterns, sometimes described as **canonical forms** (though the canonical form sometimes includes other factors than syllabic division). In English the pattern consonant-vowel-consonant, or vowel-consonant, is most frequent (*gener-al;* the syllable is said to be **closed** when it ends in a consonant sound, **open** when it ends in a vowel sound). In other languages, such as Spanish, Italian, Japanese, Indonesian, the preferred pattern is consonant-vowel (*ge-ne-ra-le, ge-ne-ral*). This leads to a basic difference of juncture and a different coloring of the vowel sounds, since a vowel in the **free position**, at the end of a syllable, tends to have greater prominence, sonority, and duration than one in the **checked position** (followed by a consonant in the same syllable). This difference in syllabification, while seldom phonemic (i.e., causing a difference in the meaning), is basic to the acquisition of a

---

[7] While the peak of sonority is generally a vowel sound, there are many languages where *l, r, m, n,* even *s, z,* can be used in a vowel function so far as syllabics are concerned: Czech *krst, pln,* where the *r* and the *l* function as peaks of sonority, or vowels.

native-speaker accent.[8] Pronouncing the foreign words or
word group in slow motion, syllable by syllable, with the
correct pauses between syllables, then gradually speed-
ing up the utterance until normal speed is attained, usually results in the acquisition of the proper vowel tone
and juncture.

Two additional language features that partake of both
a phonetic and a phonemic nature are free variation and
the question of permissible sound combinations in any
given language.

Free variation occurs when two possible pronunciations are equally acceptable. *Either* with *ee* of *feet* or *i* of
sigh; tomato with *a* of *fate* or *a* of *father; with* with *th* of
thing or *th* of *this* are cases in point. There is more than
a suspicion that, where free variation occurs, it represents
the coexistence of two or more social (class) or dialectal
(local) forms whose separate origins may have been forgotten. But tracing origins is properly a function of the
historical, not of the descriptive linguist. The latter simply records the fact of coexistence and goes on to describe
the existing forms.

Sound combinations, particularly **consonant clusters**,
and the positions in which they can occur, differ from
one language to another. English admits a final consonant
cluster such as that of *desks, pests,* which many other
languages would not tolerate, but rejects such initial clusters as the *nr-* of Russian *nravit's'a* ("to please") or the
sdr- (pronounced *zdr-*) of Italian *sdraiarsi* ("to lie
down"). Since these clusters are admitted in other positions in the word, or in word sequences (u*nr*avel,
his *dr*awl), the learner may be advised to pronounce the
English word or sequence, omitting the sound or sounds
that precede the desired cluster.

We may note that, though the phonemic scheme of a

[8] If you persist in pronouncing the Spanish *ge-ne-ral* with the syllabic division of English *gen-er-al,* you will be understood; but you
will forever sound like a foreigner.

language and its permissible sound combinations are what they are, there is nothing to prevent one language from "borrowing" ("appropriating" seems a better word in this case) the sounds and permissible combinations of another in loan words, thus giving the foreign sound or combination what amounts to naturalization. English, for example, does not have the velar unvoiced spirant of German *ach*, but this does not prevent most people from pronouncing the name of Bach correctly. Two sound combinations that English does not permit in initial position for native words are *ts* and *shm*. Yet the name of the *tsetse fly* and the Yiddish borrowing *schmo*, or the German family name *Schmidt*, are correctly handled by cultivated and even uncultivated English speakers.

These illustrations exemplify a broader, universally valid consideration. There is no sound or combination of sounds of one language that cannot be correctly acquired and used by the speaker of another language, granted the necessary outlay of time, attention, and effort.

21. MORPHEMICS

The traditional grammatical concepts are based largely upon the system originating with the ancient Greek grammarians, who were describing their own highly inflected language. The Greek grammatical categories included such items as number, gender, and case, which applied to nouns, adjectives, and pronouns; also tense, mood, voice, person, and number, which applied to verbs. The structure of ancient Indo-European languages such as Sanskrit, Greek, Latin, and of a good many of the modern ones, notably Slavic, Lithuanian, and, to a lesser degree, German, permits a neat, scientific division of words into **parts of speech** (nouns, adjectives, pronouns, verbs, adverbs, articles, prepositions, conjunctions, interjections), based not merely upon the meaning of the words but upon their function, behavior, and form. The noun has forms and a mode of functioning that clearly set it apart from the adjective, and both are in turn distinguished from the verb. This clear-cut distinction among parts of speech is largely due to flectional endings and internal flections which are peculiar to each of the main individual parts of speech.

It was only when the grammatical system of the old Indo-European languages was applied to languages of different families, such as Chinese or the American Indian tongues, or even to languages of the same family which, like English, had evolved away from the original pattern, that it was realized that the system itself was not universally applicable to all tongues without discrimination. Modern descriptive linguistics has attempted and is attempting (though not altogether successfully up to the present time) to create a new grammatical system and terminology which may either be applicable to all languages or at least serve to give a more satisfactory description of most tongues of the inflectional, agglutinative, and isolating types, as well as some idea of the way in which polysynthetic languages work.[9]

The morpheme, previously defined as the minimal unit of meaning, and subdivided into free and bound, according as it can be used in isolation or only in union with another morpheme (see p. 18), is characteristic of this new system of grammatical classification.

But before undertaking to discuss the morpheme it will be well to state that, corresponding to the phone in phonemics, there is a basic unit, or raw material, of morphemics. That unit is the **morph**. The morph has been defined as a pronounceable series of phonemes which *could* function as a morpheme in the system of a given language. This means that, so far as English is concerned,

[9] For a definition and description of these various structural types of languages, with examples, see Section 10, Language Classification.

a sequence of phonemes such as *sab* or *lund* could be morphs, though they are not morphemes, having no meaning in English. But they could fit easily into the phonemic structure of English. They "sound" like English. A sequence such as *shmorpf*, on the other hand, could not function as a morpheme in English, save by being borrowed as a loan word.[10]

The **morpheme** was previously defined as the smallest unit of meaning, or minimum meaningful unit. It may further be described as a meaningful series of phonemes which is not further divisible save with destruction or alteration of meaning. If I take a sequence like *posts*, I can subdivide it into two morphemes, *post* and *-s* (the latter conveys the accessory meaning of plurality). It is obvious that I cannot further subdivide *-s*. As for *post*, there is no possible logical subdivision. If I try *po-st*, I can give the first the meaning of "the name of an Italian river," which changes the meaning; I can do nothing with *-st*. If I try *p-ost*, I will have an unusable *p-* and an *-ost* that can serve only as a combining form for "bone," again changing the meaning. *Pos-t* gives me two unusable forms. *Post* must therefore be kept intact. It has a definite meaning and answers the definition of a morpheme.

The morpheme is not necessarily monosyllabic or even syllabic. The *-s* morpheme that denotes plurality is a phoneme, but it is not syllabic, while in *Monongahela* or *crocodile* we have morphemes of many syllables. The same phonemic sequence may constitute different morphemes: *post*, for example, has numerous morphemic values, as in *post office, to post a notice, to establish a post*. While phonemes are realized only through their allophones, morphemes are relatively constant and stable.

With regard to free and bound morphemes, some mod-

---

[10] This definition has the added merit of illustrating that languages are far from utilizing all of their permissible combinations of phonemes. Plenty of room is still left for language expansion and growth.

ern linguists prefer to use the term **formant** for the free
morpheme, and to reserve the term "morpheme" for the
bound variety, or the one that carries an accessory notion. If we use traditional grammatical terminology, then
"formant" or "free morpheme" is roughly equivalent to
"root" or "stem," while "bound morpheme" (or "morpheme" pure and simple, as opposed to "formant") can
be equated to "inflectional ending" or "internal change."

The reason for preferring "formant" and "morpheme"
to "free morpheme" and "bound morpheme" is that, while
free and bound morphemes work out well for languages
where bare roots are used as separate words (as in English *mail,* which may be used in isolation, or to which can
be attached such bound morphemes as *-ed, -s, -ing*), it
does not work out so well for Latin or Greek or Russian,
where roots are seldom used in isolation.[11] In the older
or Bloomfieldian classification, English *mail* would be described as a free morpheme, since it can be used by itself, *-ing* as a bound morpheme; but Latin *mūr-* and *-us*
would necessarily both be bound morphemes, since
neither can be used by itself. On the other hand, if we
use "formant" for both English *mail* and Latin *mūr-,* and
reserve the term "morpheme" for English *-ing* and Latin
-us, we have an additional advantage: we can bring in
the traditional idea of a root conveying the basic meaning, as against a secondary element (morpheme in the
more restricted sense) that merely modifies that meaning or indicates how the word is used.

For what concerns the traditional parts of speech, modern structural linguists still recognize them, but they base
their classification of words on a combination of function
and form rather than on meaning or etymology. This
means that they describe rather than define.

An English noun, for example, would be *defined* in a
traditional grammar as "the name of a person, place or

[11] In Latin, *mūr-,* the root of the word for "wall," cannot be
used by itself but requires the addition of *-us, -ī, -ō, -um,* etc.

thing." In a descriptive or structural grammar a noun would be *described* as a word that can be used in certain specific functions or positions and assumes certain forms. A noun can be used as subject or object of a verb, or after a preposition: "The — goes home"; "I see the —"; "I am going with the —." In addition, the noun is capable of indicating plurality by adding *-s* or *-es*, and shows the possessive relation by adding *-'s:* "The — goes"; "The —s go"; "This is the —'s book." An English verb characteristically forms its third person singular by adding *-s*. It forms its present participle by adding *-ing*, and its past and past participle by adding *-d* or *-ed* or *-t*, or by making an internal change. An adjective regularly stands before a noun or after a copulative verb ("The — man"; "The man is —"); also, it shows comparative and superlative degrees by adding *-er* or *-est*, or by prefixing *more* or *most*, but is otherwise uninflected.

The foregoing examples are greatly oversimplified, but they will serve to give some idea of the principles underlying the new method of classification of the parts of speech. The structural method of classifying parts of speech is based essentially on form and function, and eschews the meaning of the individual word. Whether this method is an improvement over the traditional one, which was based essentially on meaning, particularly in its application to the Western languages, is still a moot question. It seems to be, however, more widely applicable, with appropriate modifications, to languages other than the Indo-European.

Just as in phonology we discovered that phonemes have allophones (different objective *sounds*, or **phones**, occurring in **complementary distribution**, or **non-contrastive positions**, and accepted by the speakers as permissible variants), so in morphemics we have **allomorphs**, or **variant forms**, used in different environments to convey the same meaning.

Traditionally, and basing oneself on written-language

phenomena, one could say that English nouns normally form their plurals by adding *-s* or *-es*, occasionally *-en* (*ox, oxen*), occasionally by changing the root vowel (*man, men*), occasionally by no visible or audible feature at all (*sheep, sheep*). Using morphemic terminology, and referring only to the spoken language, one could say that the *-s, -z,* and *-iz* pronunciations of most plural endings (*books, legs, boys, sizes*) are all allomorphs occurring in complementary distribution (*-s* where the noun ends in an unvoiced consonant, as in *books; -z* where the noun ends in a voiced consonant, a vowel, or a semivowel, as in *legs, ladies, boys; -iz* where the noun ends in an *-s* or *-z* sound, as in *glasses, sizes*). The *-en* of *oxen,* the vowel change in *goose, geese, foot, feet,* the zero change[12] of *sheep* and *deer,* are then labeled exceptional allomorphs of a single, universal, plural-indicating morpheme. They occur only in the case of certain specific nouns and are easily catalogued. Since the terminology and methodology used in the morphemic description are purely descriptive, all historical references as to why certain nouns behave in one way and others differently are avoided. The descriptivist is merely describing what occurs in the present-day stage of the language.

English verbs are traditionally divided into two classes, weak and strong. In written form, weak verbs form the past and past participle by adding *-d* or *-ed* (*work, worked; love, loved*). Strong verbs generally change the vowel of the root (*sing, sang, sung*) or make other changes which may or may not involve the addition of an ending (*speak, spoke, spoken; bring, brought, brought*).

Transferring the concept of morpheme and allomorph to verbs, one could say that the *-d* or *-ed* written ending of weak verbs (which phonetically comes out as *-t, -d,* or

[12] The term ZERO CHANGE is used when there is no apparent change in form from the singular to the plural (*one sheep, two sheep*), or from the present tense to the past (*Now I put this book on the table; yesterday I put this book on the table*).

id: wrap, wrapped, pronounced *wrapt; love, loved; light, lighted*) resolve themselves into allomorphs of the same past-indicating morpheme, with a positional variant *-t* after unvoiced consonants, another positional variant *-d* after voiced consonants and vowels, a third positional variant *-id* after spoken *-t* or *-d*. Past forms characterized by a change in the internal vowel (*write, wrote; sing, sang*) are then described and classified as additional allomorphs of the same past-indicating morpheme. Note again the zero allomorph of such verbs as *put, bet, hurt.*

22. MORPHOPHONEMICS

Allomorphs may be purely morphological or grammatical, as with the *-en* of *oxen,* which does not depend on any phonological factor.[13] But they may also be phonologically conditioned, as when we use an *-s* sound after an unvoiced consonant, but a *-z* sound after a voiced consonant or vowel. Under these circumstances the change is described as **morphophonemic**, or involving a morphological factor which is conditioned by a phonological factor. The morphophonemic change occasionally affects the root morpheme or formant as well as the bound morpheme or ending (*knife, knives; path, paths; house, houses,* with the unvoiced final consonant of the singular changing to its voiced counterpart in the plural, while the ending likewise assumes the voiced form *-z* or *-iz*). There is no question that the *kniv-* of *knives* is an allomorph of *knife,* occurring only in a special environment, which in this case is the plural form (note that it does

---

[13] The vowel change of *man, foot,* to *men, feet* is likewise purely morphological but comes under the heading of REPLACEMENT (a difference of phoneme in the word stems of two grammatically distinct forms). *Feet* shows a REPLACIVE form instead of the usual *-s* suffix. SUPPLETION is a complete change in the form of a stem, as when *went, was* are used as the past forms of *go, be; worse* is the SUPPLETIVE comparative of *bad.*

not appear in the possessive singular: *the knife's edge*).
Nevertheless, *kniv-* must now be considered as a bound
instead of a free morpheme, paralleling the *mūr-* of
Latin, since it cannot occur in isolation.[14] To take another example, the *duke-* of *dukedom*, the *duch-* of
duchy, and the *duc-* of *ducal* may be considered allomorphs of a single formant. But if we prefer to speak of
free and bound morphemes, then *duke* is a free morpheme, but *duch-* and *duc-* can be considered only as
bound allomorphs.

In all cases where there are allomorphs, whether of
the purely morphological or of the morphophonemic
type, it is desirable to select one as the **base form** and
describe the others as variants. If we describe the negative prefix *in-* of *inept, indecent,* as the base form of a
morpheme indicating negation, then the *im-* of *impossible* would be a variant; so would the *ing-* often heard
in *incapable, ingratitude*.

Morphophonemic phenomena occur not only within individual words but also in word groups, where they involve syntax. Such phenomena are described in the traditional terminology as cases of **syntactic phonology**.[15] The
term **sandhi**, borrowed from Sanskrit grammar, is also
occasionally used.[16]

[14] But if we restrict the term "morpheme" to those forms which
convey secondary or accessory meanings, *knife* will be considered
a formant, with an allomorph *kniv-*.

[15] The phenomenon is one which affects pronunciation, therefore it is phonological. At the same time it occurs only in certain
given sequences of words, therefore it is syntactical.

[16] Among the more familiar phenomena of syntactic phonology
or sandhi is the one called LIAISON, or linking, in French grammar.
Here we have *les livres*, with the *-s* of *les* silent before consonants,
as against *les oncles*, where the *-s* of the article is not only linked to
the following vowel sound but is pronounced as a voiced *z* because
it finds itself in intervocalic position. Another example is Spanish
vaca, where the initial *v-* is sounded as a bilabial plosive *b*, opposed to *la vaca*, where by reason of intervocalic position the sound
shifts to that of a bilabial fricative. Examples of English sandhi
alternants are such abbreviated forms as appear in *I'm, it's, we're,*

23. GRAMMATICAL STRUCTURE: SYNTAX

The syntactical terminology evolved by the descriptive linguists is both involved and unstandardized. It reveals a preoccupation with universality (applicability to all types of languages) and a tendency to use traditional terms (such as "subject," "predicate"), in combination with such innovations as "immediate constituents" and "endocentric" or "exocentric structure."

Exocentric structure normally involves what the older terminology would call complete sentences ("I am here," "I hit him"), while **endocentric structure** is applied to groups of words fulfilling the functions, respectively, of nouns ("the big red book"; "language and thought in action"); of verbs ("was being told off"; "should have been seen"); of adjectives ("up-to-date"; "down-to-earth"); or of adverbs ("forty-five years ago"; "in a moment or two").

A **construction** is, in one definition, a significant group of words or morphemes, among which there exists direct connection ("the old man who lives there," "the old man," or, simply, "he"); in another definition, it is "a pattern for building composite forms of a specific form-class out of immediate constituents of specific form-classes." This calls for a definition of "form-class" (or "constituent class") and of "immediate constituents."

A **form-class** or **constituent class** includes those words and groups of words which have the same **privilege of occurrence**; that is to say, can occur in the same construction pattern, and may be substituted for one another and still make sense. A group such as "man who lives there" and a single word such as "dweller" would belong to the same form-class, since they could be placed in the

---

where the ABSOLUTE or basic form of the morpheme is *am, is, are,* respectively.

same spot within a given construction. So would a group
such as "at his son's house" and a single word such as
"there."[17]

A **constituent** is defined as any word entering into a
larger construction. An **immediate constituent** is one of
two or more constituents (or **components**) out of which
a construction is formed. In a sentence such as "the
houses of this man are white," the immediate constituents
would be "the houses of this man" and "are white"
(roughly, what the traditional grammar would describe
as the subject with its modifiers and the predicate with
its modifiers). To isolate "this man are" and call it an
immediate constituent would be incorrect, despite the
fact that the words occur in sequence. In "hothouse
flowers," *house* goes with *hot,* not with *flowers;* but in
"hot housewarming," *house* goes with *warming.*

Constituents may be **continuous** or **discontinuous**. In
"the man did come," *did* and *come* are continuous constituents of the verbal expression. In "Did the man
come?" they are still constituents of the verbal expression,
but they are discontinuous.

Transformation, in the structural sense, is defined as
"a statement of the structural relations of a pair of constructions, treating the relation as a process." Transformation would be involved in the change from an affirmative
to a negative or interrogative sentence ("The man is
coming"; "The man isn't coming"; "Is the man coming?").
One of the various constructions (normally the affirmative sentence) is called the **input**. It is altered to produce
a variant (negative or interrogative construction), which
is called the **output**. Rules are then formulated for ob-
taining various outputs from the original input. These
rules often vary, according to the language used and the

---

[17] Here traditional terminology would describe our first example
as a "noun" or "anything that behaves like a noun," with all its
modifiers, including relative clauses, while our second example
would be defined as an "adverb" or "adverbial phrase."

circumstances. In English, to form the negative output of the affirmative input "The man is coming," we add *n't* to *is;* but to form the negative output of the affirmative input "The man walked away," we must insert *did,* add *n't* to *did,* and change *walked* to *walk* ("The man didn't walk away"). Taking French instead of English, we could start with an affirmative input "L'homme est ici" ("The man is here"). There are two alternative ways of producing an interrogative output for that type of sentence in French. One is to prefix *est-ce que* to the affirmative input ("Est-ce que l'homme est ici?"); the other is to repeat the subject after the verb in pronoun form ("L'homme, est-il ici?"). Once we have stated all the rules for changing from the affirmative to the negative, or to the interrogative, or to any other form of the sentence we may want, we have a complete transformation.

The expression **head**, or **head word**, is often applied by descriptive linguists to the center of the construction. In "the new houses now being built," *houses* is the head, and *the, new,* and *now being built* are called **attributes**.

The expression **function words** is frequently used in reference to "small words," such as English *the, a, some,* which act purely as structural markers and are frequently omitted in headlines, but whose absence can cause some confusion. In "The water is pure," the presence of the article *the* particularizes the water and restricts it to a given body of water, while in "Water is pure," the absence of an article generalizes water. It goes without saying that the use or non-use of these function words varies from language to language. In Russian and Latin, for example, there is no definite or indefinite article, and it is therefore impossible to make the distinction between particular and general that appears in English, save by the use of circumlocutions or different constructions. In English we establish a twofold distinction between what is near and what is at a distance by the use of *this* and *that.* Spanish establishes a threefold distinction between what is near the speaker (*este*), what is near the person addressed (*ese*), and what is far removed from both (*aquel*). The fact that English once had the same three-fold distinction (*this, that, yon*) pertains to historical but not to descriptive linguistics. French, by way of contrast, ordinarily makes no distinction at all; *ce livre* may mean, indifferently, "this book" or "that book."[18] There are some American Indian languages which establish a five- or sixfold distinction, using different words to indicate what is out of sight, what is altogether in the past, etc.

The advantages of the new syntactical terminology over the traditional are not altogether obvious; but it is possible that it may have wider applicability to languages of different types.

24. VOCABULARY

The descriptive linguist is interested in vocabulary from a functional rather than from an etymological or semantic point of view, both etymology and semantics being prime concerns of the historical linguist. Hence, in descriptive linguistics, the concept of the word is largely bound up with that of the morpheme, which has already been discussed. **Lexicology** is then defined as "the total stock of morphemes in the language, and their combinations."[19]

From the structural standpoint a **word** is defined as

[18] French may make a distinction, if the speaker feels the need to distinguish, by adding *-ci* or *-là* to *livre;* but in practice this occurs only in a minority of instances.

[19] Notice, however, that semantics cannot be altogether avoided by the structuralist, since the concept of the morpheme is intimately bound with meaning. Any reference to historical transformations of meaning and their causes, however, lies beyond the realm of purely descriptive linguistics.

"a segment of a sentence bounded by successive points between which pausing is possible" (the pausing does not necessarily have to take place, however). In a sentence like "The houses are being built," it is theoretically possible for me to pause after *the,* or *houses,* or *are,* or *being,* or *built;* but a pause between *hous-* and *-es,* or *be-* and *-ing* would give my utterance an illogical flavor.

The **sentence** itself is then defined as "a succession of words plus intonation morphemes," which makes the two definitions slightly circular, since "sentence" appears in the definition of "word," and "word" appears in the definition of "sentence." To exemplify both definitions at once: in "Do you want this book?" it is theoretically possible to put a pause after every word, though this is not normally done in ordinary speech. The sum total of segments between which pauses are permissible (words), plus the pitches, junctures, and intonations required by the meaning, are then said to form the sentence.

While the structural concept of a word differs from the traditional, it has the advantage of wider applicability to a larger number of language structures. Without going into either polysynthetic or highly inflexional languages, note the contrast between English "by giving him two of them" and its Italian equivalent *dandogliene due,* where five "words" of English are rendered by a single "word" in Italian. From the traditional standpoint, it would be a little difficult to decide whether *dandogliene* is a single word (as the spelling would seem to imply) or a combination of three separate words, *dando glie ne* (as indicated by the meaning). Structurally, the Italian form would be rated as a single word, since no pause is normally possible between the three components.

A distinction is made between a word that is a complete grammatical form (**lexeme**) and one that is not. The *want* that appears in "I want some water" is a lexeme. So is the *wants* in "He wants some water"; but the *want-* that is a part of the lexeme *wants* is not itself a lexeme,

even though it may coincide in form with the earlier
want. To put it another way: the first *want* is both a free
morpheme and a lexeme. The second *want-* is a free
morpheme (it could be used in isolation in a different
connection), but it is not a lexeme in this specific instance. The status of a lexeme depends upon its specific
use in a specific sentence, while the status of a free morpheme is absolute and not determined by its specific use.
The *-s* of *wants* is, of course, a bound morpheme and can
under no circumstances be a lexeme.

A concession is made in descriptive linguistics to semantics in the term **idiom**, which is defined as a word or
a group of words having a special meaning which is not
inherent to or determinable from its component parts.
White paper, for example, has in combination a special
diplomatic significance that does not appear in either
white or *paper,* and is an idiom when used in that special
diplomatic sense. But if *white paper* is used in its more
customary acceptance ("Let me have a sheet of white
paper") there is nothing idiomatic about it. "Look out"
used in the sense of "Be careful" is an idiom; it is not an
idiom if I say, "Look out the window." Idiomatic com-
posites normally have to be learned as a whole, since
there is nothing in the individual morphemes that go to
make them up to indicate the special meaning they
carry when they are combined. Idioms, of course, vary
from language to language, as exemplified by the Frenchman who stuck his head farther out of the window of
the railroad coach when his American traveling compan-
ion shouted "Look out!" because they were approaching
a tunnel. The story goes on to relate that the Frenchman,
yanked back by his coat collar, thanked the American,
but then added: "But why did you tell me to look out
when you really wanted me to look in?"

Ordinary productive suffixes which have an established
pattern of combination (like the *-ish* of *Spanish, yellow-
ish,* etc.) sometimes produce idioms when they are com-

bined in novel and unusual ways (the teen-agers' "I'll meet you five-thirtyish").

Close in nature to idioms are those expressions or forms in one language which have no precise counterpart in another, like the German *Geschwister* to include both brothers and sisters. On the other hand, English has the word *parent*, which may be used for either gender, while German *Eltern* can be used only in the plural. Spanish *padre*, which in the singular can mean only "father," may in the plural mean not only "fathers," but also "parents."

Lastly, reference may be made to two terms popularized by De Saussure and best left untranslated from his original French, *langue* and *parole*, though they are sometimes rendered as "language" and "speech."

Langue is that aspect of language which is inherited or institutional, a complete, homogeneous grammatical system used by an entire community. **Parole** is an individual's use of language to convey messages. *Langue* is independent of the individual speaker and exists, so to speak, in the abstract; this is what we mean when we speak of, say, the French language. *Parole* is peculiar to the speaker and corresponds to, say, De Gaulle's own personal use of the French language. It is fairly obvious that *langue*, being an abstraction, has realization only in someone's *parole*. One might even compare *langue* with the phoneme (an ideal, abstract entity), and *parole* with the allophone (a living, spoken, objective reality).

PART III

Descriptive Linguistics: Methodology

25. PHONEMIC AND MORPHEMIC ANALYSIS[1]

The primary concern of the descriptive linguist is the sounds and the grammatical forms of the spoken language. Hence his methodology will normally eschew written material and, particularly, pre-existing, traditional grammars. These are in part based on older and superseded stages of the language. They take the language's written form as their base of operations, referring to it all spoken-language phenomena. In any event they are seldom constructed in accordance with scientific observation and deduction.

The analytical methodology of the descriptive linguists was especially developed in connection with the study of languages of so-called "backward" groups, where there was no written form of the language, no previous attempt at grammatical description, in fact no possibility of getting at the language in any other way.

A rudimentary form of descriptive methodology is followed by laymen who acquire a foreign language by ear, directly from native speakers. Other attempts at this methodology were made by early missionaries who codi-

[1] Excellent descriptions of this methodology appear in Hockett, 102–11 and 274–76, and in Gleason, 271–311 and 65–91. The reader is referred to these works for a more extended discussion.

fied the tongues of the groups with which they came in contact into primitive grammars and vocabularies for purposes of religious instruction and Bible translation. But the earlier of these attempts were largely frustrated by the then prevailing linguistic philosophy that all languages should be made to fit into one universal mold, patterned after the structure of Greek and Latin, instead of following the pattern of the language under consideration. The contribution of the modern descriptive linguist lies in his knowledge of phonemic and morphemic principles, which permit a far more detailed and precise description of the language than can be gained by the untrained ear and hit-or-miss methods.

The descriptive linguist's work lies overwhelmingly in the field of living languages, where it is possible to secure the services of native speakers, technically known as **informants**. The desirable degree of education of the informant is a relative matter. In the case of languages of "backward" groups, the question of education does not enter. For languages of civilized groups, those informants can be selected who best represent the stratum of language that it is desired to record and systematize. If one wants to describe French as spoken by the country's most educated classes, it will be well to select highly cultured informants, such as college professors, lawyers, physicians, government employees; if one wants to record the language of the Paris slums, apaches and their gun molls will do very well; if one wants something in between, one can pick up a few bakers, butchers, and servingwomen. In any case, with the use of living native informants one has what is described as **field conditions**. These are in contradistinction to **philological conditions**, which characterize the work usually done by historical linguists, whose main sources of information are documents, inscriptions, and other non-living material.

The twin processes of **gathering** and **collation** begin with questions designed to elicit from the informant or informants how certain things are said in their language. Usually one goes from short, simple words to longer expressions and complete sentences. The answers are transcribed in some sort of phonetic transcription, the more detailed the better, or recorded on tapes or disks, or both.

Once a sufficient body of material has been gathered, the linguist's work of deduction starts. On the basis of his specialized training in phonemics, he must determine which **contrasts** or **oppositions**[2] are relevant in a given environment and which are not. He then must separate the true phonemes of the language from the allophones. By the time he is through he should have a complete picture of the phonemic structure of the language and of the allophones of each phoneme, together with clear statements of the conditions under which the allophones occur.

To exemplify: if American English, considered as an unknown and unwritten language, were to be subjected to a process of phonemic analysis, the linguist would differentiate among the phonemes by using the technique of **minimal pairs**, two words phonetically identical in all respects but one, such as *sit* and *fit*, or *sit* and *set*, or *sit* and *sip*. If the phonetic difference involves a difference in meaning, he knows that he must make provision for two different phonemes in his phonemic scheme of the language. Everything else being equal, the *s* of *sit* and the *f* of *fit* yield two altogether different meanings. Hence provision must be made for /s/ and /f/ as two separate phonemes in the American English scheme. On the other hand, he would observe a slight phonetic difference between the *p* of *pit*, that of *spit*, and that of *sip*, and would

---

[2] For the use of these terms in the phonemic sense, see pp. 50, 77. Two words identical in all respects but one are placed in contrast or opposition to each other. If the single difference makes a difference in the meaning, we have separate phonemes. If the meaning remains unchanged despite the use of one sound for the other, we have allophones of the same phoneme.

at first be in doubt whether these three similar yet different sounds constitute separate phonemes in the language. But as his samples accumulate, he would soon reach the conclusion that the sounds occur in complementary distribution, are never in contrast or opposition to one another, and may therefore be considered as allophones of a single phoneme. His ultimate phonemic scheme of the language would then indicate a phoneme /p/ with three possible allophones, occurring under specific conditions.

If the unknown tongue to be analyzed were Italian, the analyst would at first wonder whether the difference in sound between *eco* and *ecco*, or between *cade* and *cadde*, or between *ala* and *alla* were of a phonemic nature or merely variant pronunciations due to individual whim. But as soon as he realized that *eco* means "echo," while *ecco* means "here is"; that *cade* means "he falls," while *cadde* means "he fell"; that *ala* means "wing," while *alla* means "to the," he would come to the conclusion that in Italian each stressed or long consonant (which Italian orthography indicates by writing it double) is a distinct phoneme from its short or single counterpart, and that therefore his phonemic scheme of Italian must make provision for each consonant sound twice, in "single" and in "double" form.

All this sounds far simpler than it actually is. A vast number of subsidiary factors will normally enter into the ultimate decision. There is the question of phonetic similarity. Are the three *p*-sounds of American English sufficiently similar in nature and point of articulation to warrant their being considered as allophones? They are. It would be quite exceptional, though not inconceivable, for /p/, a labial, and /k/, a velar, to function as allophones of the same phoneme, in complementary distribution.[3]

[3] There are some obscure languages where this happens. Also, it happens in historical evolution, as when Latin *aqua, lingua,* with labialized velar /kw/, /gw/, turned into Rumanian *apă, limbă,* with labial /p/, /b/. But remember that the descriptive linguist is

But then note that English /n/ and /ŋ/[4] are similar in nature and are sometimes, though not always, in complementary distribution, as when the /ŋ/ sound appears in *anchor* (by reason of assimilation to the following velar), but not in *enter*. Note also that /n/ can occur initially, while /ŋ/ cannot, which would seem to point to some sort of complementary distribution. But here the determining factor in setting up /n/ and /ŋ/ as separate English phonemes is their contrast in minimal pairs, such as *kin* and *king*. *Phonetically*, Italian also has both sounds: [n] in *dente*, [ŋ] in *bianco*. But in Italian no minimal pair can be found where the two sounds are in **contrast** or **opposition**.[5] Therefore, in the Italian phonemic scheme the two sounds must be rated as allophones of the same phoneme. All of which shows that the various clues have to be studied and balanced against one another.

Numerous pitfalls in phonemic analysis are pointed out by Gleason. Among them are **over-differentiation** and **under-differentiation**, both caused by the analyst's own speech habits. An English-speaking analyst might be tempted to merge Arabic /k/ and /q/ under the heading of a single phoneme, like the English velar sounds in *kin* and *cool*,[6] though the semantic contrast between *kalb*, "dog," and *qalb*, "heart," should set him straight. On the other hand, an Arabic-speaking analyst might erroneously differentiate the single unvoiced velar plosive of English, which has separate allophones before front and back vowels (*kill* vs. *cool*) into two imaginary

---

not concerned with historical evolution, but only with the state of the language at one given time.

[4] The symbol /ŋ/, taken from the International Phonetic Alphabet, represents the sound of *ng* in *sing*.

[5] I.e., where they yield different meanings, everything else in the two words being equal.

[6] These are mere positional variants, or allophones, of a single English /k/ phoneme. The first occurs before front vowels, the second before back vowels.

English phonemes, until he noted the utter absence of
satisfactory minimal pairs.

There is also the possibility of wrong **segmentation**.
Phonetically, English *ch* of *church* and German *tsch* of
Deutsch are quite similar. But the English **neatness of
pattern**, or symmetry in the phonemic structure, seems
to call for a single phoneme. English shows a complete
series of palatals: /č/, /ǰ/, /ʃ/, /ʒ/, /ʎ/, /ɲ/;⁷ while in
the German pattern a single phoneme /č/ would stand
isolated in the palatal row, save for /ʃ/. Hence it is
preferable, though not compulsory, to interpret German *tsch* as a sequence of two phonemes, /t/ and /ʃ/.
The term **suspicious pairs** is used for pairs of sounds
which seem to be phonetically similar and hence could
be allophones of the same phoneme.

Phonemic analysis is also often troubled by the factor
of **free variation**, exemplified by *with*, which some American speakers pronounce with voiced *th* (/ð/), others
with unvoiced *th* (/θ/). In the case of certain languages
there is also the complication of **tones**, which have full
phonemic value instead of being merely suprasegmental.
Here Gleason suggests two useful tests. One is the **monotony test**, where words having the same tone are uttered
one after the other, producing a monotonous effect; if a
word with a different tone is inserted into the series, the
monotony is broken.⁸ The other is the setting up of

⁷ The IPA symbol č represents the sound of *ch* in *church;* ǰ represents the sound of *j* in *jet;* ʃ represents the *sh* of *show;* ʒ represents the *s* of *pleasure;* ʎ represents the *lli* of *million;* ɲ represents
the *ny* of *canyon.* For the last two sounds, many phoneticians prefer the composite notations *lj* and *nj*, which are more accurate for
what concerns the English sounds. Note also that many phoneticians, disregarding "neatness of pattern," prefer to treat /č/ and
/ǰ/ as affricates, or composite sounds (/t/ + /ʃ/, /d/ + /ʒ/).

⁸ In Gleason's study of Ewe, a West African language which has
three tones, high, middle, and low, various words of one syllable
were put in sequence and the native speaker was asked to pronounce them. If all the words in the series had the same tone, the
result was a monotonous, singsong effect. Where the tone of a given
word was still uncertain, it was inserted into the sequence. If it

frames, which means placing the words in juxtaposition with a series of other words, such as numerals, whose tones are known.[9]

The extensive use of tape recorders in phonemic field work has greatly simplified the analyst's labors, since it permits the objective recording of actual speech sounds to supplement a transcription often tinged with subjective features from the analyst's hearing and background. But even the tape recordings must eventually be referred to the analyst's ear and interpretation, so their main value is one of convenience.

Special reference must be made at this point to phonemic transcriptions of standard languages. While the phonetic transcription is an objective representation of the sounds, the phonemic transcription is based upon the speaker's consciousness of differences, and the distinctions he subjectively makes. This means that what is a satisfactory transcription of one local brand of a language such as English is not necessarily a hundred per cent accurate for another local variety. The vowel sound of *lot, not, pot* is, objectively and phonetically, [a] in the mouth of the average American speaker, but [ɒ] or [ɔ] in the mouth of the average British speaker.

This in turn accounts for the fact that one linguist's phonemic transcription will not always coincide with that of another linguist. Each tends to use and transcribe his own local forms of speech. To the average British linguist, and in the average British transcription, the vowel sound of *leave, feel,* etc., is represented by [i:] (a long, pure

"rhymed" in tone with the others, whose tone was known, it was assigned to that tone class. If there was a break in the monotony, it was tried with a different tone group until it fitted into the sing-song.

[9] A noun whose tone is still uncertain is coupled in turn with each of the numerals from one to six, whose tones are definitely known. It is then heard to ascend, descend, or be on the same level with each of the numerals, and can easily be assigned to its proper tone class.

vowel); to most American transcribers, it is represented by [ij] (the pure vowel sound of *bin* followed by a *y* off-glide). Most transcribers warn their readers of this unavoidable injection of their own familiar dialectal features in their transcriptions.

The process of morphemic analysis is identical with the one described above, save that the analysis bears on morphs, or possible minimal units of meaning (see p. 58), which have to be resolved into separate morphemes and allomorphs. In actual practice, phonemic and morphemic analysis often go side by side rather than in sequence, with the analyst's observations recorded separately but contemporaneously as the study progresses.

Here again, if there is a definite contrast in meaning, it is safe to assume the presence of separate morphemes. But if the two morphs convey the same meaning and are used in complementary distribution, they will be rated as allomorphs of the same morpheme. The *-ing* of *working* and the *-ed* of *worked,* conveying different meanings, are separate morphemes; but the spoken *-t* sound that appears in *worked,* the spoken *-d* sound that appears in *filled,* the vowel change from *find* that appears in *found,* even the zero change from present-tense *put* to past-tense *put,* all convey the identical past-tense meaning, and may therefore be rated as allomorphs of a single past-indicating morpheme.

Gleason reasonably suggests that a **base-form** for the grammatically significant morpheme be selected, with the other forms considered as **replacives**. With the base-form selected on the basis of frequency of occurrence, we would then set up the spoken *-d* of *filled, toyed, dallied,* as the base-form of the past-indicating morpheme, and describe the *-t* of *worked* and *stopped,* the *-id* of *ended,* the vowel change of *found,* the zero change of *put,* as replacive allomorphs.[10]

---

[10] See Section 22, Morphophonemics, footnote 13, for the difference between a replacive and a SUPPLETIVE. The latter involves a complete change of form, as when *went* is used as the past of *go*.

All sorts of morphophonemic factors, especially of assimilation and dissimilation, enter into morphemic analysis. The allomorph is often conditioned by surrounding phonemes, which are equally often themselves affected (Italian *amico*, plural *amici*, with palatalization of *c* by reason of assimilation to the front vowel of the plural-indicating morpheme *-i;* or the negative prefix *in-* of English *intransitive*, which usually becomes a spoken /iŋ/ in *incapable*, being drawn into the velar orbit by the following velar consonant, and which becomes a spoken and even written *im-* in *impossible*, because of the assimilative pull of the following labial *p*).

The final steps in analysis are the establishment of syntactical rules and the preparation of a vocabulary, both in accordance with the descriptive principles and methodology outlined above.

Syntactically, for example, the analyst must determine the form-classes of the language he is analyzing; the rules of transformation for forming such constructions as the negative and interrogative forms of a sentence; the distinctions which are inherent to the language under consideration (see Section 23, Grammatical Structure: Syntax).

From the standpoint of vocabulary, the analyst will have to draw up a list of the total stock of morphemes in the language, along with their possible combinations, determine the possible lexemes of the language; the idioms; the productive prefixes and suffixes (see Section 24, Vocabulary).

The final product of the analyst's labors will be a descriptive grammar of the language under consideration, as described under the next heading.

26. CONSTRUCTING A DESCRIPTIVE GRAMMAR

By the time the phonemic and morphemic analysis of the language under consideration is completed and the appropriate structural syntactic features have been added, the analyst has at his disposal a descriptive grammar of the language. It must be stressed that the descriptive grammar is not a "use" grammar in the ordinary school text sense of the word, but rather a reference grammar on which a use grammar can be scientifically based.

The descriptive grammar will present an exact list of all the significant phonemes in the language, with their allophones and a statement of the circumstances under which each of the latter appears. It will also give a description of the language's suprasegmental phonemes (intonation, stress, juncture). On the basis of this precise, scientifically formulated information it will be possible to construct, in presentation lessons, a series of pronunciation drills and exercises that will take into account the true phonetic and phonemic difficulties of the language, concentrating on those features which are likely to give most trouble to the learner who approaches the language from the background of another tongue. This process is often aided by presenting in the descriptive grammar parallel phonemic structures of the two languages for purposes of comparison. It is then easy to touch lightly upon those features which both languages have in common and to concentrate on points where they differ. A Spanish-speaking student of English can, for instance, be drilled on the phonemic difference between the vowel sound in *leave* and that in *live* until he has thoroughly overcome his natural tendency to merge the two into a single imaginary phoneme. Conversely, an English-speaking student of Chinese can be drilled intensively on the phonemic difference in Chinese between the *p* of *pit* and that of *spit,* which he tends to regard as a single phoneme. A student of Italian can be given intensive training in the phonemic distinction between a single and a double consonant. All this, however, will appear in the use grammar based on the descriptive grammar rather than in the descriptive grammar itself.

Since the phonemic analysis of the descriptive grammar is based squarely upon the spoken tongue, its description will be one of sounds (or phones) and their function, not a description of letters of the alphabet and what sounds they represent. It is perfectly legitimate, of course, even from the descriptive viewpoint, to bring in statements of this type: "The phoneme /e/, which we have just described with its two allophones, or positional variants, [e] and [ε], usually appears in French spelling in one of the following guises: é, è, ê, ai, ei." What the descriptive grammar will not do is to say: "French written *e* is pronounced in such and such a fashion, depending on whether it bears an acute, a grave, or a circumflex accent, or no accent mark at all." The progression is from the spoken to the written form, not the other way round.

While the phonemic transcription is normally more economical of space than the phonetic, which represents the sounds as they occur objectively, it requires a thorough knowledge of positional variants (allophones) of the various phonemes. The learner can be told: "The French phoneme /e/ has the closed allophone when it is final in the syllable, the open allophone when it is followed by a consonant in the same syllable," but that is not quite as good, from the beginner's standpoint, as a clear-cut indication of the two sounds by the use of two separate symbols, [e] and [ε]. The application of full descriptive principles to use grammars for the beginner must be circumspect, and based on circumstances and needs.

The grammatical material, both morphological and syntactical, is presented by the descriptive grammar in the same fashion. Here again, occasional comparison between the functioning of morphemes in the two languages can be useful. Among the uses of the descriptive grammar is the fact that the learner of a foreign tongue is quickly undeceived as to what he considers to be the relative ease and simplicity of his own language. Speakers of English who think that all there is to plural formation in their language is the addition of a simple -*s* or -*es* are often surprised to note the multiplicity of spoken-language allomorphs that go into English noun plural formation (/-s/, /-z/, /-iz/, vowel change, /-en/, zero), often with morphophonemic modification of the root morpheme, as in *knives* or *houses*. They are also surprised to note that, while English verbs do not have many inflectional endings, they often involve the tricky combination of numerous separate verbal free morphemes (*do, does, did, has, had, will, would, should, must*).

This process of comparison, however, does not have to appear in a descriptive grammar, which is constructed mainly for specialists, who are already aware of the problems and pitfalls.

27. CONSTRUCTING A LINGUISTIC ATLAS

The construction of linguistic atlases antedates the most modern findings in descriptivism and bears largely upon the element of vocabulary, which is rated as secondary by the descriptivists. It nevertheless follows a methodology that can only be described as descriptive, and is an excellent example of work under field conditions. Though originally put into operation by historical linguists for purposes in the main historical, it sets the pattern for practically all descriptive field work.

The linguistic atlas was primarily devised as a guide to the living dialects of a language, and arose largely as a result of the controversy between the Neogrammarians and the Neolinguists of the nineteenth century (see Section 48, The Nineteenth Century). In their attempt to prove the infinite variety of language and its lack of submission to strict norms of sound change, the Neolinguists pointed to the multiplicity of local dialects of such countries as France and Italy, and undertook to demonstrate their point by actually charting those dialects. When all was said and done, they had neither proved nor disproved their main contention, since each dialect can and should be viewed, linguistically speaking, as a separate language, subject to its own sound laws, and not at all to those of the "national" language. Once initiated, however, linguistic atlases became a powerful tool of descriptive linguistics in their own right. They cast light upon the existing language forms of a country's various localities; they are on occasion of great aid to historical linguists in figuring out what probably happened in the past, when documentary evidence is unsatisfactory or insufficient; and they supply the geolinguist with precious information concerning the status and extent of the world's languages, their availability and replaceability in given areas. Their stress upon present-day, spoken-language phenomena and their use of field techniques, however, place them squarely within the descriptive rather than the historical or the geolinguistic field.

Field workers are sent out to various selected localities of an area which has been marked for charting, with the precise mission of eliciting from local native speakers the way in which they render a carefully predetermined series of words, phrases, sentences, even concepts. (The less cultured the speakers the better, since the more educated speakers of the area are likely to be influenced by their knowledge of and respect for the national, literary language.) In the case of picturable objects, pictures are often used, so that the informant may not be influenced by the form of the word used in the question. The statements of the informants are then either transcribed in phonetic notation, or recorded on tape, or both. At the collation stage, each word, phrase, or expression is entered upon a large separate map of the area. The linguistic atlas of France, for instance, contains one separate large map for *horse*, as the word appears in spoken use in some five hundred different French localities, another map for *dog*, another for *cat*. The sum total of all the maps gives us a fair cross section of any one of the five hundred local dialects, particularly for what concerns vocabulary but also, in connection with the longer expressions, for grammatical structure. It is then perfectly possible to construct a descriptive grammar of each of those local dialects by following the principles of phonemic and morphemic analysis outlined previously.

The linguistic atlas thus acts as a ready reference work which the linguist can consult at his ease, instead of going out and doing his own field work in the locality in which he is interested. Such direct field work, however, is often done in connection with special problems.

One of the drawbacks of the linguistic atlas is that it is chronologically unstable, since the local language changes, often more rapidly than the national. Sometimes the survey is conducted again after the lapse of a certain number of years, and the new results are compared with the old, giving us a semihistorical picture of the intervening changes in the speech of a given community.

The term **linguistic geography** is applied to dialect studies based on the linguistic atlas. This is an unfortunate choice, since to most laymen the term would rather imply linguistic distribution, or what we term geolinguistics.

PART IV

Historical Linguistics: Basic Terminology

28. POINTS OF CONTACT WITH DESCRIPTIVE LINGUISTICS AND GEOLINGUISTICS

Descriptive linguistics may be described as fundamentally static. Language in general, or a particular language, is outlined as it appears at a given point of time, which is not necessarily the present.

Historical linguistics is basically dynamic. It studies language in its changes, and change across both time and space is an inherent characteristic of all language and languages. The changes occur in all divisions (phonemic pattern, morphological and syntactical structure, vocabulary), but not at a uniform rate or in accordance with a predictable pattern. These language changes depend upon general historical factors, and while they can be descriptively studied, with mere statements of what changes have occurred, they cannot be divorced from the historical events which occasioned them.

While the main function of descriptive linguistics is to describe and that of historical linguistics to outline language changes, it is often difficult in practice to keep the two separate. Practically all the terminology presented under the descriptive heading is applicable to the historical branch.

The concepts of standard language, dialect, patois, jargon, slang, enter both fields, and geolinguistics as well (see Section 16, Literary Language, National Language, Dialects, Colloquial Forms, Slang; and Section 42, Dialects and Local Variants; Class Languages). A **standard language** is the speech form which has official recognition and is used by the more educated speakers (the King's or Queen's English of Britain, also known as the Received Standard, is a good sample). Often the standard language is merely a sublimated local dialect, which at first received official recognition because it was the dialect of that part of the country where the court was situated (Parisian French), or the dialect of a group that had gained military predominance (Castilian Spanish), or the dialect of a region that held literary pre-eminence (Tuscan or Florentine Italian).

Dialects are localized speech forms, diverging to a greater or lesser degree from the standard tongue but recognizably (sometimes only through historical origin) forming a single unit with it. **Patois** refers to a highly localized dialect form, often that of a single village; the patois does not appear in written form, while the dialect often has a long and flourishing literature. **Jargon** is the specialized vocabulary of a given class or calling. Gobbledegook (also called federalese or officialese), pedagese, gangsterese are all samples. **Slang** is a substandard form, used by the less educated classes, which is widespread if not nationwide (*ain't, I laid on the bed, swell, lousy, scram* are samples); one can distinguish various degrees of slang by the names of **colloquialisms, vulgarisms, substandard speech**.

The justification for including these items under the historical heading is twofold. They are more frequently discussed by historical than by descriptive linguists; secondly, some descriptivists refuse in practice to recognize their separate existence, defining language as any existing speech form, high or low.

Specifically historical are the following terms:

Monogenesis—the theory that all languages stem from a single common ancestor.

Substratum—the underlayer of an earlier speech form used by the original inhabitants of a region, which is supposed to mix with and modify the language of incoming conquerors, as when one speaks of the Iberian and Gaulish substratum in the Latin brought by the Romans to Spain and France.

Superstratum—a kindred term; the language of incoming conquerors that gives way to the language of the conquered, but modifies it, as when the Franks and Longobards gave up their own Germanic tongues and adopted the Latin of the Roman Empire, but contributed words and perhaps phonological tendencies and even speech sounds to what later became French and Italian.

Adstratum—a term sometimes used to include both substratum and superstratum.[1]

Reconstruction—the attempt to build up a hypothetical Indo-European parent speech from a comparison of the historically attested descendants. Reconstruction can also be applied to other unrecorded languages believed to have existed, as well as to individual unattested forms of known languages, such as Latin or Gothic; *sagja or *sagwja, the hypothetical Germanic ancestor of English *say*, is not attested; reconstructed forms are usually preceded by an asterisk in linguistic works.

Sound Law (or **Lautgesetz**)—a theory to the effect that, if a certain sound change becomes operative in a given area and at a given period, the change will work

---

[1] *Languages in Contact,* a term popularized by Weinreich, is occasionally used as a quasi synonym for adstratum. However, the implication of languages in contact is rather to the effect that the two languages coexist as separate entities, even while they influence each other. Adstratum, substratum, and superstratum rather imply the disappearance of one language, even while it leaves its trace in the other.

universally, unless extraneous factors come into play.[2] Opponents of the theory point to divergent developments in words that should have developed similarly, and prefer to speak of sound-change tendencies; but supporters claim that in these cases definite factors, such as learned influences, foreign or dialectal borrowing, or analogy, caused the deviation.[3]

Analogy—the occasional and unpredictable tendency of a word or form to be pulled out of its natural orbit of development by the attraction of another word or form with which it has a real or fancied resemblance (the past tense of *help* was once *holp;* but the fact that the majority of verbs form the past by the addition of a spoken -*t*, -*d*, or -*ed* suffix rather than by change in the internal vowel caused *helped* to be created and used).

Simplification—a term often, but perhaps erroneously, used in connection with a change in a given language whereby inflectional endings are dropped and their function is taken up by additional words or other devices (the disappearance of the Latin case system and its replacement in the Romance languages by word order and prepositions; or the similar phenomenon attending the transition from Anglo-Saxon to modern English).[4]

Two branches of study, both dealing with the written form of a language as it appeared at times from which no spoken records are available, are **epigraphy** (the study of inscriptions and their interpretation) and **paleography** (the study of ancient and medieval documents inscribed on papyrus, parchment, and other soft media).

[2] E.g., Indo-European initial *p* appears in Sanskrit, Greek, and Latin as *p*, but it appears in Germanic as *f*. Compare Latin *pes, piscis, pater* with English *foot, fish, father*.

[3] For example, English *paternal*, as opposed to *fatherly*, is borrowed from the root of Latin *pater; podiatrist*, as against *foot*, is borrowed from the root of Greek *pous-podos*, while *pedal* is borrowed from the root of Latin *pes-pedis*.

[4] The question legitimately arises whether an analytical compound such as *I shall love* is "simpler" than Latin *amabō*, or whether *the book of the boy* is a simplification of *the boy's book*.

29. PHONOLOGICAL AND ANALOGICAL CHANGE

Phonetics and phonemics deal primarily with the description of sounds or phonemes in the living language spoken by living speakers. For the historical transformation of such sounds and phonemes in the past there is a terminology which is only partly applicable to descriptive linguistics.

In the historical transformation of a language it is not merely possible but customary for the phonemic pattern to change, sometimes drastically. Whether the changes occur piecemeal and are largely unrelated to one another, or whether, as some structuralists hold, the pattern is transformed, so to speak, harmoniously, as a whole, so as always to maintain some semblance of symmetry, is still an open question.

It will be noted from a mere glance at English spelling that certain phonemes which the language once had (such as the velar spirant indicated by the *gh* of *night*) have been lost, and that even the traffic rules of permissible combinations have been changed (spellings like *know* and *gnaw* indicate that English speakers once admitted such spoken combinations as *kn-* and *gn-* in the initial position, something that their descendants no longer handle with ease).

Some of the terms of descriptive linguistics come into play in historical linguistics, but with relation to changing patterns of sounds and grammatical forms. Among static (descriptive) items that often determine the nature of a given change may be mentioned **vowel quantity** (the distinction between a long and a short vowel) and **vowel quality** (degree of openness or closeness of a vowel; see p. 41).

Phenomena connected with accentuation (change

from a predominance of pitch to a predominance of stress; shift of accent from one to another syllable of the word) are often of paramount importance in historical linguistics. We have reason to believe, for instance, that many of the transformations from Latin to the Romance languages (such as the change in the stressed vowel of *tenet,* which becomes French *tient,* Italian and Spanish *tiene*) were originally due to the intensifying of the stress element in speech.

Intervocalic position for consonants, particularly plosives, as against **initial, final,** or **protected medial position** (as when *t* is preceded by another consonant) often makes for an entirely different development (note the different development of Latin intervocalic *t* in *amata,* as compared with *terra, tenet, porta.* The first becomes French *aimée,* while the others go on to French *terre, tient, porte*).

Many of the terms used as nouns in descriptive phonology assume in historical phonology the form of verbs, then go on to produce new abstract nouns: diphthong; diphthongize; diphthongization:

Diphthongization—the turning of a monophthong into a diphthong (Latin *tenet* to Romance *tient, tiene*).

Palatalization—shifting the point of articulation of a sound into the palatal zone (Latin *centum,* pronounced with the velar sound of *k,* becomes Italian *cento,* with the palatal sound of *church*).

Vocalization—turning an original consonant (usually *l*) into a vowel sound (the *l* of Latin *alba* has its point of articulation pushed farther and farther back until it turns into the *u* of French *aube,* at first pronounced as *w,* later merging with the preceding *a* to produce the modern closed *o* sound).

Labialization—turning a labialized velar (*qu, gu*) into a pure labial (*p, b*), with loss of the velar element (Latin *aqua, lingua,* to Rumanian *apă, limbă*).

Sonorization or **voicing**—turning an unvoiced consonant into its voiced counterpart (Latin *amata*, with unvoiced dental plosive *t*, becomes Spanish *amada*, with *d* pronounced at first as a voiced dental plosive, later as a voiced dental fricative; the ultimate step in this process is complete disappearance of the consonant, which we observe in the transition from Old French *amede* to Modern French *aimée*).

Processes opposite to the ones mentioned are often indicated by the prefixes *de-* or *un-*. Latin *quinque* to Italian *cinque* is a good example of **delabialization** followed by palatalization; the labialized velar *qu-* first loses its labial element and becomes *kinque;* then the velar *k*, brought into immediate contact with the front vowel *i*, is shifted forward into the palate to narrow the gap between the two points of articulation. Latin *grandem* turning into the *grant* of Old French, with an unvoiced *t* that is still heard today in such linkings as *grand homme*, is a sample of **unvoicing** of voiced consonants in the final position. Another is Latin *novem* to French *neuf*.

Nasalization is the throwing of a vowel resonance into the nasal passage in anticipation of a following nasal consonant that itself often disappears, as again illustrated by Latin *grandem* becoming Old French *grant*, modern French *grand*. **Denasalization** may also occur, as when French *bonne*, at first pronounced with nasalized *o* followed by *n*, loses the nasal quality of the vowel.

Rounding of vowels may occur, as when the *ū* of Latin *lūna*, phonetically [u:], turns into the *u* of French *lune*, phonetically [y].

Simplification of "double" consonants (Latin *communem* to Italian *comune*), and **gemination**, or doubling, of single consonants (Latin *publicum* to Italian *pubblico*, or Latin *aqua* to Italian *acqua*) may occur in the same language development, though the trend is more generally one-way (Spanish, for example, simplifies practically all Latin double consonants). Let us recall in this connection that **double consonant** is really a misleading term, borrowed from the written language. In speech, the consonant sound is merely lengthened in duration if such lengthening is possible, which is the case if the consonant is anything but a plosive. Since the plosive cannot be lengthened at its point of actual utterance, what is lengthened is the holding period of the road block before the plosive is released. This happens in languages that have true spoken "double" consonants, like Italian and Japanese. In such languages the difference between a single and a double consonant is phonemic and makes for a difference in meaning (Italian *eco,* "echo," *ecco,* "here is"; *cade,* "he falls," *cadde,* "he fell"). In drawing up a phonemic chart of Italian, each "double" consonant must be counted as a separate phoneme from its "single" counterpart. In English a double written consonant is normally purely orthographic and etymological, and makes for no phonetic or phonemic difference (*abbot, redden* would be pronounced the same, so far as the consonant sounds are concerned, even if they were spelled with single *b* and *d;* even in compound words like *unnamed* there is normally open juncture (a very brief pause of silence) between the two separately pronounced *n*'s).

Some other terms used frequently in historical linguistics:

Ablaut (or **apophony**)—the changes occurring in a vowel sound according to the position of the musical pitch in the parent language, or of the stress at a later period (English *sing, sang, sung* represent ablaut variations reflecting conditions in the parent language where the accent was on the root or on preceding or following syllables later lost). A modern example of ablaut variation is the Spanish radical-changing verb *dormir,* where *o* is retained wherever unstressed, but turns to *ue* when stressed, as in *duermo.*

Umlaut (or **metaphony**)—the fronting of a root vowel in anticipation of a front vowel in the ending, as in German *Satz,* plural *Sätze.* English plurals of the type of *foot, feet* go back to an umlaut phenomenon caused by a front vowel in an ending later lost (**fōtiz* was the original Germanic plural of *fōt;* the *ō* of the root was fronted to *ē* in anticipation of the *i* of the ending, so that by the time Anglo-Saxon appeared the form *fēt* as the plural of *fōt* was already established).

Assimilation—making two unlike sounds alike; the Indo-European *nd* indicated by Latin *spondeo* is in Germanic changed to *nn* (Anglo-Saxon *spannan,* English *span,* German *spannen;* the Cockney pronunciation of *Lunnon* for *London* and vulgar American *wunnerful* for *wonderful* are modern examples).

Dissimilation—making two like sounds unlike; Latin *peregrinum,* with two *r*'s in close sequence, changes into French *pèlerin,* with *l-r* instead of *r-r.*

Syncopation—the disappearance of an unstressed vowel, generally due to increase in stress elsewhere in the word. Latin shows such double forms as *calidus, caldus; dominus, domnus;* the second of each pair is a syncopated form. *Int'resting* for *interesting* is a present-day instance of syncopation.

Haplology—the disappearance of an entire unstressed syllable, due to the same causes as above: Latin *civitatem* to French *cité,* Italian *città;* English *till* from *until.*

Apheresis—the disappearance of an initial vowel: *mid* from *amid.*

Prothesis (or **prosthetis**)—prefixing of an initial vowel, usually before a consonant cluster of which *s* is the first element: Spanish *especial, escudo, estrella,* from Latin *specialem, scutum, stella.*

Epenthesis—the placing within the word of an extra sound, usually to facilitate pronunciation: Latin *camera* undergoes syncopation in French and becomes *chamre;* then *b* is inserted to ease the transition from *m* to *r,* and *chambre* results.

Anaptyxis—epenthesis of a vowel: French borrows

Scandinavian *knîf*, but finds it expedient to insert an
anaptyctic vowel between *k* and *n;* the result is *canif.*

Paragoge—the addition of a vowel at the end of a word:
Latin *amant* becomes Italian *aman,* but Italian, prefer-
ing vocalic to consonant endings, adds a paragogic *o,*
and *amano* results.

Rhotacism—the change of another sound, usually *l* or *s,*
to *r:* an original *blanco* becomes *branco* in Portuguese;
early Germanic *auso,* a form which appears in Gothic,
ultimately becomes *ear* in English, *Ohr* in German.

Lambdacism—the less frequent change of another
sound (usually *r*) to *l:* dialectal Tuscan *polta* for Italian
porta.

Metathesis—transposition of sounds within the word:
French *moustique* from Spanish *mosquito.*

Yod—the name of a letter in the Hebrew alphabet rep-
resenting the semivowel value of *y* (a voiced glide).
While the term **yodization** does not appear in English
dictionaries or linguistic writings (*yodisation* is, however,
used in French), it could well be coined to betoken the
process whereby a front vowel in hiatus (see below)
turns into a yod, which palatalizes the preceding consonant: Latin *vīnea,* pronounced in three syllables, with
the full vowel *e* in hiatus before *a,* turns into *vinya,* pronounced in two syllables, and ultimately becomes French
vigne, Italian *vigna,* Spanish *viña.*

Hiatus—the position wherein a vowel stands before another vowel, without an intervening consonant, and does
not form a diphthong with the following vowel, as in
naïve, Noël, or Latin *habeo.* This position calls for a slight
pause of silence (internal open juncture) between the
two vowels, each of which is to be distinctly uttered.
This causes hardship to the speaker, who must interrupt
his breath stream, then resume it; he finds it much easier
to turn the first vowel into a glide.

Parisyllabic—a term used in connection with languages
having declensional systems, to indicate nouns and ad-

jectives that have the same number of syllables in all or most of their case forms (Latin *mūrus, mūri, mūrō, mūrum,* etc.). Nouns having a shorter form in the nominative and accusative than in the other cases (Latin *pectus,* but *pectoris, pectori, pectore,* etc.) are called **imparisyllabic**.

Consonant shift (or **sound shift**, or **Lautverschiebung**) —a term used in Germanic philology to refer to the two sets of changes whereby, for instance, a primitive Indo-European root **d-nt* (Latin *dentem,* Greek *odont-,* Sanskrit *danta*) first became *t-nth* (Anglo-Saxon *tonth,* later English *tooth*); then, by a second consonant shift appearing only in High German, turned into the *z-nd* of Old High German *zand,* which ultimately became the modern German *Zahn.*

Vowel shift—often used to refer to the series of changes in the long vowels of English, which began about the time of Chaucer and ended in the Elizabethan period.[5]

Oxytone, **paroxytone**, **proparoxytone**—bearing the stress on the last, penult, and third from the last syllable, respectively.

30. MORPHOLOGICAL AND SYNTACTICAL CHANGE

A language is said to be **synthetic** when it gathers numerous units of meaning within a single word or word group, **analytical** when the separate meanings are ex-

---

[5] This shift in the original long vowels of English, which were pure vowels, led eventually to the creation of diphthongs which are still popularly labeled "long vowels" today. For example, an original Old English *bitan,* with a long *i* pronounced like the *ee* of *green,* turned into the /bajt/ heard today; *hūs,* which sounded like *hoos,* became the modern *house,* which is phonetically /haws/; *stān,* which had the *a*-sound of *father,* became *stone,* phonetically /stown/. The diphthongs in question underwent numerous intermediate stages before they reached their present phonetic form.

pressed by words that can be used in isolation (free morphemes; see p. 18). A synthetic arrangement would be
typified by *impossible* in English, *esperaré* in Spanish;
corresponding analytical arrangements would be *no can
do, I shall wait.* The extreme in analysis is offered in the
isolating languages of the Chinese type; the extreme in
synthesis by polysynthetic (incorporating) languages of
the type of some American Indian tongues or of Basque;
inflectional and agglutinative languages are strung out in
between.

It is perfectly possible for a language to change its
typology in the course of its history and pass from a synthetic to an analytic structure, or vice versa. The first
change is more common than the second, at least for the
languages with whose history we are better acquainted.
English, for example, starting out with the synthetic, inflectional structure of Anglo-Saxon, historically drops
many of its endings, replacing them with auxiliaries,
prepositions, devices of word order, etc. The transition
from Latin to Romance presents similar features, particularly for what concerns the structure of the noun.
The transition from Sanskrit to Hindi is attended by a
change from a highly inflectional to a largely agglutinative structure. From the descriptive standpoint, one
could say that the superanalytical, isolating structure dis-
plays a preponderance of free morphemes, while the
supersynthetic or polysynthetic structure shows a preponderance of bound morphemes.[6]

The mechanics of transition from synthetic to analytic
generally involve a fall of endings and a resulting merger
of declensional and conjugational forms that were once
separate. Whether this fall of endings is occasioned by a
subconscious desire on the part of the speakers to "sim-
plify" their language or is connected with an increase of

----

[6] E.g., English *I shall go,* where each of the three morphemes is
free, as against Latin *i-b-ō,* which has three bound morphemes
(see p. 18).

stress accent on other parts of the word, leading to a slurring and confusion of the endings and to their ultimate disappearance, is still a debatable issue.

There is also the question, linked with the insoluble problem of the origin of speech, whether all languages originally consisted of isolated words (free morphemes), later combined into longer words composed of bound morphemes, the separate identity of whose parts was later lost. Few present-day Frenchmen who utter the word *aujourd'hui* are conscious of the fact that it was originally *ad illum diem dē hōc diē,* so that this hypothetical process of prehistoric synthesis from analysis is at least a possibility.

Without going into the traditional grammatical terminology of Indo-European languages of the inflectional type (most of this terminology can be got from a good traditional Latin grammar), it may be worth while to refer to **declension** and **conjugation**. **Declension** is the system that appears in connection with nouns, adjectives, and pronouns of the Indo-European languages, whereby the form of the word changes in accordance with its function in the word group, as well as with other subsidiary concepts, such as number and grammatical gender. **Conjugation** is the system of similar changes occurring in verbs, in accordance with factors of person, number, gender, tense, voice, and mood. A **paradigm** is an example of a declension or conjugation, showing a word in all its possible inflected forms (e.g., *boy, boy's, boys, boys'*).

31. LEXICAL CHANGE: DERIVATION, COMPOSITION, COINAGE, BORROWING

The normal tendency of vocabulary is to grow and multiply. This is due to the growth and multiplication of human activities in the course of history. New objects, qualities, actions, and concepts demand names for themselves as they appear, and these names are supplied in a variety of ways.

There is also, though to a lesser degree, the possibility of loss of words. As an object, concept, or action becomes obsolete, the word that betokens it may also undergo **obsolescence**, until it disappears from use and survives only in the dictionary under the label of **archaism**. This happened to Middle English *yclept* and *hight;* many Anglo-Saxon words have disappeared even from the dictionary, as have numerous Elizabethan words, such as *begeck*. It is quite safe to assert, however, that for every word that becomes obsolete and disappears ten new words spring up.

The creation of new words falls under several distinct headings:

Derivation is the formation of a new word by taking an existing root (formant, or free morpheme), and combining it with prefixes and suffixes (bound morphemes). Examples are *childish* from *child, befog* from *fog*. The new words formed in this fashion are **derivatives** of the earlier words. The **augmentatives**, **pejoratives**, and **diminutives** much favored by some languages are for the most part the result of derivation (Spanish *hombrón,* "big man," from *hombre;* Italian *libraccio* "bad book," from *libro;* English *lambkin* from *lamb*).

Composition is the putting together of two roots (or free morphemes): *railroad* out of earlier *rail* and *road;* Italian *ferrovia* out of *ferro* and *via; breakfast* out of *break* and *fast*). Here **compound** words result.

Back-formation (occasionally called by its German name, **Rückbildung**) appears when a word is formed from another by cutting off a real or supposed suffix (*peddle* from *peddler, buttle* from *butler,* French *cri* from *crier*). This change normally involves the transformation of one part of speech into another (noun to verb, verb to noun, etc.). One could, by exercising the imagination, form the verb *to rambunct* from the adjective *rambunctious.*

Shortening is the cutting down of a word (*mike* from *microphone*), often with the creation of a new meaning (*cab* from *cabriolet, Miss* from *Mistress, mend* from *amend*). Akin to this process is that whereby alphabetic abbreviations are used as regular words (*M.C.,* or *emcee,* for *master of ceremonies; C.B.'s,* or *seabees,* for *construction battalions; Anzac* for *Australia New Zealand Army Corps*).

Coinage is the creation of a word out of thin air, so to speak, often by a known individual whose creation meets with favor (Gelett Burgess' *blurb*). Sometimes the coinage is really a blend of two pre-existing words, like *smog* (*smoke* and *fog*), *motel* (*motor* plus *hotel*), or Clare Boothe Luce's *globaloney* (earlier, the term **portmanteau words** had been devised for some of Lewis Carroll's creations). Equally often the coinage is of the **echoic** or **onomatopoetic** variety (imitating or symbolical of a sound heard in nature: *fizz, tick-tack, meow, buzz*).

Functional change, a process much used in English (*contact* used as a verb), far less in some other languages, where the parts of speech are recognizable by their form, adds to the vocabulary only in its operation, not in its word stock. Here an existing word, previously used in only one grammatical function, acquires, without change in form, the function of a different part of speech. However, the various functions are still distinguished by the behavior of the word (in *mail* used as a noun, there is a characteristic *-s* plural; if the word is used as a verb, it will take on such characteristic endings as *-s, -ed, -ing;* if used as an adjective in *mailbox,* it will be invariable).

The last but largest source of vocabulary growth is **borrowing** from other languages. Some languages take more from their neighbors, some less, but all take something. The vocabulary of English is less than twenty-five per cent of native Anglo-Saxon stock, and over seventy-

five per cent borrowed, from the Scandinavian of the
Danes, the French of the Normans, the Latin and Greek
that had begun to infiltrate the tongue of the Anglo-
Saxons even before they reached the British shores, and
have continued to infiltrate English throughout the rest
of its history down to the present; as well as from many
languages, European, Asian, African, American Indian,
with which English speakers have had contact.

In borrowing, two processes are possible. The borrowing language may take a word and adapt it to its own
sound-and-form scheme, as when Old French *verai*
("true"; modern French *vrai*) is turned into *very;* in this
case we have a **loan word**. Or the borrowing language
may literally translate into native words the separate constituents of the foreign word, in which case we get a
loan translation. English *expression,* taken directly from
Latin *expressio,* is a loan word; but German *Ausdruck,*
from the same Latin source, is a loan translation.

Contamination or *blending* occurs when two words
from different sources are blended into a single word;
this happened when Germanic *hoch* mixed with Latin
altum (both words meaning "high"), to produce the
halt of Old French which later became *haut.*

The process of **semantic change** (change in a word's
meaning) may enrich the vocabulary to the extent that
the old meaning stays on along with the new. This happens in the case of *liberal,* where the old meaning "de-
sirous of freedom from excessive government" is confused with a more recent "advocating more government
control in private affairs." More frequently, the old meaning drops out of circulation, as when *silly,* originally
"soulful" (cf. the German cognate *selig,* "blessed"), gradually shifts over to "foolish" (**pejoration** of meaning); or
nice (from Latin *nescius* and French *niais*), originally
meaning "ignorant," "foolish," acquires pleasant connota-
tions (**enhancement** or **amelioration** of meaning).

Additional terms connected with vocabulary change are:

Cognates—words in two different languages that have a common origin, though not necessarily identical meaning at the present time: English *rent* and French *rente* ("income"), or English *knight* and German *Knecht* ("serf").

Doublets—two or more words stemming from the same original word, showing different stages of popular or learned development, like *frail* and *fragile, bishopric* and *episcopacy*. **Popular development** means that the word has been in spoken use from the time of its inception and has undergone all the sound transformations normal to the language. **Learned development** means that the word has been taken, for scholarly or literary use, from the classical vocabularies and adapted to the borrowing language with a minimum of change. Some words, described as **semilearned**, show arrested development: Latin *spiritum,* carried out to its normal French outcome, should have given *éprit* or *épri;* as a fully learned word, it should have given *spirite;* the *esprit* that actually appears in modern French shows that the word went through normal popular language transformations down to the fourteenth century, then "froze."

Popular (or **folk**) **etymology**—the process whereby the popular mind creates a false though plausible association: English, borrowing French *écrevisse,* turns it into *crayfish* and even *crawfish; surloin,* meaning "above the loin," is turned into *sirloin* on the basis of an altogether spurious account to the effect that a king liked it so well that he knighted it.

Overcorrection—the process of the mind that leads some people to say "between you and I" because they are self-conscious about "it's me," or "he spoke with you and I" because they fear the social opprobrium attached to "you and me never went there."

PART V

Historical Linguistics: Methodology

32. WRITTEN RECORDS

It is difficult to establish a chronological priority between descriptive and historical linguistics. The former, in its attention to the nature and problems of language in general, may be said to have its roots in the speculations of the ancient Greek philosophers regarding the nature of language. For what concerns its other aspect, that of the description of individual languages, it goes back to the early efforts of Chinese, Indian, and Greek grammarians. But the philosophers, in addition to philosophizing about the nature of language, also speculated as to its origin, and this activity may be styled embryonic historical linguistics.

Throughout antiquity and the Middle Ages the two branches of linguistics, if we wish to use that term, operated side by side. On the descriptive side may be ranged grammars, manuals for the instruction of pilgrims and travelers to foreign lands, and statements concerning the universality of grammar and grammatical concepts. On the historical side are the legends concerning the origin and evolution of languages, and the earliest attempts to classify languages into groups. Needless to say, what went on was done for the most part without the benefit of either accurate information or a method that could in any way be described as scientific.

When the scientific procedures of observation and deduction finally reached the field of language, around the end of the eighteenth century, the historical aspect of language quickly took the upper hand. In a sense it seemed to be more of a factual procedure to investigate a language's growth and evolution on the basis of historically attested documentation than to worry about the principles that might underlie all language. Also, that portion of descriptive linguistics which appeared practical at the time (the term descriptive linguistics did not yet exist) seemed well taken care of by existing grammars and dictionaries of a highly normative, prescriptive type. The stress upon the written aspect of language was everywhere paramount. The spoken language was viewed as a fleeting, deceptive thing, and that part of it which was stable and worth knowing about was consigned to writing. It is therefore not surprising that the original steps in scientific linguistics were taken on the historical and written-language side. The two main procedures of historical linguistics, the comparative method and the method of internal reconstruction, are overwhelmingly based on the use of written documents. By its very nature, historical linguistics depends on written material as much as descriptive linguistics depends upon the utterances of living speakers.

The written materials show a multitude of forms. There are inscriptions carved on stone, on rocks, on mountainsides. There are clay tablets inscribed with wedge-shaped instruments, and wax tablets inscribed with a stylus. There are documents on papyrus, parchment, paper, written with a brush, quill, pen, or pencil. There are typewritten and printed pages. All serve as records of human thought, but with one essential difference. While some written records, which are basically picture writing, bypass the spoken language and attempt to symbolize thought and experience directly, others use speech as an intermediary. Pictographic, ideographic, or logographic writing, as it appears in modern Chinese, seems at first glance to have no connection whatsoever with the spoken language, since the written symbols do not purport to convey spoken-language sounds. They do, nevertheless, represent spoken words, in the order in which they would normally be placed in speech. This means that some information concerning the spoken tongue, even if it is only of a syntactical nature, is conveyed by logographic writing. Once we have the word-for-word translation of a string of Chinese symbols, we know the order in which Chinese would arrange its words in speech.

The syllabic-alphabetic writing common to the greater part of the world goes much further. It endeavors to represent, more or less perfectly, the spoken sounds of the language, and to convey information not merely on how the words should be arranged but on how they should sound.

It has already been pointed out (see Section 12, Writing) what drawbacks are inherent in using written forms as testimony of living speech. The historical linguist, while he uses all written material at his disposal, must forever guard against the tendency to accept its testimony at its face value. On the other hand, it is possible to push skepticism too far. In the case of any script based on syllabic or alphabetic principles, we can safely assume that there was in origin, making due allowance for ignorance of modern phonemic principles on the part of the constructors, the intention of portraying faithfully, and by a symbol-for-sound or symbol-for-syllable correspondence, the actual sounds of the spoken language. It is the business of the historical linguist to find out whether the latter changed while the former remained fixed, and to what extent the two ultimately diverged.

The quasi-cryptographic techniques used for deciphering an unknown script, determining whether it is logographic, syllabic, or alphabetic, and transcribing it, are in a field by themselves.[1] Once the transcription is effected, the work of interpreting it from the standpoint of meaning begins. Last comes the correlating of the text with the probable speech habits of the group that produced it.

The problems are enormously different in the cases of the different languages, and so are the procedures used to solve them. One may cite a few popularly known examples. In the case of the Rosetta Stone, which gave us our key for ancient Egyptian, the investigators had at their disposal three parallel texts, one in Egyptian hieroglyphic characters (normally used on stone), another in a more cursive version of the same characters, generally appearing on papyrus, the third in Greek. Greek being known, it was only a matter of time before the secret of the Egyptian characters was revealed (actually, it took more than two decades). First step in decipherment was to isolate the characters appearing in royal names, readily identifiable because they were enclosed in *cartouches*, and transcribing them with the aid of their Greek equivalents.

Etruscan, a language written in an easily decipherable alphabet, which is the direct ancestor of the Roman, has not yet been properly interpreted because of the lack of a satisfactory bilingual inscription. Whatever the internal reconstructors may say, it helps mightily to know what the message means!

When we come to later documentation, such as Roman inscriptions and Vulgar Latin dated documents on parchment, the problem shifts. Here it is normally easy enough to figure out the transcription and the meaning. The basic problem is to what extent the inscription or document

---

[1] Two fascinating works describe the techniques used in deciphering the scripts of unknown languages. They are: J. Friedrich, *Extinct Languages* (Philosophical Library, New York, 1957), and P. E. Cleator, *Lost Languages* (John Day, New York, 1959).

reflects the spoken tongue of the period. Does our mass of inscriptional and documentary evidence give us a true picture of the evolution of Latin toward and into the Romance languages? Here the testimony of the documents must be weighed against the known starting point and finishing point of each word and form, and our pieced-together knowledge of what went on in between.

One of the fascinations of linguistics, particularly of the historical variety, is its similarity to detective work, the picking up and use of clues, the stringing together of bits of evidence. In linguistics, the mystery often remains unsolved, as it does in crime detection. But there are rules of evidence and methods for the proper use of clues, as will appear later.

33. THE COMPARATIVE METHOD

Where full documentary evidence is lacking, there is another possible procedure which came into vogue at the time of the great historical linguists of the late eighteenth and early nineteenth centuries (Jones, Bopp, Rask, the Grimm brothers). Basically, the comparative method consists in laying side by side the earliest attested forms at our disposal of various languages we suspect are related, and examining them in comparison. From this examination two things should result: the degree of relationship among the various languages thus examined, if any; and the form most likely to have existed in the common ancestor from which they all supposedly sprang. It can, by the way, be rather safely assumed that languages that show sufficient similarity in their grammatical structure and basic vocabulary, and which draw closer together the farther back they are pushed in time, all stem from a common ancestor.

The picture looks something like this:

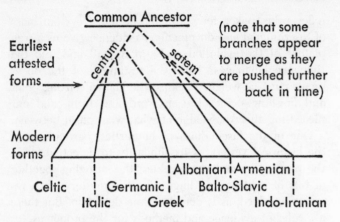

(Reverse the picture to get the methodological procedure instead of the historical progression.)

When we lay side by side, as the early nineteenth-century historical researchers did, forms from the early languages of a group suspected of being related (Sanskrit, Greek, Latin, Gothic, early Slavic, early Celtic), it quickly becomes obvious that these languages have two things in common: a basic grammatical structure and a basic primitive vocabulary. One more thing becomes clear from a comparative study of numerous words containing a given phoneme: there is among these languages a phonological correspondence, whereby what appears, say, as an initial *p* in some of them appears as an initial *f* in others, as an initial *h* somewhere else, and as an initial blank elsewhere.

This permitted the historical linguists to set up charts of regular phonological correspondences among the languages and to predict with some degree of assurance that if initial *p* appears in the Sanskrit, Greek, Latin, and Slavic word, there will appear an initial *f* in the Germanic, *h* in Armenian, and the complete fall of the initial phoneme in Celtic. Outside of its value as evidence of intimate relationship among languages later labeled *en bloc* Indo-European, these charts also permit some speculation as to what the original parent language may have been like. By taking a cross section of the grammatical structures, particularly where they largely coincided, of the vocabulary, and of the predominance of one phoneme in the chart of correspondences, the researchers were able to reconstruct, at least hypothetically, the appearance and forms of the parent language, of which no written records were extant. Comparison may therefore be said to lead to **reconstruction**, which is in itself a technique and a method.

By the same token, however, the comparative method demonstrated that, while there was an intimate relationship among a large number of languages, others were seemingly excluded. Although English, German, Scandinavian, the Romance languages, the Slavic tongues, the languages of Persia and northern India, Greek, Albanian, Armenian, and certain other tongues that underwent extinction at an early date clearly fell within the Indo-European group, no membership in the family was demonstrable for Hungarian, Finnish, Turkish, Arabic, Hebrew, Chinese, Japanese, and a multitude of other tongues. But many of these seemed themselves to form separate language families, subject to similar laws of comparison. Side by side with the Indo-European family, there were soon set up other families—the Hamito-Semitic (ancient Egyptian, Coptic, modern Berber, for the Hamitic sub-branch; ancient Akkadian, Phoenician, modern Hebrew, Arabic, Amharic, for the Semitic); the Ural-Altaic (Hungarian, Finnish, Estonian, for the Uralic or Finno-Ugric sub-branch; Turkish, Mongol, Uzbek, Tungus, Manchu, for the Altaic).

In this fashion it became possible to classify genetically a majority of the large and important languages of the world, both past and present. Some languages failed to respond to the comparative method, notably the languages of backward groups that did not possess a written form and a historical tradition. But even here, working largely by a purely descriptive methodology, the specialists have of late managed to make surprising progress in both classification and reconstruction, so that today a much better understanding exists of the grouping and past history of American Indian and African Negro languages than it seemed possible to hope for a century ago.

34. THE GENETIC CLASSIFICATION: INDO-EUROPEAN AND NON-INDO-EUROPEAN LANGUAGES

What results primarily from the comparative method is, obviously, a classification and affiliation of languages according to genetic lines. It was the comparative method that permitted the historical linguists to determine with certainty that such languages as Armenian and Hittite should be classed as Indo-European, despite the vast amount of change and mixing they had undergone. It is the comparative method that permits the linguist today to assert that English is an Indo-European language of the Germanic branch and not, as many educated laymen believe, a mixture of Germanic and Romance.

Perhaps the first fruit of comparative research was to permit the segregation of languages of the Indo-European family from others, which were later determined to fall into several family classifications of their own. In the Indo-European field, where similarity of basic grammatical structure and basic vocabulary combined with regular schemes of sound-correspondences to establish basic kinship, it was quickly observed that the eight branches that survive in modern times (Celtic, Germanic, Italic, Greek, Albanian, Balto-Slavic, Armenian, Indo-Iranian) seemed to subdivide themselves into two major groups by reason of a special phonetic difference. Celtic,

Germanic, Italic, and, generally, Greek and Albanian display, under certain circumstances, velars, and are joined in this by extinct Tokharian, while Balto-Slavic, Armenian, and Indo-Iranian show sibilants in the same positions (a simple example of this is the *centum* of Latin, *hekaton* of Greek, *cet* of Irish, *hundred* of English [in English, the initial *h* represents the Germanic outcome of an original *k*-sound]; as against the *sto* of Slavic, the *šiṁtas* of Lithuanian, the *çata* of Sanskrit, the *satem* of Avestan). This led to a further classification of Indo-European into **centum** and **satem languages,** with an assumption of a prehistoric division of the original speakers of Indo-European into two main groups, an eastern and a western. Although this theory had to be revised later, when Tokharian, a geographically eastern Indo-European language, was discovered to belong to the *centum* group, the subdivision still remains, as it supplies a convenient basis for classification.

Similar phenomena, brought out by comparison, in which two or more groups share a given feature to the exclusion of others, have given rise to other theories. There is, for example, the theory of a Celtic-Italic unity continuing beyond the point of separation of the western languages, based upon the fact that both groups are subdivided into "*p* and *q* languages."[2] Similar phenomena have lent themselves to the formulation of theories of a Germanic-Slavic period of continued unity, and even of a split in the Italic group, with Oscan and Umbrian showing features in common with Germanic, which would lead Latin and Faliscan to form the Italic group all by themselves, with the possible addition of Sicel. But definite conclusions seem unwarranted by the available evidence, though the theories form interesting topics of discussion.

[2] In the Italic group, Latin has *quis, quīnque,* but Oscan has *pis, pumpe,* for "who" and "five"; in the Celtic group, Irish has *cuig, ceathair,* but Welsh has *pump, pedwar,* for "five" and "four."

Lately the comparative method has been largely responsible for the attribution of the Minoan so-called Linear B inscriptions to the Greek subfamily, with the attendant supposition that they represent a much earlier variety of Greek (roughly, 1400 B.C.) than the Homeric poems (c. 800 B.C.), which had hitherto been looked upon as our earliest recorded samples of Greek. As new discoveries come to light they are subjected to the comparative method, and new theories are formulated on the basis of the outcome of the comparison. Sometimes the new evidence supports an earlier unproved theory (as in the case of Kurilowicz's study of the Hittite laryngeals, supporting the earlier theory of De Saussure to the effect that all Indo-European roots show the pattern consonant-vowel-consonant); sometimes it has the opposite effect.

Among all the language families the Indo-European is the one that has received by far the greatest attention, and in which the most definite conclusions have been reached. For this there are two good reasons: one is the availability of early written records, permitting extensive comparative studies; the other is in the nature of the interest that attaches to the language group that has the most extensive body of speakers (about half of the world's population speaks languages of the Indo-European family), and that has made the most far-reaching contributions to the world's civilization.

A very close runner-up, in antiquity of records (in fact, its records go farther back than those of the Indo-European family) and in contributions to civilization, but not in numerical strength, is the Hamito-Semitic (together with a third sub-branch, Kushitic, spoken in Ethiopia and nearby regions). Here the Hamitic branch is represented by ancient Egyptian and by modern Coptic and Berber (among the Berber dialects in use today are the Tamashek of the Touaregs, the Shilh and Kabyle of North Africa, the now extinct Guanche of the Canary

Islands). It is believed that at one time Hamitic languages covered all of North Africa and were spoken by the ancient Numidians and Libyans, until they were partly replaced by the Semitic languages imported first by the Phoenicians (the Punic of Carthage) and later by the Arabs. The Semitic branch of the family includes such distinguished ancient members as Akkadian (the tongue of the Babylonians and Assyrians); Phoenician, with its Carthaginian offshoot, Punic; Hebrew and the related languages of the Old Testament region (Aramaic or Syriac, Moabite, etc.); Arabic; and the Amharic and Tigre of Ethiopia, originally imported from South Arabia. Here again, by reason of the abundance of historical records, the comparative method has permitted a relatively precise classification and description, and Hamito-Semitic philology, spurred by general historical interest, is practically on a par with Indo-European.

For other language families, historical studies are more difficult. There is only one family, the Sino-Tibetan, whose antiquity and civilization are established as at least on a par with Indo-European and Hamito-Semitic. But here the nature of the written language, which has no direct link with sounds, but only with concepts, is a powerful deterrent to comparative and historical studies. Yet the ingenuity of researchers in the field has led to some sort of reasonable reconstruction of the evolution of Chinese and its related major languages, Thai, Burmese, and Tibetan, largely through the evidence of rhyming dictionaries and borrowings in Japanese and Korean. Something similar ought to be possible for Japanese-Korean, but little has materialized to date. The languages of the Uralic and Altaic families show relatively late records, as do the Caucasian tongues, the Malayo-Polynesian languages of Indonesia, the Philippines, Madagascar, Samoa, New Zealand, and Hawaii, while for the Dravidian family of southern India the evidence is still somewhat obscure. The written-record situation becomes almost hopeless in the case of American Indian, African Negro, native Australian, and Papuan languages. To this paucity of written evidence must be added the lack of interest, displayed until recently, in the languages of groups that have contributed little or nothing to Western civilization —which, again until recently, and rightly or wrongly, was considered paramount.

Despite the priority of historical linguistics in the field of linguistic research, and the very solid progress made in the course of the last two centuries, an enormous amount of work remains to be done, even in the best-explored fields. Discovery of new written-language evidence goes on all the time, and as the new evidence comes to light the comparative method is brought into play and leads to the revision of numerous tentative hypotheses. Where written records are unavailable, the comparison of living languages is often of tremendous value, and it is here that the descriptive and historical methodologies enter into the most intimate and fruitful collaboration.

35. THE METHOD OF INTERNAL RECONSTRUCTION

Internal reconstruction is normally used in combination with the comparative method, wherever possible. But there are cases where no comparison is available. In Etruscan research, for example, linguists have been able, without benefit of a bilingual Rosetta Stone or of a kindred language, to determine with some degree of assurance, from the way words are used in Etruscan itself, which are used as nouns, which as verbs or adjectives, and even to figure out a tentative scheme of declensions, case endings, and verb endings.[3] This still does not cast

[3] See A. Trombetti, *La lingua etrusca*, Firenze, 1928; M. Pallottino, *La lingua etrusca*, Firenze, 1936; M. Pei, "Etruscan and Indo-

upon the language the light that would be there if the meaning of the words were known, but it is at least a beginning.

Sometimes internal reconstruction and internal history are ingeniously put to work even in connection with obscure points in some of the better-known languages. The quantity of the *e* in Latin *lectus* and Latin *tēctus* is not revealed by either the conventional Roman spelling, which seldom gives indication of vowel length, or by the scansion of Latin verse, which normally solves our doubts on this point. Latin scansion goes by quantity, but it is the quantity of the syllable, not of the vowel, that counts (a syllable is long if it contains a long vowel, but also if it contains a short vowel followed by one or more consonants in the same syllable). The Romance development, however, shows French *lit* and Italian *letto* with open *e*, and these outcomes normally occur if Latin *e* is short; but French *toit* and Italian *tetto* with closed *e*, outcomes which are normal when Latin *e* is long. We are therefore confidently able to state that Latin *lectus* had a short *e*, Latin *tēctus* a long *e*. It would be possible to verify this conclusion by comparing the Latin words with cognates in the other Indo-European languages, but that would involve the comparative method, whereas our problem is solved by the internal evidence of Latin and its descendants alone.

Internal reconstruction was used by De Saussure in positing a second vanished consonant for Indo-European roots that exceptionally appeared with a single consonant (the normal pattern of such roots is consonant-vowel-consonant). Later, with the discovery of Hittite, an extinct member of the Indo-European group, the reflexes of the vanished consonants were found, attesting the correctness of the earlier hypothesis.

European Case Endings," *Studies in Romance Philology and Literature,* Chapel Hill, 1963.

36. GLOTTOCHRONOLOGY AND LEXICOSTATISTICS

Here we have a methodology that purports to tell us at what point in history two related languages diverged, by taking a cross section of their vocabularies as they appear today, charting the proportion of words still held in common, with more or less identical meanings, and of words that differ, and then, through a somewhat complicated mathematical calculation, establishing the length of time it would take to effect the difference.

The trouble with this methodology is that it is far too subjective and inaccurate. To begin with, what represents a reasonable cross section of vocabulary, and who is to determine what types of words shall be included and which excluded? Secondly, what ground do we have to assume that the differences actually correspond to a time schedule, unless these same vocabulary segments are compared all through the history of the two languages? Word meanings are notoriously unstable; if the same word continues to exist in the two languages, what degree of semantic change shall we accept as constituting a difference sufficient to permit us to say that they no longer correspond and are to be counted in the minus rather than in the plus column? Add to this that the compilers of lexicostatistics normally display a deplorable ignorance of the languages they are dealing with and of their historical development as well as their present status.[4]

The stage of civilization achieved at the time of separation is materialistically and systematically ignored. It is, for example, a commonplace that there is far greater agreement in meaning of words among the Romance

[4] See my review of Lehmann, *Historical Linguistics*, in *Modern Language Journal*, March 1963.

than among the Germanic languages, simply because the former have a common background of achieved Roman civilization, while the latter parted company when still at the barbarous level. The result is that *pedicure*, or some similar form, will be common to all the Romance languages, while German *Fusspflege* is meaningless to the English speaker, despite the fact that he has in his language the etymological equivalents of the German elements, *foot* and *ply*.

There would be a way of handling this methodology in scientific fashion, but it would involve a detailed comparison of all features of the two or more languages, phonological, morphological, and syntactical as well as lexical.[5] If this precise methodology were applied, we would have as numerical coefficients the exact degrees of divergence of one language from another. We would be able to establish, for instance, that Sardinian diverges from Classical Latin far less than Rumanian does; we would know the precise degree, expressed in numerical terms, of the divergence of each of the two from the parent language; and we would even have at our disposal the precise degree of present relationship between the two modern varieties. These percentages could then perhaps be worked out on the basis of known historical facts so as to reflect chronological factors. But so long as the methodology is applied, as it has been in the past, by the hit-or-miss method of fastening upon one or two phenomena that happen to catch the fancy of the individual linguist, while he completely overlooks all other phenomena, it will not serve any purpose save that of arousing controversy. Glottochronology and lexicostatistics are merely the latest manifestations of a basically unscientific methodology.

[5] See Pei, "A New Methodology for Romance Classification," *Studies in Romance Philology and Literature,* Chapel Hill, 1963.

PART VI

Geolinguistics: Basic Terminology and Problems

37. THE FUNCTION OF GEOLINGUISTICS

Descriptive linguistics devotes itself basically to the study of language in the abstract and to the description of specific languages in their phonemic, morphemic, syntactical, and lexical features. Historical linguistics deals with the evolution of language and languages, and the reconstruction of unattested parent languages on the basis of a comparison of the features of recorded descendants. Neither of the two traditional linguistic branches has for its specific function the study of the languages of the present-day world, their relation to geography, their distribution, or their significance from a political, economic, and cultural standpoint.

This situation is reflected in the manner in which these items are treated in existing manuals of descriptive and historical linguistics. A few pages, usually contained in a single chapter, are devoted to an enumeration of speakers of present-day languages and their geographical distribution; or the information may be scattered among various chapters as something coincidental and secondary, either to the structure of the languages themselves or to their historical evolution. Seldom if ever is any mention made of those characteristics which are of the greatest practical importance, not merely for the technician of linguistics, but for the average educated layman.[1] The subject of global linguistics is seldom if ever treated in ordinary language courses in high school or college, which take up languages in isolation and center their attention on grammatical and literary features. Therefore the average educated layman emerges from his higher studies either with a distorted and exaggerated sense of the importance of the one or two or three foreign languages he may have studied, or with complete ignorance of the role played by the various languages in the world of today.

That this could be the case at a time when nations, particularly our own, led a life of relative isolation is

[1] Taking seven representative works in the fields of descriptive and historical linguistics, here are the proportions of number of pages devoted to what may be even in small part properly described as geolinguistics to the total contents of the works: L. BLOOMFIELD, *Language* (1933): 31 pages out of 564 (pp. 57-73, "Languages of the World," with some figures for speaking populations; pp. 281-96, "Written Records"). L. H. GRAY, *Foundations of Language* (1939): 0 or 123 pages out of 530 (the figure of 123 is attained if one chooses to view as geolinguistic material of sorts pp. 295-418, dealing with the Indo-European and the non-Indo-European languages; but while these are genetically and structurally classified and described, nothing is said about their present-day status or speaking populations). E. H. STURTEVANT, *An Introduction to Linguistic Science* (1947): 0 pages out of 173. C. HOCKETT, *A Course in Modern Linguistics* (1958): 22 pages out of 621 (pp. 539-49, "Writing"; pp. 587-98, "Appendix of Language Names"); no figures or present-day data. H. A. GLEASON, *Introduction to Descriptive Linguistics* (revised edition, 1961): 32 pages out of 503 (pp. 408-38, "Writing Systems" and "Written Languages"; pp. 457-79, "Some Languages and Language Families"); no figures or present-day data. W. LEHMANN, *Historical Linguistics* (1962): 33 pages out of 295 (pp. 17-50, "Genetic Classification of Languages"); no figures or present-day data. J. P. HUGHES, *The Science of Language* (1962): 71 pages out of 305 (pp. 73-144, "The World's Languages," "Language and Writing"); some figures and geolinguistic data, particularly in the first of the two chapters mentioned. Since our seven works have been arranged in order of chronological appearance, it is of interest to note that only the earliest and the most recent contain material that fully coincides with our criteria of geolinguistics.

understandable. It is not understandable in the world of the late twentieth century, with its extremely rapid and widespread means of communication and transportation, its cultural and commercial interchanges, its precarious political situations which no longer affect a single country or area but are reflected in the far regions of the earth. It is no longer conceivable in the present-day world that a cultured layman should continue to believe that Spanish is the language of Brazil,[2] or wonder whether a newspaper he sees on a newsstand is printed in Russian or in Polish.[3] There is crying need for a form of instruction that will acquaint students of language with at least a knowledge of what major languages appear over the globe, where, by whom and by how many they are spoken, what their implications are in terms of political, economic, and cultural developments. Without endeavoring to turn the student into a speaker of all major languages, something that is manifestly impossible, this type of study should at least acquaint him with their outstanding spoken and written features, for purposes of identification if nothing else.

This highly practical type of information forms the basis of geolinguistics in its more elementary reaches. It is at least as important for the college graduate to know that Portuguese is spoken in Brazil, that Chinese, in its various dialects, has over six hundred million speakers, that German and Russian, more than French or English, can now be used as substitute languages in Hungary and Czechoslovakia, as to know the difference between a sound and a phoneme, or to know that Rumanian is de-

[2] A magazine ad with a picture purporting to show Brazilian scenes has one of the natives exclaiming *"Bueno!"* Another, dealing with Portugal, labels the local bull ring *Plaza de Toros*. A large prize was won on a quiz program by a contestant who was the only one to know that Portuguese, not Spanish, is the language of Brazil.

[3] I was asked this question by a very learned colleague whose scholarly attainments include a thorough knowledge of Latin, Greek, French, German, and Italian.

scended from Latin, and Latin in turn from Indo-European.

In its more complex and scientific reaches, geolinguistics goes in detail into the languages of the various areas of the earth, how they can be utilized or replaced, what they represent from the practical viewpoint of the military man, administrator, scientist, technician, missionary, or Peace Corpsman. By reason of the highly flexible mobility of these and other classes, it is not sufficient to give them a crash program in the languages of a single area.[4] They must have some knowledge of other areas to which they may be suddenly shifted. Above all, there should be available detailed studies and statistics on the languages, literacy, and educational status of the various areas of the world, with trained geolinguists who keep abreast of the often rapid changes in the field. This information is far more technical than appears on the surface and cannot be acquired overnight. It does not follow, save in a very indirect way, from a study of either descriptive or historical linguistics, but forms a special field of its own.

While some of the terminology of geolinguistics coincides with that of descriptive or historical linguistics, there are a good many terms which seldom appear in traditional linguistic works.

An **indigenous language** is the native, popularly spoken tongue of a given area, such as Bengali in northeastern India and East Pakistan, or Navajo on the Navajo Reservation. It may or may not coincide with the **national** or **official language**. The former is a language which is nationwide, like English in the United States, or which the national government is endeavoring to install as a na-

[4] An Army colonel of the writer's acquaintance was assigned to Sa'udi Arabia and told to study Arabic at the U. S. Army Language School. Less than two months later his orders were countermanded and he was assigned to Korea. He was also ordered to drop Arabic at once and enter a Korean class.

tionwide language (like Hindi in India, or Tagalog in the Philippines, indigenous to only a part of the inhabitants, but which the governments are trying to impart to the entire population); it may even be a language which receives a limited measure of governmental recognition, but need not be used in official documents or inscriptions, like Rumansh in Switzerland. An **official language** is one which must appear in official documents and be used at meetings of government bodies (German, French, and Italian are official languages in Switzerland; French and Flemish in Belgium; English and Afrikaans in South Africa; English and French in Canada). The official language is not necessarily the indigenous language of the entire area in which it is official; in fact it may not be an indigenous language of the area at all (like English in Puerto Rico, co-official with Spanish). The picture of official and national languages is a constantly shifting one, while indigenous languages, though subject to long-term change, have far greater stability. In East Pakistan, for instance, Urdu, indigenous to West Pakistan, was the sole official language, but Bengali is the indigenous tongue; as a result of popular agitation, Bengali was made co-official with Urdu.

The colonialism of past centuries gave rise to the phenomenon of **colonial languages** (or **colonizing languages**, or **languages of colonization**), which were often the sole official languages in the areas dominated by the colonizing powers. In this fashion English became the colonizing and official language of India, superimposing itself over the numerous indigenous tongues. The **superimposed**, colonial language often remains in existence after the disappearance of the colonizing power and frequently remains as the official language, or one of the official languages, of the newly independent country (English in Nigeria and Ghana, French in the new nations that have arisen out of French West and Equatorial Africa, are illustrations).

126 INVITATION TO LINGUISTICS

More subtle is the process whereby a language imposes itself as an **area** or **regional language**, as Russian has done in eastern Europe, or English and French in various areas of the world where they are neither indigenous nor official. In these areas the indigenous language tends to become a **satellite language**, subject to all sorts of influence from the dominant area language, from which it borrows words, expressions, and constructions, though retaining its individuality and status as a separate language. This often results in a **linguistic sphere of influence**, where the tongue of the dominant group is widely spoken and understood, and affects the satellite tongues.

At times the language of colonization turns not only into the official but also into the national and indigenous language, by a process of **linguistic replacement**. This has happened with English in North America, Australia, and New Zealand, with French in the Canadian Province of Quebec, with Spanish and Portuguese south of the Rio Grande. The original indigenous languages may then tend to disappear, or they may live on in a state of **symbiosis**, or peaceful coexistence, with the new tongue, like Quichua in Peru, Aymará in Bolivia, Tupi-Guarani in Paraguay. Seldom do the two languages merge into one on a basis of parity, though there is usually extensive borrowing of words and forms from one to the other. There may also be, however, the creation of a **pidgin** or **creole language**, in which the incoming tongue predominates but makes abundant concessions to the speech habits of the original inhabitants. The process of pidginization or creolization may be quite slight, as in the Afrikaans of South Africa, which is still basically Dutch, or it may be heavy, as in Melanesian English Pidgin or Haitian French Creole. Pidgins may not only become relatively stable; they may also turn into national and official languages, as has been the case with Afrikaans and with Maltese (basically Arabic, but with a heavy

Italian superstructure). Much more unstable are the **pidgins of immigration and naturalization**, which tend to disappear in a generation or two, like Italian, Yiddish, and other **immigrant dialects** in the United States. In these forms there is normally the creation of two separate but highly unstable speech forms: the immigrant's mother tongue, distorted by the addition of numerous words and expressions from the language of the receiving country, but retaining its original phonemic pattern and adapting to it the borrowed words and expressions,[5] and the immigrant dialect, in which the language of the receiving country is heavily mispronounced and otherwise mishandled by the immigrant.[6] **Absorption** takes place when the second generation goes over to the language of the receiving country, handling it as an indigenous tongue; but absorption can also result when the original natives go over to the language of colonization, as has happened with numerous people of Indian stock in such countries as Mexico and Brazil, who now speak nothing but Spanish and Portuguese. Or absorption may work in reverse, as when the Germanic-speaking Goths and Franks, entering the Roman Empire, turned into speakers of Vulgar Latin and proto-Romance, though contributing heavily to the new Romance vocabularies. The French-speaking Normans were likewise absorbed into the body of English speakers in the centuries that followed the Norman Conquest, though they made their influence heavily felt in the subsequent development of English.

A **liturgical tongue** is one used primarily in religious services, like Latin in Roman Catholic areas. Such a

---

[5] Note Italian immigrant dialect *u bebí*, "the baby," with southern Italian dialect phonemes and even shift of stress; also *sciabola* for "shovel" and *cotto* for "coat."

[6] This process forms the basis of all our immigrant dialect comedy of past decades, now fortunately on its way out. Notice, however, "With soap it's loaded!"; "It gives him a right he should talk that way?"

tongue often deeply affects the spoken language of the area where it appears and contributes many words and forms of expression to it.[7] Arabic, as the sacred tongue of the Koran, is widely spoken and understood in Moslem countries that are not Arabic-speaking, such as Iran and Pakistan.

Often a tongue is singled out by reason of its cultural merits and is widely studied and used in countries to which it is not indigenous. The role of French as a diplomatic tongue and a language of general cultural intercourse throughout most of the world over a period of several centuries is well known; while it may at one time have been based in part upon military and political predominance, its role today is almost purely cultural.[8] Persian likewise serves as a **cultural tongue** in many Moslem countries. Often the liturgical and cultural features are blended, so that it is difficult to disentangle them. Latin, starting as a superimposed colonial language, then becoming an indigenous tongue in the western Roman Empire, continued as a liturgical and cultural language long after the Empire's fall, and is still used in both capacities today.

A **koine**, or **compromise language**, is a linguistic form that combines the features of several related dialects and eventually emerges as both an indigenous and an official language. The ancient Greek dialects merged into such a koine, which was used in the later Greek classical period and during the thousand years of the Byzantine Empire. Standard literary Italian probably arose by the same process, and may be described as a koine. So may the Bahasa Indonesia which is now the official language of the Indonesian Republic, replacing an older, unofficial

[7] For example, the widespread use among Italian speakers of phrases like *Hodie mihi, cras tibi* instead of the Italian *Oggi a me, domani a te.*

[8] At the Congress of Vienna, after Napoleon's downfall, French, the language of the *defeated* nation, was the sole official tongue.

trade language, Malay (sometimes described as Bazaar Malay).[9]

The concepts of **primary**, **secondary**, **auxiliary**, and **substitute language** are basic for practical geolinguistics. The primary language of a country is, usually, its indigenous, national, and official tongue, the one that enjoys government recognition and is used in documents and communications, besides being taught in the schools. But often there is a secondary language known by a large proportion of the population and usable in many situations. Such is still to some extent the case with German in Hungary, Czechoslovakia, northern Yugoslavia. An auxiliary or substitute tongue is one which may be used in special situations and even in official circles. French is thus used in the North African Arabic-speaking countries which were at one time French possessions (Algeria, Tunisia, Morocco).

Linguistic distribution refers to the way in which a language is spread over various regions of the earth. English, French are tongues of widest distribution; Portuguese, Spanish, Arabic, German to a lesser degree; Russian, once restricted to the Soviet Union, is making a bid to become a tongue of wide distribution in eastern Europe. Italian, Chinese, Hindustani, Bengali, Indonesian, Japanese are largely restricted to their own local areas. A language may have a wide **diffusion** factor but may also be subject to **dispersion** when removed from its original environment. Such is the case with Italian, widely diffused by emigration throughout the world, but normally lost in the second or third generation of its emigrated speakers.

Bi-, **tri-**, **multilingualism** are terms that describe situa-

[9] In the old Malay, which was used in what today is Indonesia, Malaysia, and other nearby regions, there were two orthographic forms, one based on English, the other on Dutch spelling (*Surabaya*, *Soerabaja*, alternative spellings of a single pronunciation). Bahasa Indonesia follows in the main the British spelling.

tions where an individual or a group speaks two, three, or more languages with approximately equal facility. Bilingualism is normally easy to achieve, provided both languages are used from early childhood and continued in later life. Theories to the effect that bi- or trilingualism is damaging to the individual's psychological development are altogether unproved. Equally unproved is the theory that bilingualism works detrimentally to the command of either or both languages. Command over language is an individual matter and not at all dependent upon the number of languages involved. The person who speaks two languages imperfectly will speak a single language imperfectly.

The **literacy coefficient** is applied to individual languages on a percentage basis, to determine what proportion of their speakers know how to read and write and are consequently accessible to communications in written form. The **nationalism coefficient** is the factor, much less objectively determinable, of the will of the speakers to have their language survive; it is often complicated by religious, racial, and other factors.[10]

There is an entire terminology that pertains to the field of constructed languages for international use, of the type of Esperanto and Interlingua. Such languages are variously described as **constructed** or **artificial** (referring to the fact that they are the product of individual ingenuity, not of spontaneous growth); **international** or **universal** (referring to their proposed function); **auxiliary** (referring to the fact that they are not meant to displace existing tongues but only to help them out);[11] and as **interlanguages** (again referring to their function

[10] Note, for example, the "will to survive" of the Hebrew language among Jewish groups, finally culminating in the adoption of Hebrew as the national language of Israel. The same will to survive was characteristic of Gaelic in Ireland. In both cases the religious factor was also present.

[11] Do not confuse with the other use of *auxiliary language* (see above).

as mediators among speakers of various natural tongues).
Among them are **modified languages** (such as Latino
Sine Flexione, where Latin is used with its normal vocabulary and word order, but without its complicated
endings and flexions, which are standardized for international purposes); **basic languages** (like Basic English, in
which an attempt is made to get along with a restricted
vocabulary, by ingenious paraphrases and combinations
of word groups); **a priori languages**, constructed without
any reference to or similarity with existing languages,
like Ro or Suma; **a posteriori languages**, constructed by
blending different living language elements, like Esperanto or Interlingua. Proposals to **phonetize** existing languages (like English Spelling Reform) are not, properly
speaking, in the same class with constructed languages,
since the proposed change applies only to the written
form.

Language identification, in spoken or written form or
both, is the geolinguistic counterpart of the structural
typology and the historical classification and affiliation.
Here, however, the purpose is essentially practical: to
be able to tell, from the sounds of a spoken language or
the appearance of a written one, which language one is
faced with. In many ways this science of language identification bears strong similarity to the "Where Are You
From?" technique whereby a speaker is localized within
a radius of ten miles of his home locality by his distinctive speech features. The ability to identify, in spoken or
written form, a language with which one is faced can
often be of great value, even if one does not speak or
understand the language.[12]

Terms which geolinguistics shares with historical or

[12] See, for instance, the author's article "What Did He Say?"
appearing in *Police* magazine, September–October 1959, dealing
with the possibility of identifying and apprehending criminals from
their speech features. This article was spontaneously requested by
the *Police* editors.

descriptive linguistics are **languages in contact** (two or more languages coexisting in contiguous areas and constantly influencing one another in their development, despite the fact that they may not at all be genetically or typologically related; Rumanian, Bulgarian, and Albanian, all Balkan languages, but of three different Indo-European groups, seem to have developed in common the feature of a postposed definite article); **focal areas**, or linguistic **prestige centers**, from which innovations spread outward;[13] **transition** or **graded areas**, which are meeting grounds of influences from two different focal areas, or where conservative and innovational features meet;[14] **relic areas**, regions of conservatism and resistance to innovations;[15] **dialectalization**, the normal **centrifugal** tendency of language to break up into diverging dialects, and the concomitant **dedialectalization**, due to the **centripetal** influences exerted by central governments, good means of communication, transportation, and education, a national consciousness, and a literary tradition; **social stratification**, or the tendency of a local speech to break up into **class languages**, based on economic and educational differences.[16] **Vernacular**

[13] During the Middle Ages, Paris, as the seat of the French court, imposed its speech forms in an ever widening circle until Parisian finally became the standard French language. Today, New York, with its radio-TV national networks, and Hollywood, with its spoken film industry, are the great radiating prestige centers for American speech and speech innovations. Their pronunciation, grammar, and vocabulary tend to be imitated by all viewers, particularly of the younger generations, regardless of the viewers' own local speech background. Something similar happens in Italy, where local dialects once predominant in their own areas are in full retreat before the national standard, with only the Roman dialect holding its own by reason of the prestige of the national capital.

[14] For instance, the "broad" *a*, characteristic of the focal area of Boston in words like *afternoon, ask, glass,* begins to turn into the "flat" *a* of New York in Rhode Island and Connecticut, but does not altogether disappear until one reaches Stamford.

[15] The Ozarks mountain dialect retains some seventeenth- and eighteenth-century English speech features.

[16] For instance, "Those men will be killed" and "Dem guys is

and **Umgangssprache** describe the language of common spoken intercourse, or colloquial tongue, which all social classes hold more or less in common.[17]

Transcription, which we have seen in descriptive linguistics in its phonetic and phonemic variants, has in geolinguistics a third application: the transformation of a written form from one standard type of writing to another, with or without adaptation to indicate phonetic or phonemic features. Transcription has its uses in permitting the rapid acquisition, in spoken form, of languages having complicated systems of writing, like the Chinese and Japanese. A straight symbol-for-symbol transcription from one alphabetic form into another (for instance, from Cyrillic or Greek into Roman) is known as a **transliteration**.[18]

38. LANGUAGES AND SPEAKERS; COUNTRIES AND LANGUAGES

Basic to the concept of geolinguistics is the determination of what languages are spoken throughout the world and what kind of people speak them. But equally basic is the determination of what languages are spoken in each individual country or political unit.

This means, in effect, a double set of statistics, acting as a check upon each other: one for languages, their

---

gonna be bumped off" could come from the same geographical area but would be used by different social classes.

[17] Here it is easy to define but difficult to exemplify, owing to the previously mentioned factor of social and educational stratification. Whenever "usage" is mentioned, the legitimate question comes up: "Whose usage?" A reasonably safe compromise is represented by the language of ordinary radio and TV newscasts, coupled, perhaps, with some of the vulgarisms of commercials ("like a cigarette should").

[18] As when we spell *Tolstoi* and *Khrushchev* for what appears in Russian Cyrillic as Толстой and Хрущев, or *Aristophanes* for Greek 'Αριστοφάνης.

distribution among areas and political units, and the numbers of their speakers; another for nations, the languages appearing in the national area of each, and the number of people speaking each one.[19]

The factor of bilingualism and multilingualism complicates the picture, which is itself quite unstable, in view of shifting population figures that call for constant revision. The most practical procedure seems to be to count twice all true bilingual speakers (by true bilingual speakers we mean people who really possess two languages to approximately the same degree, and use them with near-native-speaker fluency). This would mean that an Uzbek-speaking inhabitant of the Asian portion of the Soviet Union who has learned Russian to the point where he speaks it well will be counted twice: once among the speakers of Uzbek and again among the speakers of Russian. For this reason there is no necessary coincidence between population census figures and speaker census figures, though in many cases the figures will be close. A delicate question is what to do with cultural speakers of non-indigenous tongues (for instance, a speaker of American English who has studied French for many years in high school and college, and handles the language reasonably well, though not with absolute native-speaker fluency). Here it seems arbitrary to set a definite standard, and approximate estimates are in order. A further discussion of this point will appear later (see Section 44, Educational Reports).

[19] To oversimplify: (a) Spanish is the national and official tongue of Spain and the Spanish colonies, of Mexico, of six Central American, three Antillean, and nine South American countries, with aggregate populations of well over 150,000,000; it is also to some degree current in areas like the Philippines, the southwestern United States, and the New York City area; (b) Spain has a population of over 30,000,000. While practically all of these speak Spanish, the native language of over 6,000,000 is some form of Catalan-Valencian; nearly 3,000,000 speak some form of Galician-Portuguese; nearly 1,000,000 speak Basque. At least 500,000 Spaniards can be reached with French, perhaps 150,000 with English.

In estimating the number of speakers of a given language the geolinguist cuts across national boundaries and even oceans. He also cuts across dialectal divides, save where the "dialect" is of such a nature as to constitute in effect a separate language, with little or no mutual understanding between the speakers of two or more such "dialects" (the dialects of Chinese are a case in point; a speaker of Mandarin and one of Cantonese generally fail to achieve spoken-language understanding, though they have a common written language of symbols to fall back upon). A language like Spanish, despite perceptible dialectal differences, can be used as a tongue of common intercourse in all the countries where it is official. It is therefore legitimate for us to set up a "Spanish language" classification and claim for it practically the totality of the inhabitants of Spain (despite Catalan, Basque, and Galician bilinguals); practically all the inhabitants of Mexico, Central America, and the Antillean nations of Cuba, Puerto Rico, and the Dominican Republic; most of the inhabitants of South America outside Brazil and the Guianas, despite the presence of numerous American Indian bilinguals and even of millions of monolingual speakers of American Indian languages.

In accordance with this methodology, we create a listing of languages, more or less extensive, but with the ideal goal of making it inclusive of all languages, major and minor, spoken on the globe. Each language is accompanied by a description of the geographical areas where the language is spoken, and by an enumeration of speakers, broken down into native speakers, to whom the language in question is a mother tongue; colonial or semi-colonial speakers (such as natives of Ghana, Nigeria, India, or Pakistan who speak English reasonably well); and cultural speakers (Frenchmen, Germans, Swedes, etc., who have acquired English in the schools or in their travels to the point where they speak it fluently, though not necessarily with native-speaker perfection).

While it is relatively easy to describe the areas in which a language appears, and to determine the number of its indigenous speakers, difficulties and complications arise in connection with the number of colonial and cultural speakers of the language, and it is in these areas that the most extensive research remains to be undertaken. The figures, once collated, are subject to constant revision. A reasonable suggestion would be that a revision appear every ten years, along with a population census.

The other procedure, serving as a check to the one just described, goes country by country. Here the problem is to determine, within each country, what languages are spoken, what their status is, how many people speak them, and in what fashion or under what specific circumstances. Taking, as a single example, a country like Spain, we would have, first, its total population; next, the figures for Spanish, Catalan, Basque, Galician, which by reason of widespread bilingualism would add up to a higher figure than the total population. Lastly, our census would include figures for those inhabitants of Spain who have acquired to a reasonable degree command over other languages, such as French, English, or German.

The combination of the two procedures should result in a body of information that would be as scientifically accurate as possible under circumstances of shifting population figures, and which could be utilized in condensed digest form by all sorts of governmental, business, scientific, and religious organizations.

This sort of statistical digest would give an accurate picture of number of speakers and language distribution. The facts of economic and industrial development for each country pertain to the non-linguistic realm, but could easily be combined with the linguistic facts to produce a picture of the geolinguistic importance of each language. This combined information would still be factual and objective, though the relative importance assigned to each of the three factors (speaking population, distribution, and economic-political potential) would necessarily have to be to some degree arbitrary. Most subjective of all would be the factor of cultural importance, but even here it is possible for certain objective criteria of measurement to be set up. One element in cultural importance, that of literacy of the speaking group, would in all events be thoroughly objective, while for literary, philosophical, and scientific output there is at least the possibility of some sort of objective measuring standard in number of books and periodicals published in each field.

39. AUXILIARY AND SUBSTITUTE LANGUAGES

One of the important functions of geolinguistic studies is the determination of those languages which can be used in various areas of the earth as substitutes for the indigenous languages, with the assurance that through them a certain percentage of the population can be reached. Since these substitute languages differ in range and use in the different countries, precise surveys are needed.

It is, for instance, of geolinguistic interest that English may be used as a substitute and auxiliary tongue in all the areas where Britain and the United States once held colonial sway, that French may be similarly used in vast areas of West and North Africa and southeast Asia, Dutch in Indonesia. But further, there are linguistic reflections of relatively remote colonization that go as far back as the days of the Spanish-American War and the First World War. Spanish is still fairly widespread in the Philippines, and German is occasionally heard in Tanganyika, Southwest Africa, and various Pacific areas.

This is because the political situation changes with far greater speed than the linguistic. Despite official efforts, it takes considerable time to change over the linguistic habits of a population or even of their cultural elite. People brought up in a given cultural tradition, such as the Indians educated in Britain, or the Africans who received their education in France or Belgium, find it quite difficult to change their mental habits, which are geared to the culture of the former colonial nation. Furthermore, in a good many cases little or no effort is made to break the cultural tradition and ties. It is likely that more English is studied at present in Ghana, Nigeria, India, and Pakistan than when Britain was in political control of those countries, and more French in the countries of the new French Union than formerly. One notable exception is Indonesia, where strong efforts are being made by the government to break the Dutch cultural tradition. There is some evidence that in Communist countries once subject to German linguistic and cultural influence some efforts are being made to lessen that influence.

The curious phenomenon of the long-range influence of colonial languages is to be observed among the Spanish speakers of the Philippines (the English influence in those islands is, of course, far more recent), and the occasional appearance of a German word in the Pidgin English of areas which were formerly German colonial possessions. In the long run it is likely that these influences will finally be erased, and there is likewise the possibility that at some future date Hindi, Urdu, and Tagalog will become so well implanted in India, Pakistan, and the Philippines as to break the English linguistic hold upon those countries. But even this is not too likely, for certain languages of former colonization enjoy a prestige and a range of practical utility, both at home and abroad, that makes their study almost imperative among those who aspire to be literate.

The auxiliary status of the several world languages in the various countries where they appear must be studied carefully and with individual attention to each area, as that status is by no means identical everywhere. It is also necessary to formulate long-range projections into the future, based on observable trends; this despite the fact that the projections are subject to drastic revision on the basis of sudden and unforeseen political changes.

40. WRITING SYSTEMS AND LANGUAGE IDENTIFICATION

The relative importance of the spoken and the written language varies from tongue to tongue and from area to area. Starting at the lower end of the scale, with languages of backward and primitive groups that have not yet evolved a system of writing, we go all the way up to the great languages of Western civilization, where the significance of the written form is practically on a par with that of speech. In between are countries with high percentages of illiteracy, and in these the importance of the written form is relatively lower; of what use will it be for a stray visitor to a remote Chinese village where the population does not know how to read and write to know the complicated system of Chinese ideographs? Under such conditions a few words or expressions of the spoken tongue are of far greater value than written-language scholarship.

Under any circumstances, however, it is important, particularly from the standpoint of language identification, for the student of geolinguistics to have some acquaintance with the various systems of writing in use throughout the world. The Western nations generally make use of the Roman alphabet, but with a few significant exceptions. Also, the form of Roman used varies considerably from language to language, with the addition of extra symbols and suprascript characters which differ from language to language and are sometimes sufficient in themselves to identify the language in written form (the

barred *ł* of Polish, the *ţ* of Rumanian, the dotless *ı* of
Turkish, the *ñ* of Spanish). There are also letter combinations distinctive of individual languages (the *szcz* of
Polish, the *ij* of Dutch, the complete series of double
vowels of Finnish). A study of alphabetic forms in the
various languages using what is basically a Roman alphabet is richly rewarding, and since such forms are in use
in countries totaling at least half of the world's population, this study will in itself lead to an important step in
identification.

Next come the scripts which are recognizably akin to
the Roman alphabet, like the Irish, Greek, and Cyrillic.
Here the situation becomes more complex for what concerns the ability to read languages that come in these
forms; but the effort involved in learning to identify them
is far from excessive. Other languages make use of alphabetic and syllabic systems of writing which are quite unlike the Western, even though they may share a common
origin. Alphabets like the Armenian and Georgian, or the
Hebrew and Arabic, the ingenious combination of alphabetic and syllabic systems that distinguishes the
scripts of Amharic and of most Indian languages based
on the Devanagari of ancient Sanskrit, the Japanese kanas, are complicated and difficult to learn for actual use,
but not too difficult to learn for purposes of recognition
and identification. Lastly come the completely pictographic and ideographic systems of languages like the
Chinese and Japanese, in which the link is not between
a symbol and a sound but between a symbol and a
thought concept; the acquisition of such forms for actual
use is almost a lifelong task, but their recognition is not at
all difficult or complicated.

It is part of the geolinguist's task to familiarize himself
with the major writing systems of the world for recognition purposes. If to this knowledge there can be added
the ability to read or transliterate, so much the better. At
any rate, the ability to recognize and identify the world's

major languages in their written form is something the geolinguist cannot dispense with, and a special course in writing systems should form part of all specialization in linguistics, and particularly in geolinguistics.

To a limited degree, and depending upon the acoustic qualities of the individual ear, there is also a well-defined possibility of learning to identify some of the major tongues in spoken form, since each language has its own distinctive phonetic and phonemic pattern. Basic instruction in the recognition of the sound patterns of a number of major languages should again form part of the equipment of the linguist, and particularly of the geolinguist, with further specialization in the languages of a given area according to the individual's requirements and for specific purposes.[20]

Practical applications of the principles of language identification are many. Aside from its obvious value in times of hot or cold war (censorship, military intelligence, soldiers in the field who must collaborate with or fight against forces speaking languages other than their own), there is the question of finding the proper interpreter for a person or the right translator for a document, which presupposes a knowledge of what language the person speaks or the document is composed in; the work of librarians faced with publications in numerous languages; there is even the matter of knowing the nationality or language background of a person with whom you are entering upon social or business relations, and thereby guarding yourself against undiplomatic utterances that you might otherwise make. Language identification, in spoken or written form, frequently is of real

[20] The most complete system of language identification to date, on a geolinguistic basis as opposed to the description of individual languages, appears in the author's *World's Chief Languages* (5th revised edition, Vanni, New York, 1960) and *Language for Everybody* (Devin-Adair, New York, 1956; Pocket Books, New York, 1958).

value in the field of crime detection and prevention (see footnote 12, above).

41. SUBSIDIARY FACTORS: CULTURE, CULTURAL SLANT, RELIGION, EFFECT OF PAST HISTORY

While all these topics impinge to some extent on the fields of descriptive and historical linguistics, they are legitimate subjects of study for the geolinguist, since they are reflected in the present status of the world's languages.

The link between language and group culture (of which language forms a part) is of particular interest to the anthropologist. The word **culture** itself is misleading, since it has two possible interpretations. In the anthropological sense, it means the sum total of the customs, habits, traditions, and ways of life of any social group, whether highly developed or backward. In the anthropological sense, all groups, however small or primitive, have a culture; and all cultures are on the same plane. In the more traditional sense, "culture" is associated with the higher manifestations of civilization, most frequently expressed through the instrumentality of the written language, and includes such items as literature, poetry, philosophy, science and scientific output, high standards of living, sanitation, communications. This semantic discrepancy between two meanings of the identical word leads to frequent misunderstandings, and for this there might perhaps be a remedy in the adoption or creation of a different word for one of the two meanings.

The culture of a nation or social group has a great deal to do with its type of language, since the latter normally reflects the group's activities. The Whorf school of metalinguistics goes further, and claims that the type of language spoken exerts a direct influence upon those activities, but this is still a matter of controversy.[21]

At any rate there is no doubt that language definitely forms a part of the group's cultural consciousness and is perhaps one of the earliest manifestations of that consciousness. The distinction between one group and other groups is often at least outwardly based on language. If you speak my language, the chances are that you belong to my group. If our languages differ, it is assumed that we belong to different groups, and we tend to behave accordingly. Hence the language is often a key to the behavior of a group and permits a forecast of the group's probable reaction to various situations. The geolinguist learns very early that it is a fatal mistake to ignore the linguistic factor in any form of intercultural relations, and that one thing he must respect above all others, along with religious beliefs, is the language of the group he is dealing with.

When we pass from backward to advanced civilizations, the linguistic factor in culture becomes even more pronounced, since language, particularly in written form, acts as the vehicle of culture, both in the anthropological and in the traditional sense. At this point account must be taken not merely of the primary culture and language of the group we are dealing with but of secondary and even tertiary cultural and linguistic factors. One nation, even though highly civilized and endowed with an abundant and rich culture of its own, may yet be under the cultural spell of another. Many European nations, in the course of the seventeenth, eighteenth, and nineteenth centuries, fell under the cultural spell of France, and this was quickly reflected in the change in many of their customs and outlooks to conform with the culture they admired. Linguistically speaking, this cultural spell is reflected in the widespread study and use of the language

[21] See B. L. Whorf, *Language, Thought and Reality* (ed. J. B. Carroll), Wiley, New York, 1956.

of the prestige culture, and this in turn leads to the creation of what might be styled a secondary language in the nation under consideration. French is said to be spoken, for instance, by no fewer than two million Italians, or one person out of twenty-five; this situation differs in its causes, but not in its effects, from the one created in a country of colonization, such as India, where an even larger percentage of the population speaks English. In the sense described above, English has of late become a highly cultural language, spreading its influence not merely to countries originally colonized by English speakers but even to lands, like Turkey and the Soviet Union, where there has never been any British or American colonization.

The religious factor must also be taken into account in connection with geolinguistics. The linguistic influence exerted by such liturgical languages as Latin in Roman Catholic countries, Arabic in Moslem lands to which Arabic is not indigenous, cannot be neglected by the geolinguist. This religious-linguistic influence normally means that the language whose speaking population subscribes to a certain faith will become interspersed with loan words and loan translations from the liturgical language, and that a segment of the population, greater or smaller, but invariably including nearly all ministers of that faith, will handle, in one fashion or another, the liturgical language as a spoken tongue. Italy might thus be described as a country whose secondary language is French and whose tertiary language is Latin.

It would be idle to insist upon the fact that past history exerts a tremendous influence upon the linguistic state of present-day countries. Yet this fact is often neglected or overlooked. There are deep-seated historical reasons why the new state of Israel selected Hebrew rather than Yiddish as its national and official tongue, and why the Irish feel the urge to set up Gaelic as a national language, while the Scots do not experience the same urge. A knowledge of a country's past history will often give valuable insights into the linguistic setup and attitudes of the present and future.

It may again be desirable to stress that descriptive linguists, historical linguists, and geolinguists, while they are interrelated and intertwined, have each their own peculiar slant on languages. To the descriptive linguist, all languages are on an equal plane, because, from the descriptive standpoint, they actually are equal and share the same basic characteristics (a phonetic and phonemic structure, a grammatical system, a vocabulary of spoken use). To the historical linguist, languages have varying importance based upon the range and availability of their previous history; a language like Greek, with its early beginnings in recorded form and its clear and documented historical development, cannot possibly be placed in the same classification with Menomini, for which there is no recorded history; to the historical linguist, Greek, despite its small number of speakers and lack of influence today, is of greater importance than Indonesian or even Russian. The geolinguist must regard languages from the standpoint of their relative importance in the world of the present and immediate future. It is idle to expect the geolinguist to regard Hopi and Zuñi as on a plane of equality with French and Spanish, languages of huge populations, vast range of distribution, and tremendous economic and political significance.

This is not a matter of making value judgments, or being linguistically subjective, or playing favorites. It is simply a matter of regarding the facts of language from a different angle and with a different perspective, as well as for different purposes. Once this principle is clearly understood, much of the acrimony that appears today among linguists of different persuasions will disappear.

42. DIALECTS AND LOCAL VARIANTS; CLASS LANGUAGES

Dialectal varieties are inherent in all speaking groups, save perhaps the very smallest; and even here perceptible idiolectic[22] differences may be noted among the speakers. This is due to the natural tendency of language, which is centrifugal, unless active steps are taken to counter it. Language, left to its own devices, will break up, both in time and in space. The changes that occur in time pertain primarily to the domain of the historical linguist. Those that occur in space are the concern of all three groups of linguists. The descriptive linguist must bring in dialectal differences to make his picture of the language he is describing complete. The historian of language must take account of dialectal differences in so far as they appear in the past and affect the evolution of the language he is studying. The geolinguist must consider these differences in the light of the language of today and their effect upon the global picture. If local differences in speech reach the point of making mutual comprehension difficult or impossible, the effectiveness of the language for purposes of communication is to that extent impaired. At the same time a study of the dialects involved becomes imperative if one wishes to know which are the truly effective means of communication in the area under study.

The border line between language and dialect is often quite difficult to trace. Mutual comprehension offers only a partial yardstick. There is often more effective communication between speakers of two standard, official languages that are genetically related (Italian and Spanish, for instance) than between two dialects of the same

[22] IDIOLECT: the speech habits of a single individual; e.g., the English language as I speak it. The term is roughly equivalent to De Saussure's *parole* (see p. 71).

official language (Piedmontese and Sicilian, or Asturian and some forms of Andalusian). This is in part due to the factors of education and literacy but is often the result of purely natural courses of development. The geolinguist's work is not completed until he has charted not merely the spatial range and number of speakers of a language but also its major dialectal varieties and their significance. The obstacle to communication presented by dialectalization is far from equal in all languages.

The educational factor leads to a social stratification of language within the same area. Generally speaking, this stratification affects primarily those compartments of language which permit wide fluctuation (vocabulary and syntax), and has a comparatively small effect, however striking that effect may seem, on phonology and morphology. This is because basic phonemic and morphemic patterns are usually held in common by all the speakers of a given area; where differences occur, they are seldom a bar to understanding, though they may be distinctive and picturesque, like the New York metropolitan area lower-class speaker's tendency to substitute *t* and *d* for the two *th* sounds, and to interchange *er* and *oi*, things that an educated speaker of the identical area would carefully eschew, or the London Cockney *lidy* for *lady*, which a London "U-speaker" would under no circumstances use.

A "class language," in the sense that the speech of one social class is incomprehensible, or nearly so, to another social class in the same area, is a rare phenomenon, though it does occasionally occur, particularly in backward areas. Normally, the fact that the social classes have to live together in the same environment and communicate with one another makes it imperative for one type of speech to be understood by the speakers of the other, purely for purposes of basic communication.

Where there is an official, national standard, the speech of the educated portion of the population tends to coincide with it (again, however, with notable exceptions). This confers upon the educated brand of speech the advantage of universality in the area, since lower-class forms succumb most easily to local dialect tendencies.

The geolinguist must take into account social and educational levels in speech, particularly when they become significant from the standpoint of communication and comprehension. At the same time, in the case of languages of large speaking groups that have attained a high measure of civilization and standardization of culture, it will be advantageous for him to fasten his attention primarily upon the national standard, which has numerous advantages: that of coinciding with the official language and the written form; that of being area-wide rather than local; that of presenting a more comprehensible variant even to the speakers of local and class dialects than most of the other local variants and class dialects of the area. It is a commonplace in countries that are heavily stratified as to both local dialects and class forms, such as Italy, that if you speak the national standard you will generally be understood, even though the answer may not come back in the same form. Furthermore, present-day tendencies are all in the direction of standardization and the leveling out of both local and class differences, with the language of radio, TV, and spoken films gaining general acceptance and being more and more used by younger-generation speakers.

Some descriptive linguists of the more theoretical variety often make the point that "language is what people speak, not what someone thinks they ought to speak." This, to their way of thinking, confers legitimacy upon local dialects, slang, substandard forms, and vulgarisms, and makes them all coequal with the standard language. Anyone disagreeing with this extreme point of view is then charged with aristocratic tendencies and value judgments.

It can readily be conceded that dialectal, slang, and

substandard forms exist and are in use. It can also be conceded that in the past such forms have often entered the standard language and become fully legitimate and official. Condemnation of such forms on quasi-moral or aesthetic grounds is a matter of individual, subjective choice. It should, however, be quite obvious that the existence of dialectal and substandard forms of speech tends to impede the flow of communication, which is, after all, the primary purpose of language. Language control is no different from any other form of social control. If it is desirable to have uniform traffic regulations so that drivers will not become confused in areas other than their own and have accidents, it is equally desirable that in a politically unified area there be some measure of linguistic unity that will minimize misunderstandings and lack of comprehension. Those linguists who advocate "leaving your language alone" and using any language forms you may please are doing a disservice to the cause of language and its basic purpose. That they implicitly recognize their error is shown by the fact that in their own writings they are most careful to avoid localisms, slang, vulgarisms, even colloquialisms, and employ a language so correct and prim that it occasionally verges on stuffiness.

PART VII

Geolinguistics: Methodology

43. CENSUS AND LITERACY STATISTICS

Primary to the purpose of geolinguistics is the enumeration of speakers of the various languages, their geographical distribution, and, to some extent, their description. From this the geolinguist can pass on to relate languages to political, economic, and other factors and to formulate estimates of the practical importance of languages and the uses to which they may be put.

This means that the primary and basic tool of the geolinguist is the population and language census. Population figures for the various countries are generally available, though they are not all equally trustworthy. Countries in which the processes of modern civilization have been going on for a considerable period of time regularly issue fairly reliable figures of their own populations and revise them periodically. In a general way these bare population figures permit us to estimate the numerical progress or retrogression of a given national language. We can, for example, total the population figures of all countries where Spanish is the official and national tongue and say that those figures represent, very roughly, the number of Spanish speakers throughout the world.

What census figures fail to indicate is the linguistic overtones and nuances, the factor of bilingualism, which heavily colors some national pictures, the auxiliary, secondary, tertiary languages of the country, the languages of minorities, which often indicate bilingualism but occasionally represent a subtraction that should be made from the figures for the national tongue.

Such information, of value and interest to the geolinguist, is occasionally supplied in the form of a rough estimate, along with population figures. This permits us to assert, for instance, that there are on British soil a certain number of Welsh speakers, that a certain percentage of them is bilingual in English and Welsh, while a smaller percentage is monolingual, speaking only Welsh. In the case of most countries, however, this information is at the most a rough estimate or an educated guess.

Far greater accuracy is needed if we are to have at our disposal a true picture of the world's linguistic state. As census-taking methods improve, and more and more countries render an accurate report concerning their populations, it would be highly desirable for the census questionnaire to include questions concerning languages spoken and understood.

Second in importance only to the population figures themselves are the literacy figures. Here again the present offering is often sketchy in the extreme, with estimates and guesswork rampant. For this there is some justification in the fact that the figures are constantly shifting and changing, with, fortunately, upward revisions that are often spectacular. Nevertheless, greater accuracy is needed.

Literacy percentages are an index of many things. They show what portion of a country's population may be reached with written materials and to what extent the acquisition of secondary and tertiary languages by a large part of the population is possible. They are also a clue to the country's potential productivity, along both material and intellectual lines. In the present-day world it is seldom if ever that high productivity and living standards are achieved by groups that are largely illiterate.

The campaigns on behalf of literacy that are now being waged all over the world should be attended by what might be styled progress reports, issued periodically and based on accurate surveys.

One important index of national literacy and intellectual productivity is supplied by the existence of newspapers, magazines, books, and other printed material. A census of such written-language media, country by country and area by area, would add materially to our understanding of the geolinguistic picture. Since mass communication by way of radio, TV, and spoken films has now reached proportions where it vies with and often outstrips the written-language medium,[1] figures on radio and TV stations and sets in proportion to population figures, and on the showing of spoken films, would tend to round out our knowledge. If such figures were to give, in addition, a breakdown as to the linguistic forms in which these activities are carried on in each area, there would be a signal further advantage.

44. EDUCATIONAL REPORTS

The question is frequently asked how many people in a given country have studied another language to the point of proficiency. The answer invariably comes in the form of a rough estimate or an outright guess. Yet it would be of great geolinguistic interest to know, with some degree of precision, not merely what foreign languages are studied in the various countries of the earth, but by what proportion of the population and to what degree of intensity, duration, and proficiency.

Here the figures are often misleading. It may be very well to say that out of our total high school and college

[1] Visitors to Chinese cities are often amazed at the blaring of radios in all public places, and attribute it to a desire to broadcast political propaganda. This may be partly true, but there is also the factor of widespread illiteracy and inability to read written signs, which makes spoken announcements imperative.

population twenty per cent have studied or are studying a foreign language, and to give the breakdown in terms of the major languages studied; then to figure, on the basis of fairly accurate school attendance statistics, how many Americans have been exposed in one way or another to a foreign language. But this sort of count does not jibe very well with that of other lands, where the course of foreign language instruction is longer and more intensive. Also it fails to take into consideration figures for private institutions, such as the Berlitz schools of language, and for home instruction, through private tutors, recordings, and other devices. Here again the inclusion of questions on linguistic abilities in the general census would be of help. Even if absolute precision cannot be attained, it would perhaps be possible to take extensive samplings of the general population, by Gallup poll methods. Of interest also would be the purpose or purposes, if any, beyond the mere accumulation of credits toward graduation, that courses of language instruction are being put to by their recipients. Even without going into excessive details, it ought to be possible to ascertain with some measure of certainty which languages are most extensively studied in the various countries and, in a general way, what the outcome of such studies is.

For such statistics, or estimates, as are actually available in this country, we are largely indebted to the Modern Language Association, which has accumulated vast sets of facts and figures in connection with its work of propaganda for foreign language study. But the resources of the Modern Language Association are limited and ought to be supplemented by official government action, of the kind that apparently can go on only when we are at war and the information in question becomes a strategic necessity.

One field of specialization for geolinguists could very conceivably be that of language statisticians, gathering, collating, and revising the facts of language in their geo-linguistic aspect, with precise statistical methods.

45. AREA AND LANGUAGE STUDIES

A good deal has been accomplished in area and lan-guage studies, though more from the standpoint of in-dividual areas than from that of the world as a whole. The area-language study is nevertheless the best example to date of embryonic geolinguistics. Here a selected por-tion of the globe is studied in detail, and the languages of the area are placed in direct juxtaposition with the other factors with which they are linked—geography, his-tory, politics, productivity, commerce, cultural outlook, even art, music, and literature. What emerges is a geo-linguistic consciousness referred to a specific area, which still lacks the sense of balance and proportion that it ought to have but is yet a vast improvement over the study of a single language, or of linguistics in a vacuum.

While intensive language courses are largely the pre-rogative of the armed forces, area-language programs are more often left to the initiative of private institutions.

It is believed, with some justification, that a good deal of area and language study goes on, under government auspices, in other countries interested in bringing about political changes all over the world. This ought to inspire us to redouble our efforts, for the sake of self-preserva-tion if nothing else. However, the area and language study should not be viewed exclusively from a military and political angle, but should also be slanted in the di-rection of commercial and economic interests and of cul-tural relations.

PART VIII

A Brief History of Linguistics

46. ANTIQUITY AND THE MIDDLE AGES

That antiquity, even in remote Biblical times, was conscious of language and language difficulties is attested by the episode of the Tower of Babel in the Book of Genesis. Here the anonymous writer, throwing his unspoken desires back into the past, envisages all mankind as having at one happy time been of one language and one speech. But man, through his foolish pride and defiance of God, lost the priceless boon of full understanding and the possibility of full collaboration that it entails, and sank into a state, viewed as deplorable, of plurilingualism. Of special interest to the linguist is the recognition of the important role that language and linguistic understanding play in social relations.

Other ancient samples of unconscious and rudimentary linguistics are the recorded use of translators and interpreters at the court of the Pharaohs, the bilingual and trilingual inscriptions carved on stone for areas that had more than one language, even a bilingual Sumerian-Akkadian dictionary of sorts.

Conscious interest in language and its problems begins with the Greek philosophers and the Sanskrit grammarians. While the former discussed the origin and nature of language, the latter went to work to codify the rules for the use of their tongue. Pāṇini's grammar of Sanskrit (c. 300 B.C.; but it contains references to much earlier works) is a jewel of precision and concision, but we are left to wonder whether it is in the main prescriptive or descriptive.

The discussions of the Greek philosophers are of interest because they foreshadow later debates. Is language something of supernatural origin, bestowed upon man by the gods? Is there an inherent link between the signifier and the signified?[1] Or does language depend upon convention and agreement among speakers that they will accept a certain linguistic symbol as having a certain semantic value, more or less common and equal to all who are parties to the understanding? From our twentieth-century standpoint, and fortified by the clear exposition of De Saussure, we do not hesitate to give our answer; but at the time of Plato and his *Cratylus* there could still be doubt and discussion.

Independently, it would seem, of the Indian grammarians, the Greeks eventually went to work and elaborated a grammatical system applicable to their own language and others of similar structure—languages with clear-cut grammatical categories, such as gender, number, case, person, tense, mood, voice, imbedded deep in their structure and readily recognizable by an observation of forms as well as of meanings and functions; languages in which the words fall into neat pigeonholes that can readily be labeled nouns, adjectives, verbs, etc.; and this not merely by reference to the way they behave in the sentence but also by the way they are structured, with endings and internal changes which are peculiar to each individual part of speech. This was the beginning of the universal grammar that continued to dominate the linguistic scene down to the eighteenth century and beyond.

[1] These terms, devised by De Saussure, indicate the thought-concept or physical object (*signified*) and the word symbol that is used in speech to represent it (*signifier*). See p. 71.

Several things are to be noted in connection with the Greek construction of a grammar. The precise description that ultimately emerged was not achieved overnight but took centuries to build up, with numerous false starts and errors of classification. This is somewhat surprising, as Greek grammar, from our modern viewpoint, is self-evident. The only reason that can be advanced to explain the slowness and clumsiness of the Greeks in achieving it is that they were too preoccupied with questions of philosophy and logic, which frequently got in the way of their scientific observations, and led them to use a deductive rather than an inductive procedure.

The grammatical structure and the grammatical categories, once achieved, were there to stay. They were inherited and applied not only by the Romans but also by grammarians of other languages of a different type, like the Hebrews and the Arabs. Fortunately the Semitic languages do not differ too much in structure from the Indo-European, so that a transfer could be effected with relative ease.

It is frequently charged that the grammatical views of the ancients were prescriptive rather than descriptive, that the ancient grammars set forth the structure of the language as it should have been spoken rather than as it actually was. It is as often forgotten that grammars, like systems of writing, are at the outset fairly accurate reflections of an existing state of affairs; but as the linguistic state of affairs changes, the grammars and writing systems do not keep pace with it, so that ultimately we have, in both grammar and writing, a reflection of an older, superseded stage of the language. There are, particularly in Latin, abundant indications that, as the language changed, the prescriptions of the grammarians tended to become crystallized. There are also abundant indications that the more educated and intelligent speakers were fully conscious of the language changes that had occurred and were occurring.[2] Still, it was held desirable to hold up the ancient models as the linguistic ideal and to look upon the innovations that were taking place in speech as vulgar aberrations to be condemned and frowned upon.

At the same time it is probable that we exaggerate the relevance and purport of these same condemnations, that they were intended to apply to the written language and to the flowery tongue of oratory rather than to everyday speech.

The fall of the Roman Empire of the West entailed a degeneration of prescriptive standards, coupled with drastic and far-reaching changes in the spoken tongue. These changes were finally acknowledged when the new Romance languages emerged in written form, at which time a new linguistic consciousness arose. Where before there had been a dividing line between "correct" and "incorrect" Latin, now Latin itself, a semi-artificial but still living tongue of scholarship and religion, was opposed to the vernaculars, the spoken dialects of the peasantry, the nascent *roman* or *romance* or *volgare* of the rising middle classes. But the process of admitting these new tongues to something resembling equality was slow. It was not until about the year 1000 that a bilingual grammar of Latin and Anglo-Saxon appeared. Codification of the rules of use for the Romance tongues was even slower, to the point where Dante could still describe his *Volgare*, in 1305, as Latin without the rules of grammar.

Throughout the entire period under consideration, from the dawn of history to the dawn of the Renaissance, languages were in constant spoken and written use. An awareness of language and language differences could

[2] Note, to cite only two instances, St. Jerome's statement to the effect that "the Latin language itself is changing daily, both region by region and with the passing of time"; and St. Augustine's remark that "it is better that the grammarians should chide us than that the people should not understand us."

be assumed, even if we did not have direct testimony to that effect. Direct references to such differences and the difficulties engendered by them, on the other hand, are relatively scanty. In works corresponding to our modern fiction (*Iliad, Odyssey, Aeneid, Chanson de Roland,* to cite four examples), the characters, obviously of different language backgrounds, converse freely and without apparent need of interpreters. This minimization of the linguistic factor, implying indifference even more than ignorance, has its parallel in early Hollywood movies. Correction and realism come later, with mature reflection.

A linguistic consciousness, in the modern sense of the term, based upon observation, analysis, synthesis, and generalization, is conspicuous by its absence. Such basically correct conclusions as are attained by the early grammarians are the result of chance rather than of method. Between the years A.D. 400 and 1000 there is little that a modern linguist would consider indicative of linguistic awareness, save for Bible translations and pilgrim phrase books, both of which have a highly utilitarian slant.

Above all, there is little in the pre-Renaissance era to indicate an awareness of language classification and affiliation, or the relationship among the languages. The Greeks, actively conscious only of their own tongue, lumped all speakers of other languages together under the disparaging label of *barbaroi*—barbarians or babblers. The Romans, showing respect for only one foreign tongue, Greek, have left us only stray references to such languages as Gaulish, Iberian, Etruscan, or Punic. Varro, the only Roman grammarian to hazard a guess as to the connection between Greek and Latin, came to erroneous conclusions. The picture, from the historical linguist's side, is an extremely discouraging one. The descriptivist comes off a little better, with descriptions of Sanskrit,

Greek, and Latin which are basically accurate, however archaic at the point when they were formulated.

47. RENAISSANCE TO 1800

Beginning with Dante's description of the ideal Italian language, in his *De Vulgari Eloquentia* of 1305, coupled with a correct genetic statement concerning the origin and relationship of Italian, French, and Provençal, and a basically correct classification of the Italian dialects, the Renaissance begins its way slowly and gropingly toward modern views of language.

The major contribution of the Middle Ages to linguistic science had been the concept of a universal grammar, applicable, with appropriate modifications, to all languages. This was in a sense only a restatement of something that had been implicit in the views of the ancients, who regarded their own dominant tongues as the only ones worthy of attention and, by extension, of universality. The medieval contribution lies in the recognition of other tongues than Latin or Greek, even if they are consigned to an inferior role. This concept of a universal grammar continued to dominate the linguistic world long after the discovery of languages radically different in structure from the classical began to cast doubts upon its validity. In a sense it may still be said to dominate the linguistic world today, because among the avowed purposes of descriptive linguistics, in the words of De Saussure, is the ascertaining of principles universally applicable to all language (and note also Whorf's attempt at constructing a new universal grammar built along modern scientific lines). The main differences between the medieval and the modern view lie in the emphasis that is placed on different linguistic elements and the predominance given to one language group over others; but the medieval writers could be excused for their methodological errors in view of their ignorance of all languages that did not belong to the Indo-European family or to one structurally similar, the Semitic, including both Arabic and Hebrew, two languages of which there was a fair knowledge among medieval European scholars.

But as European horizons widened, first with the Crusades, then with the voyages of discovery and exploration, notice had to be taken of new and strange languages, Far Eastern, African, American Indian, to which the old familiar grammatical concepts could be applied only by the forceful process of fitting a square peg into a round hole.

It is difficult to say precisely when it dawned upon the Renaissance mind that these newly discovered languages were in conflict with the theory of a universal grammar, at least as it had been formulated up to that point. At all events there was a considerable flowering of descriptive grammars of new tongues, as well as of the old ones. There began to appear discussions, often distorted by ignorance of the facts, concerning the classification and affiliation of languages. There also began to appear discussions concerning language standards, the problem of a national tongue vs. dialects, and of what might be described as class languages.

It is an interesting fact that research and investigation, however methodologically unsound, however based on erroneous principles, advanced contemporaneously along many fronts. The Renaissance mind was an inquiring one. It wanted to experience, experiment, and know, getting away as far as possible from the timeless aspects of the Middle Ages, when all that really mattered was eternity, and the things of this world were purely coincidental.

This process, continued down to the end of the eighteenth century, bore abundant fruit, though not of invariably high quality. By the year 1800 much of the groundwork had been laid, and the only thing still lacking was a sound methodological approach that would give some guarantee of scientific precision. Practically all known languages had been in some fashion or other described, even if some of them had been forced by violence into an Indo-European mold. Progress had been made in the matter of language classification, though many rough edges remained to be smoothed, and incorrect hypotheses based on guesswork or individual leanings roamed the field. A great deal of documentary evidence had been gathered, which would serve the purposes of historical research into the evolution of languages. Some modern issues, such as that of correctness and incorrectness of language, and that of dialectal forms and literary standards, had been squarely posed. Above all, a linguistic consciousness had been aroused and a linguistic interest created. All that remained to bring into being was a sound methodology.

48. THE NINETEENTH CENTURY

Even before the close of the eighteenth century Sir William Jones had presented to the world of scholarship his ideas on the intimate relationship of Sanskrit and Old Persian with Latin, Greek, Celtic, and Germanic. This study was the forerunner of the comparative method, which was to dominate the linguistic world for the next hundred years and more.

Jones himself did not establish the method, though he suggested it. But it quickly followed, in the works of Schlegel, Rask, Bopp, Grimm, and Verner. Basically, the method was simple: get the earliest attested forms and words of each Indo-European branch, lay them side by side, describe their similarities and differences, and establish, by a sort of majority vote among them, the probable form of the parent language. Of course this methodology could not be followed until it had been established and accepted that Latin, Greek, Sanskrit, Old Slavic, Old Celtic, etc., belonged to the same family of languages and had a common ancestor. For the core of this pronouncement, made in precise and definitive form, we have to thank Jones, though the bulk of the demonstration was supplied by the later writers. The comparative methodology was later extended to individual branches of Indo-European (for instance, the Romance languages, issuing from a common ancestor, Latin; and even to groups of languages seemingly unrelated to Indo-European, but connected among themselves, such as Akkadian, Phoenician, Hebrew, Aramaic, and Arabic, all of Semitic stock). What grew up was a science of comparative linguistics, or, as it was more generally styled then, comparative philology (the fact that the earliest attested samples of words, forms, and constructions all came from written-language documents lent itself to this description).

Very little of what was later styled descriptive linguistics appeared in the nineteenth century. It was tacitly assumed that the historical interest was paramount. Comparative studies led, if anything, to the discarding of the last vestiges of the traditional belief that all languages stemmed from a common ancestor. The idea of establishing principles that would be applicable to all language failed to arise, therefore. Geolinguistics, of course, was not even thought of. Down to the end of the century and beyond, it was taken for granted that the only languages worthy of serious consideration from a practical standpoint were the great tongues of Western civilization, which had also turned into the great tongues of colonization. It was no accident that constructed languages attempted during this period, including Esperanto, give little attention to the question of proportional representation among the world's great language groups but limit their "internationality" to the Germanic, Latin, Romance, and Greek fields, with occasional but scanty Slavic participation.[3]

The harmonious unity of linguistic thought in the nineteenth century was brusquely broken by the angry controversy that arose between the proponents of absolute regularity in sound change (Neogrammarians, or Junggrammatiker) and those who held that language change is largely a matter of individual whim (Neolinguists). This quarrel was ultimately patched up by a compromise formula to the effect that there is regularity in sound change provided other factors, such as analogy and learned or dialectal borrowing, do not interfere with the working of the so-called "sound laws." Despite its unpleasant aspects, the controversy was of value because it centered attention on dialectal forms and the speech of groups hitherto held inferior and unworthy of scholarly consideration. Since dialects are partly unrecorded in their historical development, this in turn led to an interest in the living languages and their dialectal ramifications. This again led to interest in the working of these living language forms under conditions of direct observation, and cleared the way for a new brand of linguistics, the descriptive, in which spoken language was paramount, documentary evidence lost a good deal of its importance, and principles applicable to all language processes began to be evolved.

Yet, despite the appearance of the first linguistic atlas in the first decade of the twentieth century, a precise formulation of descriptive linguistics as a separate branch had to wait until the posthumous publication, in 1916, of De Saussure's *Course in General Linguistics,* in which

[3] Note, however, the preoccupation of Monsignor Schleyer, creator of Volapük, a constructed language, with the convenience of the speakers of Chinese, to the point where *r* is eliminated from the sound-scheme of his creation because the Chinese cannot pronounce it.

the boundaries between the two branches of linguistic science are precisely and unmistakably set forth.

49. THE TWENTIETH CENTURY

Centuries, in the sense of eras, do not always coincide chronologically with a year that ends in two zeros. In practically all respects, sociological, economic, and cultural, the nineteenth century may be said to go on beyond the year 1900 to the outbreak of the First World War, since which the world has never been the same. Historical linguistics continued, of course, after the publication of De Saussure's work, and continues today. But it is dogged at every step by its younger and more vociferous partner, descriptive linguistics. The balance of power had now shifted from comparative research into the history and prehistory of the Indo-European languages to the description of individual languages, not all of them by any means Indo-European, and many of them quite obscure, but which nevertheless were illustrative of the processes common to all languages.

In America especially, descriptive studies were slanted in the direction of the languages of obscure American Indian groups, with abundant field work paralleling that of European researchers in the dialects, and the evolution of a practical methodology for the study of unwritten languages without a historical background. Early pioneers in the field were such men as Boas, Sapir, and Bloomfield, and their work is continued today by a host of younger and enthusiastic disciples. The European extension of the descriptive principles was more theoretical and, in a sense, philosophical, with Jespersen attempting to lay down principles for progress in language as it evolves from a more synthetic to a more analytic stage, the Prague School developing its highly structuralistic, quasi-symmetrical approach, the Copenhagen School working on an attempt to reduce language and language evolution to a series of quasi-mathematical formulas, the Soviet School of N. Y. Marr placing its stress upon language as a class manifestation.

Historical linguistics, while displaced from its nineteenth-century post as sole holder of the field, has been by no means dormant. Both in Europe and America, much work has been done in recent years. European Indo-Europeanists such as Meillet, Hrozný, Kuriłowicz, Benveniste, and Pokorny, Romanicists such as Menéndez-Pidal, Rohlfs, Bourciez, Brunot, Von Wartburg, Entwistle, Paiva Boleo, Cintra, Monteverdi, Migliorini, Devoto, have carried the work of their predecessors to new heights; while in America we have had the highly significant works of men like Sturtevant, Kent, Bolling, Buck, Conway, and Whatmough. In very recent times attempts have been made to link descriptive methodology with historical subject matter (Martinet, Hoenigswald) and to reconstruct linguistic history on glottochronological bases. Even the field of monogenesis has not been neglected.[4]

While historical pursuits are still perhaps in the lead in Europe, descriptivism prevails in America. As for geolinguistics, that is still in its budding stage, yet there is little doubt that full recognition will come to it as a third partner when its practical importance and right to separate existence are fully demonstrated and official interest centers upon it.

[4] A. Trombetti, *L'unità d'origine del linguaggio* (Bologna, 1905) and *Elementi di glottologia* (Bologna, 1922–23); A. Cuny, *Etudes prégrammaticales sur le domaine des langues indo-européennes et chamito-sémitiques* (Paris, 1924); B. Collinder, *Indo-uralisches Sprachgut* (Uppsala, 1934).

50. LOOKING AHEAD

Long-term predictions are invariably risky, because events have a way of swinging history into new and unexpected channels. Linguistics is no exception. Such prognostications as are here offered are made with full realization of the fact that the unforeseen always holds sway over future events.

On the basis of present trends it seems safe to prophesy a rosy future for the study of languages in the United States, one of the few countries in the world where that study was in jeopardy until not too long ago. Since languages form the subject matter of linguistics, this, too, should progress satisfactorily, as it always has in other countries that never underwent isolationistic phases.

At the present time descriptive linguistics is definitely in the saddle. When people mention linguistics without further qualification, it is almost always understood that the linguistics is of the descriptive, structural variety. Descriptive linguistics does and should form the basis of linguistic studies, but there is the danger that it may be overstressed. Its contributions to knowledge have been in the main along the line of phonetic and phonemic description, the most objective among the divisions of linguistics, and the one most susceptible of precise scientific procedures and measurements. In the field of morphology and syntax there is considerable doubt whether the descriptive methodology and terminology offer great advantages over their historically determined predecessors. When it comes to vocabulary, descriptivists generally abandon the field to their historical colleagues, and it is as well that this should be so, particularly for what concerns etymology. For what concerns semantic studies, words go to join morphemes and grammar in the beloved doctrine of usage, which justifies all uses and abuses.

It is perhaps this theoretical and one-sided slant on the problems of linguistics that presents the greatest menace to harmony in the linguistic world and to the progress of linguistic studies. From a purely descriptive standpoint, the descriptivists are of course justified in thinking of all language and all languages as being on an equal plane. But there are three other viewpoints to be considered, all equally based on fact and reality: the historical, the geolinguistic, and the sociological. From the viewpoint of the historicist, all languages cannot be on the same plane; some encompass far greater historical interest than others. Geolinguistically speaking, account must be taken of the difference in practical importance of individual languages and of different types of languages.[5] Sociologically, and from the point of view of the average man, there are prestige and non-prestige, U and non-U types of language, which make their influence felt when it comes to employment, preferment, social status. One cannot blind oneself to these realities merely on the basis of an equalitarian theory built upon a reality of a different order.

In addition, descriptivists ought to realize that the unnecessary complications with which they surround their science are not conducive to its popularity or spread. Too often has the complaint been voiced by students of linguistics that they do not understand what it is all about. Not all these complaints can be written off as due to insufficient preparation or scanty intellectual equipment. The burden of responsibility rests upon the spreaders of a science that aims at gaining converts and followers to make that discipline available to all who are duly qualified, through the use of a standardized, reasonable ter-

[5] The geolinguist, for instance, need not apologize for the fact that he devotes more attention to French, Russian, and Chinese than to Ojibwa, Tibetan, and Fula. He is fully within his rights, also, when he describes the Indo-European languages as of greater *practical* importance than the tongues of the Australian natives.

minology and presentation, and a cessation of insistence on trifles.

Otherwise, the field of productive descriptive linguistics has barely been scratched. Ample work yet remains to be done, particularly in the description of individual languages and the refinement of techniques. It is the descriptive linguist who is most concerned with mechanical equipment and mechanical aids to language learning and language research, and this presents a vast, entrancing, fruitful field.

At present far too few areas have been charted by linguistic atlases. Note, for example, the need of a comprehensive linguistic atlas of the Spanish-speaking world, and of French-speaking areas not contiguous to France, such as Quebec and Haiti, and the former French and Belgian possessions in Africa. This is a field that calls for the best efforts of descriptive linguists. Revision of existing atlases is also a crying need. This sort of work, done by descriptive linguists in accordance with their most modern methodologies, will be of signal help to historical linguists and geolinguists as well.

Historical linguistics is, more than either of the other two branches, a pursuit of the hobby type. What we find out in connection with the past history and evolution of language and languages will, generally, not be applicable to the practical field of language learning and language teaching, nor will it otherwise put money in anyone's pocket. At the most, it may be said that lessons learned from what has happened in the past may have their applicability to what happens in the present or will happen in the future. But that could in itself be of some practical merit.

The historical linguist should learn to repress fancy and rely more on evidence and facts. Here he has much to learn from his descriptive colleague. His branch of the science is definitely a part of general historical studies and ought to be viewed as such. There is the possibility

of strict application of historical methodology, involving
the proper weighing of available evidence and the fer-
reting out of additional proof. Since historical linguistics,
while the least practical, is perhaps the most picturesque
branch of linguistics, and the one that makes the greatest
appeal to the layman's imagination, it will never be
threatened with extinction. Lacking, at least on the surface, the more forbidding aspects of descriptive linguistics, it makes its appeal to the popular fancy, as evidenced by the fact that there are few popular magazines
that do not have a section on word power and word
derivations.

The problems yet to be solved in historical linguistics
are innumerable. This is true even of those areas where
the greatest amount of work has been done in the past,
such as the Indo-European and Semitic. Genetic affiliations, the evolution of languages where the written evidence is scanty or difficult to follow (or even where it is
abundant), the problem of monogenesis, the interpretation of ancient languages that have so far defied the efforts of the researchers, all lie before the prospective historical linguist and invite him to exert greater efforts.

One task that particularly needs doing is a truly scientific study of the vocabularies of the major languages
to determine the percentage, nature, and sources of loan
words in each; this to satisfy the curiosity not merely of
the linguist but of the historian. The links between historical linguistics and history need very much to be tight-
ened, and linguistic change placed in its proper historical
perspective.

The field of geolinguistics is the most promising, because it is the one where the least amount of organized
work has been done. The problems of geolinguistics have
so far been viewed by the linguistic specialists as ancil-
lary to the other two branches, instead of being treated
in an organic and practical fashion. Materially speaking,
geolinguistics promises to be the most rewarding of the

three fields. But it also calls, more than the others, for concerted effort on the part of such external agencies as government and industry, which have until recently failed to realize to what an extent geolinguistics can assist them in the solution of problems they consider basic. It is in this area that the greatest progress can be achieved and linguistic science yield its most practical fruits. All linguistic scientists worthy of the name should by this time have come to a realization that sciences do not exist in a vacuum and that, while you can have pure-research scholars who are unconcerned with practical applications, these practical applications exist in every known field of science and are not to be scorned.

From time to time pleas are voiced for the reunification of linguistics, and a bridging of the gap that has slowly been developing between the descriptive and the historical branches. Attempts have been made to foist a descriptive methodology and terminology upon the historical division of linguistics.[6]

It is of course true that there should be harmony and collaboration among the linguistic branches. It is equally true that there should be a cessation of the ideological battles caused by the insistence of the followers of each branch on viewing the problems of the others through their own colored glasses.

However, no useful purpose will be served, in this writer's opinion, by any attempt to merge once more into a single discipline, with an identical methodology and terminology, what De Saussure so clearly proved to be a divided field. Descriptive linguistics, historical linguistics, and geolinguistics each have their own problems, their own subject matter, their own procedures and nomenclatures, which have been evolved through a long period of trial and error and which are best suited to each branch.

[6] See especially H. M. Hoenigswald, *Language Change and Linguistic Reconstruction,* University of Chicago Press, Chicago, 1960.

Attempts to follow descriptive methods in connection with purely historical problems merely complicate their solution and lead to a situation where it takes ten involved pages to explain what is simply and clearly set forth in one. Any attempt to lead descriptive linguistics back to a nineteenth-century point of view and methodology will prove equally unsuccessful. Nor will it do any good to heap scorn upon geolinguistics and say there is no need for it as a separate discipline; the astounding lack of achievement in this field under the handling of historical linguists first, of descriptivists later, gives clear indication of the need for special treatment by specialized experts.[7]

On the other hand, it was the geolinguistic aspect of linguistics that aroused, during the last World War, such government interest as there was, and led to the creation both of the Media Analysis Bureau and of the ASTP courses in languages for the armed forces. The government was interested in the practical, not the theoretical or historical aspects of language. It wanted to know what languages were in use throughout the world, who and how many spoke them, how they could be used, and to have at its disposal a fairly large number of trained people who could speak and understand them, as well as a smaller number of experts who could recognize and identify them. All this was clearly neither descriptive nor historical linguistics, but geolinguistics.

The three related disciplines will achieve their best results if they are allowed to proceed side by side as separate but equal partners, sharing their findings and applying what is applicable of one another's methodology and terminology and points of view. Anything beyond this will result in compulsion, inefficiency, and waste.

[7] See footnote 1 in Part VI.

International
Phonetic Alphabet

THE INTERNATIONAL PHONETIC ALPHABET

CONSONANTS

	Bi-labial	Labio-dental	Dental and Alveolar	Retroflex	Palato-alveolar	Alveolo-palatal	Palatal	Velar	Uvular	Pharyngal	Glottal
Plosive	p b		t d	ʈ ɖ			c ɟ	k g	q ɢ		ʔ
Nasal	m	ɱ	n	ɳ			ɲ	ŋ	N		
Lateral Fricative			ɬ ɮ								
Lateral Non-fricative			l	l			ʎ				
Rolled			r						ʀ		
Flapped			ɾ	ɽ					ʀ		
Fricative	ɸ β	f v	θ ð s z ɹ	ʂ ʐ	ʃ ʒ	ɕ ʑ	ç j	x ɣ	χ ʁ	ħ ʕ	h ɦ
Frictionless Continuants and Semi-vowels	w ɥ	ʋ	ɹ				j (ɥ)	(w)	ʁ		

VOWELS

	Front	Central	Back
Close	(y ʉ u) i y	ï ʉ	ɯ u
Half-close	(ø o) e ø	ə	ɤ o
Half-open	(œ ɔ) ɛ œ	ɐ	ʌ ɔ
Open	(ɒ) a	a	ɑ ɒ

(Secondary articulations are shown by symbols in brackets.)

OTHER SOUNDS.—Palatalized consonants: ƫ, ᶁ, etc. Velarized or pharyngalized consonants: ɫ, đ, ᵶ, etc. Ejective consonants (plosives with simultaneous glottal stop): pʼ, tʼ, etc. Implosive voiced consonants: ɓ, ɗ, etc. ɼ fricative trill. ɘ, ɞ (labialized θ, ð, or s, z). ƪ, ƺ (labialized ʃ, ʒ). ƫ, ɕ, ʑ (clicks, Zulu c, q, x). ł (a sound between r and l). ʍ (voiceless w). ɪ, ʏ, ʊ (lowered varieties of i, y, u). ɜ (a variety of ə). ɵ (a vowel between ø and o).

Affricates are normally represented by groups of two consonants (ts, tʃ, dʒ, etc.), but, when necessary, ligatures are used (ʦ, ʧ, ʤ, etc.), or the marks ͡ or ͜ (ʦ͡ or ts͜, etc.). c, ɟ may occasionally be used in place of tʃ, dʒ. Aspirated plosives: pʰ, tʰ, etc.

LENGTH, STRESS, PITCH.—: (full length). ˑ (half length). ˈ (stress, placed at beginning of the stressed syllable). ˌ (secondary stress). ˉ (high level pitch); ˍ (low level); ˏ (high rising); ˎ (low rising); ˋ (high falling); ˎ (low falling); ˆ (rise-fall); ˇ (fall-rise). See Écriture phonétique internationale, p. 9.

MODIFIERS.—˜ nasality. ̮ breath (l̮ = breathed l). ̬ voice (s̬ = z). ʻ slight aspiration following p, t, etc. ˌ specially close vowel (e̝ = a very close e). ˏ specially open vowel (e̞ = a rather open e). ˌ labialization (n̫ = labialized n). ̪ dental articulation (t̪ = dental t). ˏ palatalization (z̧ = ʑ). ˔ tongue slightly raised. ˕ tongue slightly lowered. ˒ lips more rounded. ˓ lips more spread. Central vowels ï (=ɨ), ü (=ʉ), ë (=ə̈), ö̈ (=ɵ), ё̈, ̈ö̈, (e.g. n̩) syllabic consonant. ̯ consonantal vowel. ʃˢ variety of ʃ resembling s, etc.

B.4.

APPENDIX II

Phonetic-Phonemic Chart
of Six Major Languages

Vowel and consonant sounds appearing in English, French, German, Spanish, Italian, and Russian are here listed with their phonetic IPA notations, of the broad rather than the narrow variety, with a description of the forms in which they appear in the orthography of each language. It must be stressed that equivalences among the languages are approximate, not precise. In a strictly phonemic transcription of any individual language, some of the symbols attributed to that language may be dispensed with when the different phones they represent are positional variants and merge into a single phoneme.

In the case of English, where there is no standard dialect, there may be considerable divergence of opinion concerning the IPA symbols to be used. In the case of Italian, where the distinction between a single and a double written consonant is generally phonemic, it has been judged unnecessary to list the "double" consonants, as they show no phonetic difference from their single counterparts beyond that of duration; they will, however, appear in a strictly phonemic chart. In the case of Russian, the three palatal fricatives ж, щ, and ш, are pronounced not with the tongue lying flat but retroflex (i.e., the tip of the tongue is curled upward so that it alone forms contact with the hard palate).

VOWEL CHART

DESCRIPTION	IPA SYMBOL	ENGLISH	FRENCH	GERMAN	SPANISH	ITALIAN	RUSSIAN
Front spread close	[i:]	i, ee, ea, ie, ei, etc.	i, î	i, ih, ie	i, y	i	и
	[i] or [ɨ]	i		i			
Front spread half open	[e]	e	é, ai / -ez, -er	e, eh, ä, äh	e	e	э
Front spread less open	[ɛ]		e, è, ê / ai, ei	e, ä		e	
Front spread half closed	[æ]	a					
Middle spread open	[a:]	o	a	a, ah, aa	a	a	a (stressed)
	[a]		a	a			
Front rounded close	[y:]		u, û	ü, üh			
	[y]		u	ü			

Front rounded half close	[ø:]	eu, oeu		ö, öh
	[ø]	eu, oeu		
Front rounded half open	[œ:]	eu, oeu		
	[œ]	eu, oeu		ö
Middle spread close	[ï]	i, ea, u, etc. (+r)		
Middle spread half close	[e:]	a, e, i, o, u (unstressed)	e	e
	[e]	u̇		
Middle spread half open	[ʌ]		a, o (unstressed)	a, o (unstressed)
				ɪ

VOWEL CHART (continued)

DESCRIPTION	IPA SYMBOL	ENGLISH	FRENCH	GERMAN	SPANISH	ITALIAN	RUSSIAN
Back rounded close	[u:]	u, oo	ou	u	u	u	y
	[u]	u, oo	ou	u			
Back rounded half close	[o:]		o, ô au, eau	o, oh	o	o	
	[o]		o, ô au, eau				o (stressed)
Back spread open	[ɔ:]	aw, au, ou, etc.		o		o	
	[ɔ]	British pot	o				
Front spread open	[ɑ:]	a	a, â				
	[ɑ]		a				

DIPHTHONG CHART

IPA SYMBOL	ENGLISH	FRENCH	GERMAN	SPANISH	ITALIAN	RUSSIAN
[ei], [ej]	a, ai, ei, etc.			ei	ei	ей=[jej]
[ou], [ow]	o, oa, etc.					
[ai], [aj]	i, ai, ei, etc.		ei	ai, ay	ai	
[au], [aw]	ou, ow		au	au	au	
[ɔi], [ɔj]	oi, oy		eu, äu	oi, oy	oi	
[iə]	e, ae, ea (+ r)					
[ɛə]	e, ai, etc. (+ r)					
[ɔə]	o, oa, etc. (+ r)					
[uə]	u, oo, etc. (+ r)					
[ja]	ya	ia	ja	ía, ya	ia	Я (stressed)
[jɛ], [je]	ye	ie	je	ie, ye	ie	е (stressed)
[jɔ], [jo]	yo, yaw	io	jo	io, yo	io	ё
[ju]	yu, you		ju	iu, yu	iu	Ю (stressed)
[ji]						е (un-stressed)
[jə]						е (un-stressed)
[jʌ]						Я, Ю (un-stressed)
[ɥi]		ui				
[wa]	wa	oi		ua	ua	
[wɛ], [we]	we	oue		ue	ue	
[wi]	wee, wi, wea, etc.	oui		ui	ui	
[wɔ], [wo]	wa, wo, etc.			uo	uo	

NASAL VOWELS AND DIPHTHONGS

IPA SYMBOL	FRENCH
[ã]	an, am
	en, em
[ɛ̃]	in, im,
	ain, aim,
	ein, en
[ɔ̃]	on, om
[œ̃]	un, um
[wɛ̃]	oin

CONSONANT CHART

DESCRIPTION	IPA SYMBOL	ENGLISH	FRENCH	GERMAN	SPANISH	ITALIAN	RUSSIAN
Glottal unvoiced plosive	[ʔ]			die ʔ Eier			
Glottal unvoiced fricative	[h]	h	h (aspirate)	h			
Uvular rolled	[R]		r	r			
Velar unvoiced plosive	[k]	c, k, ck, q ch	c, qu	k, ck, q g (final)	c, qu	c, ch, q	к, г (final)
Velar voiced plosive	[g]	g	g, gu	g	g, gu	g, gh	г
Velar unvoiced fricative	[χ]			ach	g (+e, i), j		х
Velar voiced fricative	[ɣ]				g (between vowels)		

CONSONANT CHART (continued)

DESCRIPTION	IPA SYMBOL	ENGLISH	FRENCH	GERMAN	SPANISH	ITALIAN	RUSSIAN
Velar voiced nasal	[ŋ]	ng		ng	ng	ng	
Palatal unvoiced fricative	[ç]			ich			
Palatal-alveolar unvoiced fricative	[ʃ]	sh, s ch	ch	sch s (+t, p)		sc, sci	Ш Ж (final)
Palatal-alveolar voiced fricative	[ʒ]	s (measure) z (azure)	j, g (before e, i)			g, gi (Tuscan only)	Ж
Palatal voiced nasal	[ɲ]	ni, ny	gn		ñ	gn	Н (before palatal vowel)
Palatal voiced lateral	[ʎ]	mil*lion*		Mil*ch*	ll	gl	Л (before palatal vowel)

Velar voiced lateral	[ɫ]	mi*lk*					ʁ (before back vowel) ʁ (final) T
Dental (alveolar) unvoiced plosive	[t]	t	t	t d (final)	t	t	т
Dental (alveolar) voiced plosive	[d]	d	d	d	d	d	д
Dental unvoiced fricative	[θ]	*th*ing			z, c (+e, i)		
Dental voiced fricative	[ð]	*th*is			d (between vowels)		
Dental (alveolar) voiced nasal	[n]	n	n	n	n	n	н

CONSONANT CHART (continued)

DESCRIPTION	IPA SYMBOL	ENGLISH	FRENCH	GERMAN	SPANISH	ITALIAN	RUSSIAN
Dental (alveolar) voiced lateral	[l]	l	l	l	l	l	
Alveolar voiced rolled	[r]	r					
Dental (alveolar) unvoiced sibilant	[s]	s	s, ç	s	s	s	с, з (final)
Dental (alveolar) voiced sibilant	[z]	z, s	z, s	s (initial + vowel or between vowels)		s (between vowels)	з
Dental (alveolar) flap	[ɾ]	r		r (in stage pronunciation)	r	r	р
Dento-labial unvoiced fricative	[f]	f, ph etc.	f, ph	f, ph, v	f	f	Ф, в (final or before unvoiced consonant)

Dento-labial voiced fricative [v]	v	v	w	v	v	В
Bilabial unvoiced plosive [p]	p	p	p	p	p	П (final or before unvoiced consonant)
Bilabial voiced plosive [b]	b	b	b	b, v	b	Б
Bilabial voiced fricative [β]				b, v (between vowels)		
Bilabial voiced nasal [m]	m	m	m	m	m	М
Bilabial semivowel [w]	w	ou (+ vowel)	j	u (+ vowel)	u (+ vowel)	
Palatal semivowel [j]	y	(vowel +) il, ill		y, i (+ vowel), ll	i (+ vowel)	Й

CONSONANT CHART (continued)

DESCRIPTION	IPA SYMBOL	ENGLISH	FRENCH	GERMAN	SPANISH	ITALIAN	RUSSIAN
Palatal rounded semivowel	[ɥ]		u (+ vowel)				
Palatal-alveolar unvoiced affricate	[tʃ] [č]	ch			ch	c (+ i, e)	ч
Palatal-alveolar voiced affricate	[dʒ] [ǧ]	j, g (+ e, i)				g (+ e, i)	
Dental (alveolar) unvoiced affricate	[ts]			z, c (+ e, i) ti (+ vowel)		z, zz	ц
Dental (alveolar) voiced affricate	[dz]					z, zz	

SPECIAL CONSONANT COMBINATIONS

IPA SYMBOL	ENGLISH	FRENCH	GERMAN	SPANISH	RUSSIAN
[ks]	x	x	x	x	
[gz]	x	x			
[ʃtʃ]					Щ

NOTES

[iː] Some of the English possible spellings for this sound are represented by mach*i*ne, b*ee*t, *ea*ch, rec*ei*ve, bel*ie*ve. German possibilities are exemplified by Mar*i*ne, *ih*nen, v*ie*l.

[ɪ] English p*i*t, German b*i*n.

[e] French parl*é*, par*l*er, parl*ez*, parlera*i*; German h*e*r, z*eh*n, S*ee*, sp*ä*t, w*ä*hlen. (The German sound is normally long [eː])

[ɛ] English p*e*t; French m*e*ttre, p*è*re, fen*ê*tre, parl*ai*s, n*ei*ge; German F*e*nster, M*ä*nner. Italian makes no spelling distinction between [e] and [ɛ]

[æ] English p*a*t.

[aː] French p*a*ge; German V*a*ter, f*a*hren, H*aa*r.

[a] American English l*o*t; French p*a*tte; German W*a*sser.

[yː] French m*u*r, m*û*r; German H*ü*te, B*ü*hne.

[y] French l*u*ne; German H*ü*tte.

[øː] French M*eu*se; German sch*ö*n, H*ö*hle.

[ø] French p*eu*; v*oeu*.

[œː] French p*eu*r.

[œ] French n*eu*f; German zw*ö*lf.

[ï] Russian c*ы*н.

[əː] English b*i*rd, *ea*rth, *u*rn, etc.

[ə] English *a*ccount, sil*e*nt, char*i*ty, c*o*nnect, circ*u*s; French l*e*; German Eck*e*; Russian х*о*рошо.

[ʌ] English b*u*t; Russian хор*о*шо.

[uː] English r*u*le, f*oo*l; French f*ou*r; German g*u*t.

[u] English p*u*ll, g*oo*d; French p*ou*r; German M*u*tter.

[oː] French r*o*se, n*ô*tre; German l*o*ben, *oh*ne, B*oo*t.

[o] French rigol*o*, *au*, b*eau*.

[ɔː] English *o*rb, *aw*ful, *au*thor, c*ou*gh; Russian хорош*о*.

[ɔ] British p*o*t; French n*o*tre; German v*o*ll. Italian makes no spelling distinction between [o] and [ɔ].

[ɑː] English f*a*ther; French s*a*bre, *â*ge.

[ɑ] French p*a*s.

[ei] English c*a*me, s*ai*l, g*a*y, h*ei*nous, b*e*y, etc.

[ou] English g*o*, l*oa*f, etc.

[ai] English n*i*ght, *ai*sle, *ei*der.

[au] English *ou*t, h*ow*.

NOTES (continued)

[oi] English oil, boy; German treu, Häuser.

[iə] English mere, seer, ear, etc.

[ɛə] English lair, heir, etc.

[ɔə] English or, oar, pour, etc.

[uə] English poor, sewer, etc.

[ju] English union, Yule, you, etc.

[ɥi] French huit.

[wi] English wee, wisp, weaver, etc.; French oui.

[wo] English water, wont.

[ã] French an, ample, en, embéter.

[ɛ̃] French vin, impossible, main, sein, italien, etc.

[ɔ̃] French on, ombre.

[œ̃] French un, humble.

[wɛ̃] French moins.

[ʔ] German glottal stop before ein.

[h] French h aspirate of la hache, seldom pronounced today.

[k] English cake, brick, quiet, chorus; French car, quatre; German Kerl, Ecke, quellen, Tag; Spanish caro, que; Italian caro, chi, qui; Russian так, снег.

[g] English good; French gant, guerre; German Gasse; Spanish gabán, guerra; Italian gola, guerra; Russian гора.

[χ] German ach; Spanish gitano, jinete; Russian хорошо.

[ɣ] Spanish pagar.

[ç] German ich.

[ʃ] English shore, sure, chandelier; French chambre; German schön, spielen, stehen, Italian scelto, sciopero; Russian хорошо, муж (with retroflex tongue).

[ʒ] English pleasure, azure; French jambon, général; Tuscan gioia, generoso; Russian жена (with retroflex tongue).

[ɲ] English onion, canyon; French agneau; Spanish año; Italian ogni; Russian они.

[ʎ] English million; German Milch; Spanish llano; Italian gli; Russian поле.

[ł] English milk; Russian слушать.

[t] German Vater, Bad; Russian там, дед.

[θ] English thing; Spanish zorra, cielo.

[ð] English *th*is; Spanish ama*d*o.

[s] French *s*e, *ç*a, *c*igale; Russian са*д*, ра*з*.

[z] English *z*ero, ea*s*y, thing*s*; French *z*éro, ro*s*e; German *s*ieben, Ro*s*e; Italian ca*s*a; Russian *з*емля.

[f] English *f*ear, *ph*ase, cou*gh*; French *f*rais, *ph*ase; German *f*ahren, *Ph*ilologie, vol*l*; Russian *ф*ёдор, *ѳ*ита, орло*в*.

[p] Russian *п*адать, зу*б*.

[b] Spanish *b*oda, vol*v*er.

[β] Spanish ca*b*allo, nue*v*o.

[w] French o*u*est; Spanish b*u*eno; Italian b*u*ono.

[j] French sole*i*l, fi*ll*e; Spanish *y*erba, b*i*en, *ll*egar (dialectal); Italian p*i*ano; Russian ма*й*.

[ɥ] French c*u*ir.

[tʃ] English *ch*ur*ch*; Spanish *ch*orro; Italian *c*elia, *ci*arlare, Russian *ч*орт.

[dʒ] English *j*et, *g*eneral; Italian *g*enio, *gi*à.

[ts] German *Z*eit, *C*icero, Na*ti*on; Italian gius*ti*zia, pe*zz*o, Russian *ц*ена.

[dz] Italian *z*avorra, ra*zz*o.

[ks] English e*x*tra; French e*x*traction; German e*x*tra; Spanish e*x*istir.

[gz] English e*x*ample; French e*x*emple.

[ʃʈʃ] Russian хру*щ*ёв (with retroflex tongue).

In Spanish, Italian and Russian, vowel length is not phonemic; lengthening of stressed vowel is a matter of emphasis, or of individual choice. Modern French tends to neutralize the distinction between [a] and [ɑ], both long and short.

APPENDIX III

Genetic Classification of the World's Main Languages

(Subdivided by family, subfamily, and individual language. Approximate figures for speaking populations are given in parentheses, in round millions where possible. Note that bilingual speakers are counted *twice*, under the heading of each language they speak. Population figures are fairly accurate for some languages, estimated on the basis of available data for others.)

I. Indo-European (1600)

    A. Germanic (560)
1. English (400; including 100 non-native)
2. German (with Yiddish: 120; including 20 non-native)
3. Dutch (with Flemish, Afrikaans, Frisian: 20)
4. Scandinavian (Swedish, Norwegian, Danish, Icelandic: 20)

(Older languages of this group include Gothic, Old Norse, Anglo-Saxon, Old High German, Old Frisian, Old Saxon)

    B. Romance (410)
1. Spanish (with Catalan, Ladino, Papiamento: 160)
2. French (with Creoles: 80; including 15 non-native)
3. Portuguese (with Galician: 90)
4. Italian (with Sardinian, Rheto-Rumansh: 60)
5. Rumanian (20)

(Older languages of this group include Latin, Oscan,
Umbrian, Faliscan, probably Sicel)

C. Balto-Slavic (330)
    1. Russian (205; including 100 non-native)
    2. Ukrainian (40)
    3. Byelorussian (7)
    4. Polish (32)
    5. Czech and Slovak (15)
    6. Serbo-Croatian and Slovenian (18)
    7. Bulgarian and Macedonian (8)
    8. Lithuanian (3)
    9. Latvian (or Lettish: 2)

D. Indo-Iranian (515)
    1. Hindustani (including Hindi and Urdu: 200;
       including 100 non-native)
    2. Bengali (85)
    3. Bihari (35)
    4. Marathi (35)
    5. Punjabi (35)
    6. Rajasthani (20)
    7. Gujarati (20)
    8. Oriya (15)
    9. Singhalese (8)
    10. Sindhi (5)
    11. Assamese (5)
    12. Other languages of India and Pakistan (Kash-
       miri, Lahnda, Nepali, Pahari, Kherwari, etc.:
       15)
    13. Iranian (Persian: 15)
    14. Pashto (Afghan: 15)
    15. Other languages of Iran, Pakistan, Afghani-
       stan, U.S.S.R. (Kurdish, Baluchi, Tadjik, etc.:
       17)

(Older languages of this group include Sanskrit and
the Prakrits, of which the chief is Pali, for India; Old
Persian and Avestan for Iran)

E. Greek (10)
(Ancient Greek comprised various dialects: Attic,
Ionic, Doric, Aeolian, etc.)

      F. Armenian (4)

      G. Albanian (3)

      H. Celtic (3)
         1. Irish (with Scots Gaelic and Manx: 1)
         2. Welsh (1)
         3. Breton (1)
      (Older languages of this branch included ancient Gaulish and the recently extinct Cornish)

II. Semito-Hamitic-Kushitic (120)

      A. Semitic
         1. Arabic (90)
         2. Hebrew (3)
         3. Amharic (with Tigre, etc.: 10)
      (Older languages of this group included Phoenician and Punic, Assyro-Babylonian [Akkadian], Aramaic [Syriac])

      B. Hamitic (Berber, Kabyl, Shilh, Tamashek, Rif, etc.: 6)
      (Older languages of this group included ancient Egyptian, Coptic, Numidian, etc.)

      C. Kushitic (Somali, Galla, etc.: 11)

III. Uralic and Altaic (85)

      A. Uralic (Ugro-Finnic)
         1. Finnish (with Estonian, Karelian, Lapp, Mordvinian, Cheremiss, Votyak, etc.: 7)
         2. Hungarian (or Magyar; with Ostyak, etc.: 13)

      B. Altaic (Turkic)
         1. Turkish (27)
         2. Uzbek, Tatar, Turkoman, Kirghiz, Azerbaijani, etc. (35)
         3. Mongol (Kalmuk, Buryat, etc.: 2)
         4. Tungus (Manchu: 1)

IV. Sino-Tibetan (750)

      A. Chinese-Thai
         1. Chinese (Mandarin, 515; Cantonese, 55; Wu, 55; Min, 50; Hakka, 20; total: 695)

   2. Thai (Siamese: 25)

B. Tibeto-Burman
   1. Burmese (20)
   2. Tibetan (7)
   3. Others (3)

V. Japanese-Korean (130)
    A. Japanese (95)
    B. Korean (35)

VI. Dravidian (130)
    A. Tamil (40)
    B. Telugu (45)
    C. Kanara (20)
    D. Malayalam (20)
    E. Others (5)

VII. Malayo-Polynesian (135)
     A. Indonesian
        1. Indonesian (Bahasa Indonesia; based on older
           Malay, which is still used in Malaysia; official
           for over 100; actually used, in either Indonesian
           or Malay form, by about 20)
        2. Javanese (45)
        3. Sundanese (15)
        4. Madurese (7)
        5. Balinese (2)
        6. Other languages of Indonesia (Batak, Macas-
           sar, Dayak, Atchin, Minangkabau, etc.: 10)
        7. Malagasy (5)
        8. Visayan (11)
        9. Tagalog (8)
       10. Other languages of the Philippines (Ilocano,
           Bicol, etc.: 10)

     B. Polynesian (Hawaiian, Samoan, Maori, etc.: 1)

     C. Micronesian and Melanesian (1)

VIII. Sudanese-Guinean (100)
      1. Hausa (15; including 10 non-native)

    2. Others (Mossi, Fula, Luba, Mandingo, Yoruba, Fanti, Ibo, Ewe, Efik, etc.: 85)

IX. Bantu (75)

    1. Swahili (10; including 5 non-native)
    2. Others (Ruanda, Sotho, Zulu, Luba, Xhosa, Ganda, Makua, Umbundu, Herero, etc.: 65)

X. Khoin (300,000)

    1. Hottentot (250,000)
    2. Bushman (50,000)

XI. American Indian and Eskimo-Aleut (Geographical Classification: 12)

    1. Quechua (6)
    2. Guarani (1)
    3. Aymará (1)
    4. Maya (1)
    5. Nahuatl (Uto-Aztec: 1)
    6. Others (including Athapaskan, Algonquian, Iroquois, Siouan, Zapotec, Mixtec, Arawak, Araucanian, Carib, Chibcha, Tupi, etc.: 2)

XII. Mon-Khmer (Vietnamese, Cambodian, Lao, Munda, etc.: 45)

XIII. Caucasian (Georgian, Lesghian, Avar, Circassian, etc.: 5)

XIV. Basque (1)

XV. Australian-Papuan (Geographical Classification: 2)

XVI. Ainu and Hyperborean (30,000)

APPENDIX IV

Chart of Forms of Writing

I. Pictographic-Ideographic

A. Chinese-Japanese

This is the only widespread form of pictographic-ideographic writing in use today. Among ancient, unrelated forms are the Egyptian hieroglyphic, hieratic and demotic; the Sumerian-Akkadian cuneiform used also by the ancient Persians; the Hittite; the Cretan; the Indus Valley scripts; the hieroglyphic systems of the Mayas and Aztecs.

II. Syllabic-Alphabetic

A. Hebrew (serves also Yiddish and Ladino; probably the modern form that is closest to the Semitic prototype).

B. Arabic (serves also modern Persian or Iranian, Pashto, Urdu, and a variety of other tongues; older forms appear in Kufic and Syriac).

C. Greek (serves modern Greek with little change of form from the ancient, which was derived from the Semitic).

D. Cyrillic (serves, in slightly different forms, Russian, Ukrainian, Serbian, and Bulgarian; derived for the most part from the Greek).

E. Roman (serves, with appropriate modifications, all Germanic and Romance tongues; Balto-Slavic languages that do not use Cyrillic; Albanian; the Celtic tongues [but an archaic form is used in Irish]; the Finno-Ugric languages; has recently been applied to Turkish, Indonesian, and Vietnamese, as well as to numerous languages of Africa and Oceania; derived from Greek, probably through Etruscan).

F. Devanagari (used by ancient Sanskrit and applied in practically unmodified form to numerous languages of northern India, notably Hindi and Bengali; appears in vastly modified form in Tamil, Telugu, Singhalese, and probably in Burmese and Thai).

G. Armenian (used by modern Armenian; probably derived from early Semitic).

H. Georgian (used by modern Georgian; probably derived from early Semitic).

I. Ethiopic (used by modern Amharic; a syllabic script probably derived from Semitic in its South Arabian version).

J. Korean (an alphabetic system, using symbols that were probably derived from Chinese ideographs).

K. Japanese Kanas (two syllabic systems, using symbols that were probably derived from Chinese ideographs).

(Among ancient alphabetic-syllabic systems are the Phoenician alphabet, used also by the Carthaginians [Punic]; the Pahlavi and Avestan of Persia; the ancient alphabets of the Italian Peninsula, chief among them the Etruscan, Oscan, and Umbrian, all derived from the Greek; the Runic of the ancient Germanic tribes, possibly derived from the Etruscan; the Oghams of ancient Celtic, which are merely systems of lines; the Gothic alphabet, derived from the Greek; the Glagolitic of Old Slavic, also from the Greek. Varieties of the Latin alphabet in the Middle Ages include, in addition to the Irish, the Merovingian and Carolingian scripts and the "Black Letter" formerly used in English and still used in German.)

APPENDIX V

Table of
Alphabetic Development

SEMITIC NAME	NORTH SEM.	HEBREW	GREEK NAME	GREEK	CYRILLIC	ROMAN
Alef	𐤀	א	Alpha	A, α	А, Я, ж	A
Beth	𐤁	ב	Beta	B, β	В, Б	B
Gimel	𐤂	ג	Gamma	Γ, γ	Г, Ґ	C, G
Daleth	𐤃	ד	Delta	Δ, δ	Д	D
He	𐤄	ה	Epsilon	E, ε	Е, Э, Є	E
			Digamma	F		F
Vav	𐤅	ו	Upsilon	Υ, υ	У, ў	V, U, Y, W
Zayin	𐤆	ז	Zeta	Z, ζ	З	Z
Cheth	𐤇	ח	Eta	H, η	И, Й	H
Teth	𐤈	ט	Theta	Θ, θ	Ѳ	
Yod	𐤉	י	Iota	I, ι	І, ї	I, J
Kaf	𐤊	כ	Kappa	K, κ	К	K
Lamed	𐤋	ל	Lambda	Λ, λ	Л, Љ	L
Mem	𐤌	מ	Mu	M, μ	М	M
Nun	𐤍	נ	Nu	N, ν	Н, Њ	N
Samekh	𐤎	ס	Xi	Ξ, ξ		
Ayin	𐤏	ע	Omicron	O, o	О, Ю	O
Pe	𐤐	פ	Pi	Π, π	П	P
Tsade	𐤑	צ			Ч, Ц, Џ	
Quf	𐤒	ק	Qoppa	Q		Q
Resh	𐤓	ר	Rho	P, ρ	Р	R
Shin	𐤔	ש	Sigma	Σ, σ,	С, Ш, Щ	S
Tau	𐤕	ת	Tau	T, τ	Т	T
			Phi	Φ, φ	Ф	
			Chi	X, χ	Х	X
			Psi	Ψ, ψ	Ж, ж	
			Omega	Ω, ω		

Additional Cyrillic Characters: Ъ, Ь, Ы, Ѣ, Ћ, Ђ

APPENDIX VI

Geolinguistic Survey of the Nations of the World

This survey is meant to be only a rough approximation. Population figures are based on 1960 United Nations estimates, with a projection into the future, based on existing trends, for the purpose of bringing them up to time of publication. The lists of languages appearing for each country are not complete but take into consideration only major languages spoken in that country.

1. NORTH AMERICA

COUNTRY	APPROXIMATE POPULATION	LANGUAGES AND COMMENTS
Alaska	150,000	(Now a state of the Union.) English, Eskimo-Aleut
Bermudas	50,000	English
Canada (including Labrador, Newfoundland)	19,000,000	English and French. French speakers, mostly bilingual, numbering perhaps 5,000,000, are located primarily in Quebec and to some extent in Ontario
Greenland	50,000	Danish, English, Eskimo

COUNTRY	APPROXIMATE POPULATION	LANGUAGES AND COMMENTS
Mexico	38,500,000	Spanish, American Indian languages (Uto-Aztec, Penutia, etc.)
U.S.A.	190,000,000	(Figure includes military and civilian personnel stationed abroad; also populations of new states of Alaska and Hawaii.) English, languages of immigration (notably Spanish, French, Italian, German, Slavic, Yiddish, etc.), American Indian languages

(English predominates on the North American continent, with about 200,000,000 speakers. Spanish, with some 40,000,000, follows. French [perhaps 5,000,000] is third. The practical importance of the American Indian languages is quite limited.)

2. CENTRAL AMERICA AND ANTILLES

COUNTRY	APPROXIMATE POPULATION	LANGUAGES AND COMMENTS
Bahamas	100,000	English
British Honduras	100,000	English, Spanish
Canal Zone	75,000	English, Spanish
Costa Rica	1,250,000	Spanish, American Indian languages
Cuba	7,250,000	Spanish
Dominican Republic	3,500,000	Spanish
Guadeloupe-Martinique	650,000	French
Guatemala	4,000,000	Spanish, American Indian languages
Haiti	4,500,000	French, Haitian Creole
Honduras	2,000,000	Spanish, American Indian languages

Nicaragua	1,500,000	Spanish, American Indian languages
Panama	1,250,000	Spanish, American Indian languages
Puerto Rico	2,500,000	Spanish, English
Salvador	3,000,000	Spanish, American Indian languages
Virgin Islands	50,000	English, Danish
West Indian Federation	3,500,000	(Includes Jamaica, Trinidad, Tobago, Barbados, Leeward and Windward Islands [Antigua, Monserrat, Saint-Christopher-Nevis, Anguilla; Dominica, Grenada, St. Lucia, St. Vincent, etc.]) English

(Spanish, French, and English predominate in this area, in the order given, with about 26,000,000, 5,000,000, and 4,000,000, respectively.)

3. SOUTH AMERICA

COUNTRY	APPROXIMATE POPULATION	LANGUAGES AND COMMENTS
Argentina	21,500,000	Spanish, immigrant languages (Italian, German)
Bolivia	3,500,000	Spanish, American Indian languages
Brazil	78,000,000	Portuguese, immigrant languages (Italian, German, Japanese), American Indian languages
Chile	8,000,000	Spanish, American Indian languages
Colombia	15,000,000	Spanish, American Indian languages
Ecuador	4,750,000	Spanish, American Indian languages

COUNTRY	APPROXIMATE POPULATION	LANGUAGES AND COMMENTS
Guiana, British	600,000	English, American Indian languages
Guiana, Dutch	500,000	(Includes Surinam and Netherlands Antilles: Curaçao, etc.) Dutch, English, American Indian languages
Guiana, French	50,000	French, American Indian languages
Paraguay	2,000,000	Spanish, American Indian languages
Peru	10,000,000	Spanish, American Indian languages
Uruguay	3,000,000	Spanish
Venezuela	8,250,000	Spanish, American Indian languages

(South America has approximately the same number of speakers of Spanish [76,000,000] and of Portuguese [78,000,-000]; the latter, however, are concentrated in a single country, Brazil. American Indian languages are far from extinct in South America; Quechua has nearly 6,000,000 speakers, spread over Peru, northern Chile and Argentina, southern Ecuador; Aymará predominates in Bolivia, Tupi and Guarani in Paraguay and Brazil, Arawak and Chibcha in the northern part of the continent. English and French are current in all Latin-American countries among the educated classes, while Italian and German, as languages of immigration, appear in the southern part of the continent [Argentina, Chile, Brazil and Uruguay].)

The Western Hemisphere as a whole shows over 200,000,-000 speakers of English, followed by some 140,000,000 speakers of Spanish, close to 80,000,000 speakers of Portuguese, and about 10,000,000 speakers of French.

4. EUROPE

COUNTRY	APPROXIMATE POPULATION	LANGUAGES AND COMMENTS
Albania	2,000,000	Albanian (with many speakers of Italian, Greek, Turkish, Serbo-Croatian)
Austria	7,500,000	German
Belgium	9,500,000	French, Flemish (the first is almost universally known, the second is the mother tongue of over half the population)
Bulgaria	8,000,000	Bulgarian; Turkish along the Black Sea coast; Macedonian along the Yugoslav and Greek frontiers
Czechoslovakia	14,500,000	Czech; Slovak is a variant of Czech; German is everywhere current; Hungarian in the southern sections; Ukrainian (Ruthenian) in the extreme east; Russian becoming widespread
Denmark	4,500,000	Danish; German current, particularly in southern section
Finland	4,500,000	Finnish; Swedish, Russian, German widespread
France	48,000,000	French; heavy bilingual minorities (Breton, Basque, Catalan, Alsatian German, Italian)
Germany	75,000,000	About 55,000,000 in Federal Republic (West Germany), 20,000,000 in German Democratic Republic (East Germany). German

COUNTRY	APPROXIMATE POPULATION	LANGUAGES AND COMMENTS
Greece	8,500,000	Greek; small Turkish, Albanian, Bulgarian, Macedonian minorities
Hungary	10,000,000	Hungarian; Slovak, German, Rumanian minorities; German widespread
Iceland	200,000	Icelandic, Danish
Ireland (Eire)	3,000,000	English, Irish (or Erse; practically all speak English, only about 1,000,000 speak Irish)
Italy	51,000,000	Italian; German and Rheto-Rumansh speakers in Alto Adige and Trentino; Rheto-Rumansh speakers in Friuli; Slovenian and Croatian speakers on Yugoslav border. All or nearly all speak Italian as well, as do Sardinian speakers in central and southern Sardinia
Luxembourg	500,000	German, French (widespread bilingualism)
Netherlands	12,000,000	Dutch; many Hollanders speak English, German, and/or French
Norway	4,000,000	Norwegian; Lapp in far north; English and German widespread
Poland	31,000,000	Polish; German linguistic minorities in western areas; Lithuanian, Russian, Ukrainian in eastern sections; German and Russian widespread; perhaps 100,000 speakers of Yiddish

Portugal (in-cluding Azores)	9,000,000	Portuguese; Spanish gener-ally understood
Rumania	19,000,000	Rumanian; linguistic minori-ties include Hungarian and German in Transylvania, Bulgarian and Turkish in Dobruja; Russian and Ukrainian fairly wide-spread, particularly along Soviet border
Spain	31,000,000	Spanish (Catalan-Valencian speakers in east, Basque speakers in northeast are normally bilingual; Gali-cian speakers in northwest are accessible through ei-ther Spanish or Portu-guese)
Sweden	8,000,000	Swedish; Lapp in extreme north; German widespread
Switzerland	5,500,000	German, French, Italian, Rheto-Rumansh (the first three are official, the last is a "national" tongue; at least 3,500,000 Swiss speak German; over 2,000,000 speak French; nearly 1,000,000 speak Italian or Rheto-Rumansh)
U.S.S.R. (in Europe)	170,000,000	This includes the Euro-pean portion of Russian S.F.S.R. (over 100,000,-000); Ukrainian S.S.R. (over 40,000,000); Byelo-russian S.S.R. (10,000,-000); Karelo-Finnish S.S.R. (1,000,000); Mol-

COUNTRY	APPROXIMATE POPULATION	LANGUAGES AND COMMENTS
U.S.S.R. (cont'd)		davian S.S.R. (3,000,000); Lithuanian S.S.R. (3,000,-000); Latvian S.S.R. (2,000,000); Estonian S.S.R. (1,000,000). Russian current everywhere; other Republics also use, as co-official languages, respectively, Ukrainian, Byelorussian, Karelian Finnish, Moldavian Rumanian, Lithuanian, Lettish, Estonian
United Kingdom	55,000,000	Including England, 44,000,-000; Wales, 3,000,000; Scotland, 6,000,000; Northern Ireland, 2,000,-000. English is current among practically entire population; Welsh speakers (perhaps 1,000,000) and Gaelic speakers (about 100,000) are nearly all bilingual
Yugoslavia	20,000,000	Serbo-Croatian, Slovenian. Heavy linguistic minorities consist of German, Bulgarian, Macedonian, Hungarian, Albanian, Turkish, Greek, Rumanian, and Italian speakers. German is quite current in areas formerly forming part of Austro-Hungarian Empire

NOTE: For Turkey, see Table 5 on Asia following. Smaller political units include Andorra (10,000: Catalan, Spanish,

French); Gibraltar (30,000: Spanish, English); Liechtenstein (20,000: German); Monaco (30,000: Italian, French); San Marino (20,000: Italian). For Europe as a whole, English is officially current in countries numbering close to 60,000,000, and widely spoken and understood elsewhere. German includes nearly 90,000,000 native speakers, and is spoken and understood by at least 20,000,000 more. French, with nearly 60,000,000 speakers in France, Belgium, and Switzerland, is widespread among the more educated classes of other European countries. Russian is the native or official language of 170,000,000, and widespread in other Communist countries. Italian gives access to nearly 60,000,000 Europeans, Spanish to over 30,000,000, Polish to perhaps 30,000,000. Other European languages that do not have much currency beyond their own borders are Hungarian, Dutch-Flemish, Serbo-Croatian and Slovenian, Rumanian, Czech and Slovak, Swedish, Danish, Norwegian, Portuguese, Bulgarian, Greek, and Finnish. But Portuguese and Dutch have vast overseas ramifications in colonial or former colonial territories, as have English, Spanish, and French. To a lesser degree, this is also true of Italian and German. Europe is a multilingual continent. Many educated Europeans have a knowledge of French, English, and/or German. Many border areas are bilingual, trilingual, even quadrilingual. The everyday necessities of peoples living together in a crowded area have led to the speaking of one or two additional languages by large segments of even the uneducated in many European countries.

5. ASIA

COUNTRY	APPROXIMATE POPULATION	LANGUAGES AND COMMENTS
Afghanistan	16,000,000	Pushtu, Persian
Burma	24,000,000	Burmese; English superimposed
Cambodia	6,000,000	Cambodian (Khmer); Laotian (Thai). Formerly a part of French Indochina; French superimposed

COUNTRY	APPROXIMATE POPULATION	LANGUAGES AND COMMENTS
Ceylon	11,000,000	Singhalese (Indo-Aryan) in south and west; Tamil (Dravidian) in north and east; English superimposed
China (People's Republic)	700,000,000	Mainland, or Communist, China. Population total includes Manchuria (about 50,000,000); Inner Mongolia (about 6,000,000); Tibet (over 1,000,000). The very approximate distribution of the major Chinese "dialects" is: Mandarin (Kuo-yü, the "national" or official tongue): well over 500,000,000; Cantonese: 60,000,000; Wu (Shanghai region): 50,000,000; Min (Fukien region): 50,000,000; Miao-Hakka (south): 30,000,000. Linguistic minorities (about 10,000,000) include Tibetan, Mongol, Manchu, Vietnamese, Thai dialects
China (Republic of)	12,000,000	Nationalist China, holding effective authority only over Taiwan (Formosa) and nearby islands. Chinese, officially of the North Mandarin variety; Fukienese more widely spoken
Cyprus	600,000	Greek, Turkish; English superimposed

Hong Kong	4,000,000	Chinese; English superimposed
India	470,000,000	Indo-Aryan tongues (Hindi, Bengali, Marathi, Gujarati, Punjabi, Rajasthani, Lahnda, Sindhi, Nepali, Bihari, Oriya, Kashmiri, Pahari, etc.) in the north and center; Dravidian languages (Tamil, Telugu, Kanara, Malayalam, etc.) in the south; scattered Munda groups mainly in the northeast; English superimposed
Iran	22,000,000	Persian, Azerbaijani, Kurdish; French and English current among educated classes
Iraq	8,000,000	Arabic, Kurdish, Turkish
Israel	2,500,000	Hebrew, Arabic; English and Yiddish widespread
Japan	95,000,000	Japanese; Ainu in Yezo; English widespread among educated classes
Jordan	2,000,000	Arabic; some French and English influence
Korea	36,000,000	Includes Republic of Korea (South Korea), 26,000,000; People's Democratic Republic of Korea (North or Communist Korea), 10,000,000. Korean; Japanese and English superimposed; Chinese widespread, especially in North Korea
Laos	3,000,000	Formerly a part of French Indochina. Laotian (of the Thai branch of Sino-

216   INVITATION TO LINGUISTICS

COUNTRY	APPROXIMATE POPULATION	LANGUAGES AND COMMENTS
Laos (cont'd)		Tibetan); Cambodian (Khmer); French superimposed
Lebanon	2,000,000	Arabic; some French and English influence
Malaysia	12,000,000	Including former British Malaya, Straits Settlements, Singapore, North Borneo, Brunei, Sarawak. Malay (Indonesian). Chinese, Mon-Khmer on mainland; English superimposed
Muscat and Oman	600,000	Arabic; some English influence
Nepal and Bhutan	10,000,000	Indo-Aryan (Nepali) and Tibetan dialects
Outer Mongolia	1,000,000	Officially, Mongolian People's Republic. Mongol, with widespread Chinese and some Russian influence
Pakistan	100,000,000	Indo-Aryan tongues, with predominance of Urdu in West Pakistan, Bengali in East Pakistan. Punjabi, Baluchi, Sindhi, and Lahnda in West Pakistan also; English superimposed
Portuguese Asia	500,000	Now restricted to Macao, since loss of Goa, Damau, and Diu to India. Chinese; Portuguese superimposed
Sa'udi Arabia	7,000,000	Arabic; some English influence

Syria	5,000,000	Sometimes united with Egypt in United Arab Republic. Arabic; some French influence
Thailand	29,000,000	Siamese (Thai); Karen (Burmese); Laotian; some English influence
Turkey (including European Turkey)	30,000,000	Turkish; some Armenian and Kurdish in eastern areas; some Greek in European Turkey
U.S.S.R. (in Asia)	57,000,000	Includes Asiatic portion of Russian S.F.S.R. (about 20,000,000); Armenian S.S.R. (2,000,000); Georgian S.S.R. (4,000,000); Azerbaijani S.S.R. (4,000,000); Uzbek S.S.R. (7,500,000); Turkmen S.S.R. (2,000,000); Kazakh S.S.R. (9,500,000); Kirghiz S.S.R. (2,000,000); Tadjik S.S.R. (2,000,000). In addition to Russian, everywhere official and current, and to the languages peculiar to each S.S.R., there are languages of Uralic and Altaic stock (Ostyak, Vogul, Cheremiss, Samoyed, Mordvinian; Yakut, Uigur, Bashkir, Tungus, Mongol); and Palaeoasiatic tongues (Chukchi, Koriak, Kamchadal, Yukagir, etc.)

COUNTRY	APPROXIMATE POPULATION	LANGUAGES AND COMMENTS
Vietnam	33,000,000	Formerly part of French Indochina. North Vietnam (Communist area, or Vietminh), 18,000,000; South Vietnam (Republic of Vietnam), 15,000,000. Vietnamese (Annamese, Muong); Mon-Khmer dialects; French superimposed
Yemen	4,500,000	Arabic; some English influence

NOTE: British possessions and protectorates in and near Arabia (Aden, Bahrein, Kuwait, Trucial, Qatar) have an aggregate Arabic-speaking population of over 1,000,000, with English superimposed. In all Arabic-speaking states Arabic is now the official as well as the national language. Hindi is making slow progress as the common language of India and is now spoken, even as an acquired tongue, by no more than half of the population. Urdu, once the official language of Pakistan, has conceded co-official status to Bengali in East Pakistan. Singhalese, the official language of Ceylon, encounters opposition from speakers of Tamil. Chinese and Russian have somewhat extended their influence, but the old tongues of colonization, English, French, Portuguese, are still very much in use.

First among the Asian languages is Chinese, with its mighty mass of speakers. Japanese, with almost 100,000,000 speakers, makes its influence felt on the mainland. Russian permeates northern Asia, despite the presence of numerous Uralic and Altaic tongues. Arabic, in addition to being the national and official language of several Asian countries, makes its influence felt as a cultural and liturgical tongue in Afghanistan, Iran, northern India.

Among the superimposed languages of former colonization, first place is held by English, which still permeates India, Pakistan, Ceylon, Burma, Malaysia, Hong Kong, Cyprus, Israel, Jordan, and parts of the Arabian Peninsula. French is still strong in Cambodia, Laos, and Vietnam. Portuguese is now restricted to Macao. Russian acts as a language of current colonization throughout the Asiatic portion of the U.S.S.R. and makes its influence felt in such border regions as Mongolia and Afghanistan.

6. AFRICA

NOTE: For the African Negro languages, the two classifications of Bantu and Khoin (or Hottentot-Bushman) languages are definitely established. Despite recent attempts, there is still no unanimity among the specialists for the languages once described as Sudanese-Guinean, a strictly geographical classification.

COUNTRY	APPROXIMATE POPULATION	LANGUAGES AND COMMENTS
Algeria and Algerian Sahara	12,000,000	Arabic; Berber (Kabyl, Tamashek); French superimposed
Angola and Cabinda	5,000,000	Bantu languages (Umbundu, Kimbundu, Chokwe, Kongo, Luanda, Ngola, Ganguela, Pende, etc.); Portuguese superimposed
Basutoland	700,000	Bantu languages (Sotho, Zulu); English, Afrikaans superimposed
Bechuanaland	400,000	Bantu (Chuana); English superimposed
British Cameroon	1,000,000	Nigero-Chad languages (Hausa, Dwala, Fula, Kanuri, etc.); English superimposed
Cameroon	5,000,000	Bantu languages (Pangwe, Bulu, Fang, Yaounde,

COUNTRY	APPROXIMATE POPULATION	LANGUAGES AND COMMENTS
Cameroon (*cont'd*)		Fula, Dwala, etc.); Ubangi; French superimposed
Central African Republic	1,250,000	Ubangi, Nuba; French superimposed
Chad Republic	2,500,000	Nuba, Arabic; French superimposed
Congo (formerly Belgian)	14,000,000	Bantu languages (Luba, Ngala, Swahili, Kongo, Ruanda, Rundi, etc.); French, Flemish superimposed
Congo Republic	1,000,000	Bantu languages (Kongo, Pul, etc.); French superimposed
Dahomey Republic	2,500,000	Ewe, Fon, Efik, Yoruba, Hausa; French superimposed
Ethiopia (including Eritrea)	22,000,000	Amharic, Tigre, Tigriña, Galla, Sidamo, Harari, Beja, Somali, etc.; Italian superimposed
French Somaliland	100,000	Somali; French superimposed
Gabon Republic	500,000	Bantu languages (Fang, Yaounde, etc.); French superimposed
Gambia	500,000	Mandingo, Wolof, Fula, etc.; English superimposed

Ghana	8,000,000	Twi, Fanti, Ga, Ewe, Ibo, Mossi, etc.; English superimposed
Guinea Republic	3,000,000	Fula, Mandingo; French superimposed
Ivory Coast Republic	3,000,000	Mossi, Mandingo, Kru, etc.; English superimposed
Kenya	9,000,000	Bantu languages (Kikuyu, Swahili); Masai; English superimposed
Liberia	3,000,000	Kru, De, Kpessi, Mandingo, etc.; English superimposed
Libya	1,250,000	Arabic, Berber dialects; Italian superimposed
Malagasy Republic (Madagascar)	6,000,000	Indonesian (Malagasy, Hova); French superimposed
Mali	4,000,000	Mandingo, Fula, Mossi; French superimposed
Mauritanian Islamic Republic	750,000	Arabic, Berber (Zenaga, Shilh); French superimposed
Morocco	13,000,000	Arabic, Berber (Rif); French superimposed
Mozambique	7,000,000	Bantu languages (Makua, Ronga, Shona, Swahili, etc.); Portuguese superimposed
Niger Republic	3,000,000	Hausa, Kanuri, Berber (Tamashek), Arabic; French superimposed

COUNTRY	APPROXIMATE POPULATION	LANGUAGES AND COMMENTS
Nigeria	37,000,000	Hausa, Yoruba, Ibo, Kanuri, Efik, Fula, Nupe, etc.; English superimposed
Portuguese Guinea	1,000,000	Fula, Mandingo; Portuguese superimposed
Rhodesia-Nyasaland Federation	10,000,000	Bantu languages (Nyanja, Bemba, Kololo, Shona, Tonga, Swahili, Zulu); English superimposed
Ruanda-Urundi	3,000,000	Bantu languages (Ruanda, Rundi, Swahili); French, Flemish superimposed
Senegal Republic	3,000,000	Wolof, Mandingo, Fula; French superimposed
Sierra Leone	2,500,000	Mende, Temne; English superimposed
Somalia (former British and Italian Somaliland)	2,000,000	Somali, Amharic, Arabic, Swahili; Italian, English superimposed
Southwest Africa	500,000	Khoin (Hottentot-Bushman); Bantu (Herero); Afrikaans, English, German superimposed
Spanish Guinea	300,000	Benga; Spanish superimposed
Spanish Sahara and Ifni	1,000,000	Arabic, Berber (Rif, Shilh); Spanish superimposed

Sudan (was Anglo-Egyptian Sudan)	13,000,000	Arabic, Nuba, Dinka, Kanuri, Nda-Kongo, Beja, etc.; English superimposed
Sudanese Republic	3,750,000	Fula, Mandingo, Mossi; French superimposed
Swaziland	300,000	Bantu languages (Swazi, Zulu); English, Afrikaans superimposed
Tanganyika	10,000,000	Bantu languages (Nyamwezi, Swahili, Nyanja, Ruanda, etc.); English, German superimposed
Togoland Republic	1,500,000	Ewe, Fon, Efik, Twi, Mossi; English, German superimposed
Tunisia	4,000,000	Arabic, Berber; French, Italian superimposed
Uganda	7,000,000	Bantu languages (Ganda, Nyoro, Swahili, etc.); English superimposed
Union of South Africa	17,000,000	Bantu languages (Zulu, Xhosa, Sotho, Chuana, Tebele, etc.); Khoin (Bushman); Afrikaans, English superimposed
United Arab Republic (Egypt)	29,000,000	Arabic, Nubian, Beja; French, English superimposed
Voltaic Republic	5,000,000	Mossi, Efik; French superimposed
Zanzibar	500,000	Swahili, Arabic; English superimposed

NOTE: Canary Islands are totaled with Spanish Sahara-Ifni; Madeira and Cape Verde Islands (Príncipe, São Tomé) are totaled with Portuguese Guinea.

North Africa, as far as the Tropic of Cancer and beyond, is linguistically Semito-Hamitic-Kushitic, with Semitic Arabic stretching from Morocco to Egypt, interspersed with Hamitic Berber (Kabyl, Rif, Shilh, Tamashek). Kushitic languages (Somali, Beja) appear in the eastern part of Africa's northern half, while the predominant tongues of Ethiopia (Amharic, Tigre) are Semitic. The rest of the African continent is divided between various groups of Negro languages geographically described as Sudanese-Guinean, and the Bantu group, with the dividing line between the two running from a little north of the Equator on the western coast to a little south of it on the eastern. The Khoin, or Hottentot-Bushman, group appears only in a restricted section of southwest Africa.

The languages of colonization are still very much alive throughout the continent, with English and French leading, followed at some distance by Afrikaans, Portuguese, Italian, Spanish, and faint memories of German from the days before the First World War. There is as yet no indication of the emergence of any African Negro language as a national tongue, though such a development may occur in the future.

7. OCEANIA

COUNTRY	APPROXIMATE POPULATION	LANGUAGES AND COMMENTS
Australia	11,000,000	English. Speakers of native Australian languages number about 200,000
Caroline, Marianas, Marshall Islands	120,000	Now taken over by U.S.A. Micronesian languages; English, Japanese superimposed
Fiji Islands	400,000	Melanesian; English, Pidgin English, Hindustani superimposed

French Oce-ania	80,000	Polynesian; French superimposed
Gilbert and El-lice Islands	50,000	Micronesian and Polynesian; English superimposed
Guam	70,000	Micronesian; English superimposed
Hawaii	700,000	Now a state of the Union. Polynesian Hawaiian spoken by only about 30,000; English, Japanese, Chinese, Korean superimposed
Indonesia	103,000,000	Coincides with former Dutch East Indies. Indonesian (Bahasa Indonesia), largely based on Malay, is official language, but spoken by minority of population. Major local languages, all of Indonesian branch of Malayo-Polynesian family: Javanese, 45,000,000; Sundanese, 15,000,000; Madurese, 7,000,000; Balinese, 2,000,000; Batak, 2,000,000; Bugi, 2,000,000; Dayak, 1,000,000; others, 29,000,000. Malay and Dutch superimposed; English fairly widespread
New Caledo-nia	100,000	Melanesian; French superimposed
New Guinea	1,600,000	Papuan languages; English, Pidgin English superimposed

COUNTRY	APPROXIMATE POPULATION	LANGUAGES AND COMMENTS
New Hebrides	60,000	Melanesian; English, French superimposed
New Zealand	2,600,000	English; Polynesian Maori spoken by 100,000
Papua	600,000	Papuan; English superimposed
Philippines	31,000,000	Languages of Indonesian branch of Malayo-Polynesian. Tagalog, official tongue, 6,000,000; Visaya, 11,000,000; Ilocano, 3,000,000; Bikol, 2,000,000; others, 9,000,000. English, Spanish superimposed
Samoa and West Samoa	200,000	Polynesian; English, German superimposed
Solomon Islands	150,000	Melanesian; English superimposed
Timor (Portuguese)	500,000	Indonesian; Portuguese superimposed
Tonga	100,000	Polynesian; English superimposed

NOTE: The colonial languages are still very much alive in this area, with English, French, and Portuguese in widespread use, though sometimes in Pidgin form. Dutch still has some currency in Indonesia, Spanish in the Philippines, German and Japanese in the territories once held by Germany and occupied by Japan during the Second World War. Among the languages native to the area, those of the Malayo-Polynesian family predominate, with the Indonesian branch holding a large lead over the other three subgroups (Polynesian, Melanesian, Micronesian). Papuan and Australian native languages are still unsatisfactorily classified.

APPENDIX VII

What Is a Scientific Linguist?

(Reprinted from the *Linguistic Reporter*, April 1963, Center for Applied Linguistics, Modern Language Association of America, Washington, D.C.)

[The following statement was prepared in March 1962 by the Center for Applied Linguistics at the request of various government agencies that have occasion to employ linguists. Although the statement has not been officially endorsed by any professional organization in the field, it has been reproduced in LANGUAGE, *Journal of the Linguistic Society of America, Vol. 38, No. 4, October–December 1962, pp. 463–64.]*

A scientific linguist (also called a linguistic scientist, a linguistician, or most commonly in the profession, simply a linguist) is a specialist in linguistics, the systematic study of the structure and functioning of languages. (A linguist in this technical sense must be distinguished from a linguist in the everyday sense of a polyglot, one who speaks several languages. Cf. *Webster's New International Dictionary*, which gives both definitions of "linguist.") A linguist is qualified by training and experience to carry out such operations as the following: (1) preparation of a full-scale description of the sounds, forms and vocabulary of a language (including unwritten languages previously undescribed); (2) comparative study of two or more languages to determine their relationships; (3) determination of the nature and range of dialect variation within a language; (4) study of the history of the sounds, forms, and vocabulary of a language; (5) development of the general theory of linguistics.

In addition to such activities, a qualified linguist is able to apply linguistic science to practical language problems by undertaking, often in collaboration with specialists from other disciplines, such operations as the following: (a) preparation of a contrastive analysis between two languages to point out the similarities and differences between them on which to base instructional materials for teaching one of the languages to speakers of the other; (b) preparation of textbooks for language learning based on linguistic analysis; (c) preparation of tests of proficiency in a language or of aptitude for certain kinds of language learning; (d) analysis of the writing system of a language to determine how closely it correlates with the pronunciation and grammar; construction of an orthography for an unwritten language; (e) preparation of materials for teaching literacy in a given language; (f) analysis of language and the preparation of programs for machine translation from one language to another; (g) working out and evaluating language policies in government and education.

In recent years linguists have come to work more and more on topics which involve other disciplines, such as anthropology (with which linguistics has had a long association), psychology, mathematics, logic, speech pathology, and sociology; cross-disciplinary fields such as psycholinguistics, sociolinguistics and mathematical linguistics are now achieving recognition, and a small but growing number of linguists are specialists in them.

Education of Linguists

Normally the education of an American linguist takes place in a regular program of graduate studies at one of the dozen or so major university centers for linguistic study in the country. Requirements for the Ph.D. in linguistics vary somewhat from one university to another, but all require an introductory course in linguistics, work in phonetics and phonemics, historical linguistics, and the study of specific languages. Most include requirements of work in morphology-syntax, field methods, Indo-European comparative studies, and at least one non-Indo-European language. A Ph.D. thesis is usually a study of the types (1)–(4) listed above. One common type consists of a descriptive grammar, with texts and vocabulary, of an American Indian language.

The overwhelming majority of American linguists, in addition to taking graduate work at a major university, have attended one or more sessions of the Linguistic Institute which is sponsored every summer by the Linguistic Society of America, the chief professional organization in the field. This summer Institute, which has been held every year since 1938 at one university or another, brings together for intensive work in the field faculty and students from all over the country and usually several distinguished linguists from abroad. Some American linguists have received their training largely outside regular university programs by work with missionary organizations, special language programs, or even self-study, but this pattern of education is becoming rarer.

Careers in Linguistics

A small but important and highly influential number of linguists are teaching in the linguistics departments of universities. A larger number teach in other departments, generally modern languages or anthropology, but occasionally in departments of psychology or speech. In recent years a steadily growing number of linguists have been employed in centers of instruction for Asian and African languages either on the teaching staff or with research projects, including the preparation of textbooks and dictionaries. A few work on research projects related to communication engineering, usually with government support.

Several government agencies, such as the Foreign Service Institute of the Department of State, hire linguists to supervise language training programs. Others, such as the Department of the Interior, have linguists to carry out research on American Indian languages, or to work in specialized fields such as the determination of geographical names for mapping and other purposes.

Linguists are employed at centers of machine translation research at a number of places in the country, chiefly in university programs with U. S. Government support, but also in private industry.

One large group of American linguists is engaged either in the teaching of English as a foreign language in the United

States or abroad, the preparation of textbooks of English, or in the planning and administering of English-teaching programs. Some of them are in positions with the United States Information Agency or other government agencies; others are with foreign governments, American universities, or other private organizations.

Another sizable number of linguists work with missionary organizations engaged in such operations as Bible translation, literacy programs, or the creation of orthographies for unwritten languages.

A Few Suggestions

Descriptive Linguistics

The function of historical linguistics is to trace the evolution of language and languages from one chronological stage to another, describe intervening stages and processes, and reveal, if possible, stages of language and languages previously unknown. Obviously there is not too much connection between this and the process of learning a modern spoken language. We can have a tremendous amount of philological and historical information about the way a language has reached its present state, and still be quite unable to speak and understand it. At the most, information of a purely historical nature will aid us with the written form of the language.

The function of geolinguistics is to present the world's languages in proper perspective, in their present-day political and economic framework, and to describe their relative importance and usefulness in various connections. Again, there is little here to aid us with learning to speak and understand the languages themselves, save in so far as our geolinguistic information is supplemented by practical demonstrations.

The function of descriptive linguistics is primarily to establish principles and norms applicable to all language; but it is also to describe individual languages accurately. Out of these descriptions can come useful principles and methods of language teaching and language learning, if the descriptions are properly and intelligently utilized. But the descriptive linguist's function is completed when he has rendered his accurate description. Beyond that point, either the descriptive linguist must turn himself into a language teacher (which he is not always qualified to do), or a qualified language teacher must take over.

The language teacher's qualifications are numerous and varied. He must himself know the language he is teaching, and speak and understand it more or less as a native. He must also have considerable knowledge of the language of the learners, so as to be able to compare the two languages, to himself if not to his students, and perceive clearly what the different points of contrast and difficulty are. He must have a trained and quick language ear, and infinite patience with explanations, but above all with repetitive drills.

All this means that no linguist, historical, descriptive, or geolinguist, is by nature endowed to impart spoken languages, though some happen to be. A language teacher need not be a linguist in any of the three senses, nor need a linguist be a language teacher.

But the language teacher should be able and willing to absorb from the linguist and apply to his language teaching whatever information the linguist may have to offer that is relevant to his job. From the historical linguist come items that tie up with the literary and cultural history of the country whose language he is teaching, and with its system of writing. The geolinguist can tell him why and in what respects his language is significant, what its ramifications and connections are, and what reasons there are to study it. The descriptive linguist can give him the most valuable information, of the kind most directly applicable to the spoken language, either in isolation or in comparison with the language of the learners.

This can be done only if the information is presented in clear fashion and in clear language, which the language teacher can readily understand. Any use of involved technical jargon will defeat the purpose. The information must bear on important, not on trifling points, preferably the major points in the phonemic and morphemic structure of the target language, and the major points of difference with the language of the learner. On the other hand, truly important points should not be ignored; often they are ignored, out of a desire to make the two languages fit into one ideal universal-grammar mold, or to put them on the same geolinguistic level, because of a mistaken sense of equalitarianism. In the case of a language that is socially and educationally stratified, the information should be such as to cover the standard language of the reasonably educated speakers, since that is the form normally imparted by the language teacher and wanted by the student, save in special situations.

Above all, the analysis must be correct, and not based upon insufficient observation and hasty generalizations. Languages are highly complex phenomena, and they are far from having that oversimplified standardization which some descriptive linguists occasionally assume. It does not suffice to collect a few semiliterate, semidialectal speakers to construct a descriptive grammar of a big language of modern civilization. If we try, we may emerge with a descriptive grammar of a few idiolects or dialects, but not with something that will satisfy the language teacher.

Under proper conditions, there can exist optimum co-operation between the linguist and the language teacher. But if the linguist allows his contribution to be tinged with doctrinaire views which may or may not be justified in a broader, panoramic, philosophical view of language in the abstract, but are only partly applicable to the specific situation or language on hand, trouble and confusion may result.

A criticism that may be justifiably leveled at descriptive linguistics is in connection with the multiplication and proliferation of terminology. For this there is explanation, but not justification, in the creative urge of young and enthusiastic men who are dealing with a relatively new field. To keep up with all the new terms devised by the descriptivists, often with dozens of names applied to what is basically the same phenomenon, would call not for a glossary or a dictionary but for an encyclopedia. Earlier attempts at constructing dictionaries of linguistic terminology, such as that of Marouzeau, or of this writer, have become hopelessly outdated within less than ten years, and this not because of changes in the historical or geolinguistic portion of the offering, but solely the descriptive portion. Another recent attempt hits upon the expedient of not trying to define terms but simply citing them in the context of the writer who has coined them; but even this needs constant updating, in addition to being unsatisfactory from a definitional standpoint. There is a crying need

for a convention of descriptive linguists called for the purpose
of standardizing and stabilizing the terminology, so that the
subject matter may become more readily accessible, particularly to beginning students. As matters stand, this writer has
noted a seventy-five per cent discrepancy in terminology between two works written by serious descriptive linguists who,
in the main, see eye to eye and are describing the same phenomena and processes.

Obscuration is occasionally characteristic of writings in this
field. This is due partly to the superabundance of terminology,
partly to the inherent ponderosity of a certain type of aca-
demic mind. "Never define in three simple, short words what
can be defined in ten lengthy and unusual ones!" seems to be
the motto of certain writers. In this the descriptive linguists
guilty of the practice are accompanied by writers in other
fields, notably psychology, philosophy, sociology, education,
and government. Since this is an individual matter, it is
doubtful that it can be cured by any universal panacea.

There has been noticeable for some time in descriptivism
a tendency toward the esoteric. The reduction of descriptive
linguistics to mathematical statements and formulas, initiated
by Hjelmslev and his Glossematics, is of no particular advantage to either linguistics or mathematics. The subject matter
of linguistics is language. If linguistics cannot make itself
clear and useful in terms of its own subject matter, without
having recourse to a science with which it has no visible connection, it seems to fail in its purpose. The same may be said
of excesses in the direction of philosophy, psychology, and
metalinguistics, based on unproved assumptions. Linguistics
should be factual, not metaphysical.

There is a tendency to go in for minutiae, and to describe
in great detail points of small relevance, interest, or utility.
While it is possible, in the main, to reproduce a general system of intonations, pitches, and junctures in a given language,
it is not possible to pinpoint it to the degree where we can
confidently assert that "there are only four pitches in American English, and they are used in such and such a fashion."
There is far too much variation among the speakers. Distinctions between "light housekeeper" and "lighthouse keeper"
may elicit wonder but convey little true information. Language

depends far too much on context for understanding to be disturbed by features that are often barely audible.

Along with this, there is a reluctance to apply some of the facts established by descriptive observation and comparison to practical problems of language learning. A few examples are in order:

1. The extraordinary importance of syllabification (the breaking of a word into its component syllables, as apart from what the descriptivists call juncture), in most Western languages other than English. It can never be sufficiently stressed that the quickest and most effective way of acquiring a native-speaker accent in such languages as Italian, Spanish, French, and even German and Russian is to break up the word into its true syllables in accordance with the syllabic pattern of the language (this, by the way, does not always coincide with the written-language rules for dividing words at the ends of lines), pronounce each syllable separately and distinctly, then gradually run the syllables together until the speed of normal speech is attained.

2. The chance similarity and nearness or absolute equivalence in point of articulation, with perhaps a few minor modifications, of phonemes which two languages represent in writing by altogether different symbols, such as the English alveolar plosives and the Italian or Spanish trilled *r* (the normal way in which English "get out of here" strikes the Italian ear is *gherare hir*). There is almost an equivalence in quality and point of articulation between the English short *i* of *it* and *bit*, slightly prolonged, and the Romance closed *e* of Italian *vedere* or Spanish *ver*.

3. The fact that one language often produces, exceptionally and accidentally, or under unstable conditions, what is a regular phoneme or phoneme cluster in another. English does not have the phonemic opposition between single and double consonants that appears in Italian, Japanese, Hungarian, and many other languages. But when an English speaker says *wunnerful* instead of *wonderful*, or a train conductor shouts in stentorian fashion "All ab-board!" the double consonant is phonetically present, and without the open juncture that appears in *unnamed*. English does not permit the appearance of an initial cluster such as *mch-* (Russian *mchat'*); but an

English combination such as *cream cheese*, with *crea-* omitted, will give the learner precisely the drill training he needs.

Lack of perspective and a false spirit of democracy are evidenced by the belief of some descriptivists that all languages are on the same plane. This may be so in the abstract, but the geolinguist, who deals with realities, not with abstractions, knows that in the foreseeable future there is no possibility of putting Menomini or Ojibwa on a plane of parity with English or Russian, save in one respect, descriptively. Historically and geolinguistically, the comparison does not hold.

The same criticism applies to the erroneous belief that one type of language is as good as another, with the consequent admonition to "leave your language alone" and let the chips fall where they may. This has been abundantly proved by the violent controversies aroused by the appearance of Webster's Third International Dictionary, constructed in accordance with descriptive principles, in which distinctions of "good" usage, standard and substandard forms, colloquialisms, vulgarisms, even slang, were largely obliterated. There is a hierarchy in types of language, just as there is a hierarchy in languages. Some carry you further than others and serve far better as means of communication, which is language's basic function. By all means let us study the dialects of the mountaineers and gangsters, either from the standpoint of pure descriptive science or for specific purposes. But let us not offer the thesis that these language forms are in all respects "equal" to the standard speech that is nationwide, though with minor local variations.

Stemming from the same ideological error is the cult of the native speaker and the belief that he can do no wrong, that "correct" and "incorrect" are terms that can be used only in connection with foreigners attempting to speak a given language. In too many respects, some of which may be purely aesthetic and subjective, but others of which are linked with the very factual basis of ease of communication, there are cases, and plenty of them, where a cultured foreign accent is preferable to a graceless, illiterate, highly dialectal native one. Americans who have no difficulty understanding Charles Boyer will have difficulty in understanding some natives of certain American regions. This does not mean that we should not strive to learn and teach languages with as nearly native an accent as possible. It simply means that the only time a full native-speaker accent is imperative is in connection with espionage work.

Some descriptive linguists find it difficult to conceal their impatience with the written form of the language. They even state that there is no written language, but only an opposition between speech, which is the true language, and writing. Aside from the fact that the written language is normally paramount to the historical linguist in his philological-linguistic research, the geolinguist can point to the tremendous importance of the role played by the written tongue in all civilized languages, and to the fact that governments all over the earth have found it expedient to attempt to eradicate illiteracy among their populations. If writing is viewed as only a symbol of speech, let us not forget that speech itself is also only a symbol of thought, neither higher nor lower in hierarchy, and that semantic transfer, the basic purpose of language, can be effected just as easily by writing as by speech, as proved by ideographic-pictographic systems, where the spoken language is almost completely by-passed.

The barely veiled sufferance with which many descriptive linguists regard their historical colleagues, whose activities antedated their own, and the geolinguists, who point the way to the most important practical applications of linguistics in the present and future, is again an individual matter, and one which it is hoped will disappear in time, as a proper balance is reached among the three great divisions of linguistics. Some descriptivists, however, need to be reminded that languages were spoken, learned, taught, studied, and discussed long before the time of Boas and Bloomfield, and that other methods of approach to the problems of language than their own are possible, and sometimes more successful. A science is a science only to the extent that it keeps an open mind and permits free discussion. Otherwise, it degenerates into a dogma.

Historical Linguistics

From its inception, historical linguistics has unfortunately
lent itself to flights of the imagination. The temptation to
link linguistic evolution with one or another historical development, and attribute a cause-and-effect relationship to phenomena that could be coincidental, is invariably strong among
historical linguists.

Yet the opposite excess, the attempt to divorce linguistic
development altogether from the life of the people who speak
the language, is equally undesirable. The cause-and-effect
relationship is there, in all instances, whatever the cause may
be. The trouble lies not with seeking to ascertain causes for
linguistic change but in predetermining the causes before all
the evidence is in. Worse yet is the tendency on the part of
some historical linguists to sift the evidence to suit themselves,
discarding that part which does not fit in with their own preconceived notions and giving undue prominence to the part
which supports their *a priori* conclusions.

It was partly as a reaction to these methodological excesses
of the nineteenth century that the new school of descriptive
and structural linguistics elaborated its own excessively mechanical point of view and methodology, which consists
mainly in placing reliance only upon directly observable facts.
But these, too, can be misinterpreted and mishandled, as has
been shown.

Once scientific linguistics had become firmly established at
the outset of the nineteenth century on the basis of recorded
documents and inscriptions, an initial observation of a generic
nature was made. The evolution of languages, particularly
in the field of sounds (phonemes had not yet been invented),
took place not in a haphazard fashion but in accordance with
a regular pattern. The scheme of sound correspondences in
the various Indo-European branches was a definite and regular one. It assumed an equally definite and regular aspect in
any branch of Indo-European that was subjected to the same
searching comparison. It seemed an established fact that if
the Latin, Greek, Sanskrit, and Slavic words for certain objects
started with *p-*, the Germanic ones would have *f-*, the Ar-

menian ones *h-*, and the Celtic would show the loss of the
initial consonant. It seemed equally established that if a Latin
word contained a *-ct-* group, its French and Portuguese descendants would have *-it-*, its Spanish ones *-ch-*, its Italian
ones *-tt-*, its Rumanian ones *-pt-*.[1] True, there seemed to be
certain exceptions, but they could usually be accounted for in
one way or another. This led a group of historical linguists to
propound the thesis of the *Lautgesetz* or Sound Law, to the
effect that in a certain area and at a certain period an innova-
tion, once begun, would affect all words showing the sound
in question, and this without exception. The laws of sound
change were given the same stringency as those of Newtonian
physics, the universality of which has lately been disproved
by Einstein and others.

This intransigent position aroused the opposition of a considerable body of linguists, a few of whom went all the way in
the other direction, that of denying all cogency to the sound
laws and claiming "the arbitrium of the individual" as the
chief force in language change. A compromise of sorts was
finally effected by a modification of the *Lautgesetz* to include
the possibility of exceptions due to such factors as foreign,
dialectal, or learned borrowing, or the working of analogy.
But it must be pointed out that, while borrowing is factual
and generally demonstrable, analogy is not, save in a few
specific instances.

In broad fashion analogy may be defined as the imitation
of one language form by another, which is thereby pulled out
of its natural orbit and subtracted from the sound law that
would normally apply to it. That this frequently happens
there is no doubt. How, why, or under what circumstances it
happens is often highly problematical. The sound-law development of Latin *frĭgidum*, for example, would call for French
frid and Italian *friddo*. What we have instead is French *froid*
and Italian *freddo*, which would be phonologically normal if
the Latin form had been *frīgidum*, with short *i* in the first
syllable. To account for the irregularity, it is advanced that
frĭgidum was frequently associated in popular speech with

[1] E.g., Latin *noctem, lactem;* French *nuit, lait;* Portuguese *noite,
leite;* Spanish *noche, leche;* Italian *notte, latte;* Rumanian *noapte,
lapte.*

rigidum ("cold and stiff," as a corpse), and was therefore made to rhyme with it. This is fairly plausible but not actually demonstrable. Analogies advanced to account for irregular phonological developments, as a matter of fact, range all the way from highly plausible and even demonstrable to highly suspect and illogical.

At all events, it may be suggested that, while analogy supplies an excellent line of defense for the believers in the stringency of sound laws, since it permits them to wave all troublesome exceptions out of the way, it has its own peculiar disadvantages. It sets up subsidiary sound laws of narrower and narrower applicability, until in many cases it almost comes to coincide with the arbitrium of the individual postulated by the more mentalistic opponents of the sound law. A more reasonable position would seem to be the postulation of sound trends not having the force of ironbound laws, to which the majority of language forms subscribe, with aberrations due to a multiplicity of causes, analogy among them. Let us not forget that for every effect there is invariably a cause; but also that it is not always easy to ascertain the cause.

The firm establishment of analogy as a recognized force in linguistic change has led to numerous abuses, of which one is the presentation of dubious analogies as established fact in textbooks and elsewhere. There is nothing wrong with offering hypotheses, but they should be carefully labeled as such until they are proved beyond a doubt.

The habit of basing sweeping conclusions upon insufficient evidence occasionally appears in the work of historical linguists. There is, for example, the theory of the ethnical substratum and superstratum, whereby changes occurring in the evolution of a given language, say Latin into French, are attributed either to earlier Celtic habits of pronunciation or to later influences of the Germanic invaders. While it is very easily demonstrable that this influence was exerted for what concerns vocabulary (French has many words specifically inherited from the Gauls, and others specifically introduced by the Franks, while Spanish has Iberian and Arabic words that do not appear in other Romance languages), the evidence that this influence extended to the sound pattern of the language is doubtful and conflicting. Yet highly reputable linguists advance this substratum influence on phonological development as an established fact, and base on it all sorts of farfetched conclusions, not merely of a linguistic but even of a historical nature.

Equally dubious is the theory of lateral areas, advanced at different times by such reputable linguists as Meillet and Bertoni. Here it is supposed that the central portion of a language area acts as the radiating center for innovations, and that the outlying parts of the area often escape this influence, and consequently display common conservative features which appear at great distances from one another. Where the Celtic and the Indo-Iranian languages, for instance, happen to hold a feature in common that does not appear in the intervening Indo-European territory, this is attributed to lateral area conservatism. Where the Hispanic languages and Rumanian show a few similar coincidences, which could well be accidental, the mass of other phenomena where they diverge is forgotten, and they are endowed with a quasi-mystical link. Romance linguists have established a kinship between centro-southern Italian and Rumanian that is based on nothing more than their common dropping of Latin final -s (to this the voicing of intervocalic surds is often added, but the evidence is weak); all other features where Italian joins the Western Romance languages while Rumanian diverges from both are overlooked. This disregard of the *total* evidence, and a fixation upon a feature or features which favor a preconceived theory, sometimes lead to the remark that historical linguistics, in contradistinction to descriptive linguistics, is a somewhat fanciful science.

One recent manifestation of this mentality is the belief in glottochronology and lexicostatistics, previously described and glaringly based on insufficient, hand-picked evidence. Another is the metalinguistics put into vogue by a brilliant but insufficiently prepared linguist, B. L. Whorf, which has for its major tenet that the type of language spoken influences the mentality and behavior of the speakers and compels them to think and act along certain lines. That this may happen in part once the language is firmly established may be true, but it is forgotten that the language is developed in the first place to suit the mentality and activities of the speakers, rather than the reverse.

Historical linguistics can be both a fascinating topic of study and a highly scientific one. It must, however, revise not so much its basic methodology as its application of that methodology, in accordance with the rules of evidence. All the relevant evidence must be carefully collated and presented, and none of it discarded or neglected merely because it suits a given theory to do so. Where, as so often happens, the available evidence is conflicting or insufficient to establish definite conclusions, hypotheses should be presented for what they are, subject to possible final verification at a later date, when additional proof appears.

Geolinguistics

The complaint is frequently voiced that we fail to mobilize and utilize the foreign speakers in our midst (some twenty million of them) for purposes of area and language instruction. While this criticism may be partly justified, we must take into account the fact that not all the foreign speakers (in fact, not even a considerable percentage among them) are qualified to impart such instruction, or even to dispense valid and accurate information concerning their respective areas and languages. While these people may occasionally be used as informants, under proper checks and balances, we must be careful not to accumulate misinformation, linguistic or otherwise, under the guise of information.

One major and partly valid criticism that may be advanced in connection with geolinguistics is that its subject matter and objectives are constantly shifting, and subject to all kinds of pressures and changes. But the same criticism may be leveled at all other branches of linguistics, save perhaps the most basic features of descriptive linguistics; and even there revisions are constantly being made. Language is by its very nature not a static but a dynamic topic of study. In any event it is perfectly possible to concentrate on the more objective and factual aspects of geolinguistics, and so to refine its methodology and procedures as to bring it in line with thoroughly scientific requirements.

The real trouble with geolinguistics is that it has not so far received the attention and support to which its importance entitles it. So far as the descriptive and historical linguists are concerned, they are far too preoccupied with their own specialties to view the geolinguistic aspect of their science as anything more than a poor relation. Government and business, which should be very directly concerned, have until now failed to display the proper interest.

It will be recalled that during the war the Office of War Information (OWI) had set up a special section, called the Media Analysis Bureau, whose precise function it was to gather the facts and figures for languages spoken all over the world and catalogue them for immediate strategic use. This study was accompanied by literacy figures, charts of language affiliations, and, of course, population figures. Even before the end of the war the bureau was dissolved and its accumulation of material dispersed. Only here and there did an occasional scholar connected with it save and publish part of the material gathered.[2]

Business, which often sets up crash programs in languages for momentary and inconsequential purposes (such as how to say "Have a Coke" in a variety of languages, or making sure that the name of a product does not have an offensive or ridiculous connotation in any of the countries where it is to be sold), comes into the picture in a serious fashion only when it needs area and language specialists in connection with its own particular requirements (Standard Oil, for example, has set up courses in Arabic, Spanish, and Indonesian, on a short-term basis, for technicians destined for service in the areas where it has oil wells). But most of these activities have been of the hit-or-miss variety.

What is really needed is an Institute of Geolinguistics, supported jointly by government and business, for the purpose of conducting research and fact-finding, and gathering a stock of information that will be available on demand to both, as well as to the linguists; and for the purpose of training area and language specialists, and even pure linguists, in areas and languages for which there is not an immediate and ready

[2] Duncan MacDougald, Jr., *The Languages and Press of Africa*, University of Pennsylvania Press, Philadelphia, 1944.

commercial demand, as there is in the areas and languages of the normal U.S. high school curriculum.

It is highly unreasonable to expect a person who is gifted in the direction of these pursuits to specialize in a language, or area, for which there is little or uncertain demand, when he knows that if he specializes in French or Spanish or German he can, if the worst comes to the worst, obtain employment as a teacher in any local high school.

The Institute of Geolinguistics should be financially prepared not only to give its specialist in a language of little demand intensive training at its own expense, but also to find him remunerative employment when his course of studies is over, or even to keep him on tap and salary as a research scholar if no such employment can be immediately found.

So far, only the armed forces and the foreign service have come up with something resembling the Institute of Geolinguistics we have in mind. But the armed forces program contemplates specialization only in a single language, and with no guarantee of subsequent remunerative employment, save in connection with the army's own possible needs, which are by nature fluctuating and cannot be banked on.

The result is a succession of crash programs, minor in the case of business organizations, major in the case of the government. Emergencies are taken care of as they arise, not anticipated and prepared for long years in advance, as they should be.

Yet the need is for a large number of geolinguists, some functioning in the role of world experts for what concerns the total global picture, others specializing as statisticians of language, still others as area and language experts in specific fields. Such specialists cannot be improvised but require long and painstaking preparation and training, and even support after they are trained, at the expense of whatever body it is that plans to use their services in a pinch.

One of the fruits of the Institute of Geolinguistics would be the accumulation of a body of information that would be reliable and readily available, with a language census, of a type similar to the one created, on a limited scale and imperfectly, by the OWI's Media Analysis Bureau in the course of the war.

A Selective Bibliography

The works listed under *a* in each division are those which the beginner can read with profit and relative ease. Works listed under *b* in each section deal with special topics. Works for more advanced study are listed under *c*. The majority of works listed are in English, but it has been occasionally necessary to include foreign works that have not yet been translated. The elementary works and a few of the others are given a two-line description, with an evaluation which is necessarily subjective.

I. *a*. GENERAL WORKS, COVERING BOTH DESCRIPTIVE AND HISTORICAL TOPICS

Bloomfield, L., *Language*, Holt, New York, 1933. A deft blend of Saussurian and Neogrammarian principles, ably but somewhat dogmatically presented.

Bodmer, F. (ed. L. Hogben), *The Loom of Language*, Norton, New York, 1944. A semisuccessful attempt at a layman's popularization, marred by the strong personal viewpoint of the editor and an excessive number of factual inaccuracies.

Entwistle, W. J., *Aspects of Language*, Macmillan, New York, 1955. A fair traditional presentation of language, with stress on the historical side.

Graff, W. L., *Language and Languages*, Appleton, New York, 1932. Somewhat outdated but still good reading.

Gray, L. H., *Foundations of Language*, Macmillan, New York, 1939. A fine standard work, particularly for the historical part. Recommended for the more serious student.

Hughes, J. P., *The Science of Language,* Random House, New York, 1962. A good, introductory, clear, and up-to-date exposition of historical and descriptive linguistics. Highly recommended.

Jespersen, O., *Language,* Holt, New York, 1922. A traditional approach, with stress on sociological factors. (Norton paperback)

Laird, C., *The Miracle of Language,* World, New York, 1953. An attempt at popularization, marred by forced jocosity and lack of original thinking. (Premier-Fawcett paperback)

Migliorini, B., *La Linguistica* (2nd ed.), LeMonnier, Firenze, 1950. A very brief but excellent introduction to the main facts of linguistics. Recommended to those who can read Italian.

Pei, M., *Language for Everybody,* Devin-Adair, New York, 1956. Presents the main facts in popular tabular form, with an abundance of maps, graphs, and charts. (Pocket Books paperback)

Pei, M., *The Story of Language,* Lippincott, Philadelphia and New York, 1949. A layman's popularization, with stress on the sociological side of language. (Mentor paperback, revised, 1960)

Sapir, E., *Language,* Harcourt, Brace, New York, 1921. A good but somewhat plodding presentation.

Schlauch, M., *The Gift of Language,* Dover, New York, 1955. Good popular style combined with sound scientific approach.

Sturtevant, E. H., *An Introduction to Linguistic Science,* Yale University Press, New Haven, 1947. Good basic presentation of linguistics, with stress on the descriptivistic point of view. (Yale University Press paperback)

Vendryes, J., *Language* (ed. C. K. Ogden), Barnes & Noble, New York, 1925. Solid but traditional presentation, with stress on the historical side of language.

Whatmough, J., *Language: a Modern Synthesis,* St. Martin's Press, New York, 1956. A straightforward presentation of facts and opinions. Not always easy, but rewarding.

I. *b*. SPECIALIZED TOPICS

Doster, W. C. (ed.), *First Perspectives on Linguistics,* American Book Co., New York, 1953. A collection of articles on various linguistic topics by A. Hill, D. Brown, W. Brown, D. Bailey, P. Roberts, D. J. Lloyd, N. Francis, and others, offering a mixture of viewpoints.

Hall, R. A., Jr., *Linguistics and Your Language* (formerly *Leave Your Language Alone!*), Doubleday, Garden City, 1960. Offers little about either linguistics or language but a good deal about the author's personal likes and dislikes. (Anchor paperback)

Saussure, F. de, *Course in General Linguistics,* Philosophical Library, New York, 1959. Establishes the first clear-cut differentiation between descriptive and historical linguistics, and clearly outlines the function of each.

Thomas, L. L., *The Linguistic Theories of N. Ja. Marr,* University of California Press, Berkeley, 1957. Outlines the viewpoints of the major Soviet linguist and his school.

Weinreich, U., *Languages in Contact* (2nd ed.), Mouton, 's Gravenhage, 1963. A serious attempt to outline the influence exerted upon each other by languages in geographical proximity and subject to similar historical and environmental factors.

Whorf, B. L. (ed. J. B. Carroll), *Language, Thought and Reality,* Wiley, New York, 1956. A series of collected, partly unrelated articles, presenting, among other things, the theory of metalinguistics and a modern attempt at a universal grammar.

I. *c*. FOR MORE ADVANCED STUDY

Greenberg, J. H., *Essays in Linguistics,* University of Chicago Press, Chicago, 1962. (Phoenix paperback)

Jakobson, R., and Halle, M., *Fundamentals of Linguistics,* Mouton, 's Gravenhage, 1956.

Martinet, A., *Elements of General Linguistics,* University of Chicago Press, Chicago, 1964.

Potter, S., *Modern Linguistics*, Deutsch, London, 1957. (Norton paperback)

Wartburg, W. von, *Einführung in die Problematik und Methodik der Sprachwissenschaft* (2nd ed.), Niemeyer, Tübingen, 1962.

II. *a*. WORKS DEALING PREDOMINANTLY WITH DESCRIPTIVE LINGUISTICS

Block, B., and Trager, G., *Outline of Linguistic Analysis*, Linguistic Society of America, Baltimore, 1942. Offers the main facts of descriptive analysis, marred by an intransigent viewpoint.

Gleason, H. A., *Introduction to Descriptive Linguistics* (2nd rev. ed.), Holt, Rinehart & Winston, New York, 1961. A serious and elaborate attempt to present the main points of descriptive linguistics.

Hockett, C., *A Course in Modern Linguistics*, Macmillan, New York, 1958. A rather deep presentation of descriptive linguistics, with excessive involvement of terminology and indefiniteness of definitions.

II. *b*. SPECIALIZED TOPICS

Bally, C., *Linguistique générale et linguistique française*, Francke, Bern, 1950.

Harris, Z., *Methods in Structural Linguistics*, University of Chicago Press, Chicago, 1951. Deeper penetration into the problems of structural analysis; difficult for beginners. (Phoenix paperback)

Jones, D., *The Phoneme, Its Nature and Use*, Heffer, Cambridge, 1950. Good outline of phonemic analysis, from British point of view.

Joos, M., *Acoustic Phonetics*, Linguistic Society of America, Baltimore, 1948. One of the standard works on the subject.

Kurath, H., *Word Geography of the Eastern United States*, University of Michigan Press, Ann Arbor, 1949. Presentation and exemplification of methodology for linguistic atlas construction.

Pike, K. L., *Phonemics*, University of Michigan Press, Ann

Arbor, 1947. One of the standard works on the subject. (University of Michigan Press paperback)

Pike, K. L., *Phonetics,* University of Michigan Press, Ann Arbor, 1944. One of the standard works on the subject. (University of Michigan Press paperback)

Pop, S., *La Dialectologie,* Duculot, Louvain, 1950 (2 vols.). Outlines in great detail the principles of linguistic geography and the construction of linguistic atlases for various types of languages.

II. *c.* FOR MORE ADVANCED STUDY

Chomsky, N., *Syntactic Structures,* Mouton, 's Gravenhage, 1962.

Dauzat, A., *La Géographie linguistique,* Flammarion, Paris, 1944.

Grammont, M., *Traité de phonétique,* Delagrave, Paris, 1951.

Hjelmslev, L., *Prolegomena to a Theory of Language,* International Journal of American Linguistics, Baltimore, 1953.

Jakobson, R., *Kindersprache, Aphasie, und allgemeine Lautgesetze,* Lundequistka Bokhandeln, Uppsala, 1942.

Kurath, H., and others, *Handbook of the Linguistic Geography of New England,* Brown University Press, Providence, 1939.

Martinet, A., *A Functional View of Language,* Clarendon, Oxford, 1962.

Martinet, A., *La Description phonologique,* Droz, Paris and Genève, 1956.

Martinet, A., *Phonology as Functional Phonetics,* Philosophical Society, London, 1949.

Nida, E. A., *Linguistic Interludes,* Summer School of Linguistics, Santa Ana, 1960.

Nida, E. A., *Morphology,* University of Michigan Press, Ann Arbor, 1963. (University of Michigan Press paperback)

Trubetzkoi, N., *Grundzüge der Phonologie,* Vandenhoek & Ruprechet, Göttingen, 1958.

III. *a*. Works Dealing Predominantly with Historical Linguistics

Kent, R. G., *Language and Philology*, Marshall-Jones, Boston, 1923. Good traditional treatment.

Lehmann, W. P., *Historical Linguistics*, Holt, Rinehart & Winston, New York, 1962. Good, up-to-date coverage of subject matter and methodology, though with a strong descriptivistic slant.

Martinet, A., *Economie des changements phonétiques*, Francke, Bern, 1955. Places historical linguistics in framework of structural evolution.

Meillet, A., *Introduction à l'étude comparative des langues indo-européennes*, Hachette, Paris, 1949. A fundamental work on Indo-European comparative linguistics.

Meillet, A., *Linguistique historique et linguistique générale* (2 vols.), Champion, Paris, 1921–36. Continues the work of De Saussure.

Meillet, A., *La Méthode comparative en linguistique historique*, Champion, Paris, 1954. Outlines the traditional methodology of comparative linguistics.

Pei, M., *The Families of Words*, Harper, New York, 1962. Traces over 200 Indo-European roots through their ramifications in various branches to their English outcomes, with elementary description of the historical process.

Sweet, H., *History of Language*, Macmillan, New York, 1900. Slightly antiquated, but still good elementary reading.

Sturtevant, E. H., *Linguistic Change*, University of Chicago Press, Chicago, 1962. A solid general manual of historical linguistics.

Weekley, E., *The Romance of Words*, Dutton, New York, 1922. Traces English etymologies in popular fashion.

III. *b*. Specialized Topics

Buck, C. D., *Comparative Grammar of Greek and Latin*, Ginn, Chicago, 1933.

Buck, C. D., *Dictionary of Selected Synonyms in the Principal*

Indo-European Languages, University of Chicago Press, Chicago, 1949.

Diringer, D., *The Alphabet,* Philosophical Library, New York, 1948. A standard work on the history of writing.

Gelb, J. J., *A Study of Writing,* University of Chicago Press, Chicago, 1952.

Partridge, E., *Origins,* Macmillan, New York, 1958. A standard work on English etymology.

III. *c.* FOR MORE ADVANCED STUDY

Finck, F. N., *Die Haupttypen des Sprachbaus,* Teubner, Leipzig, 1923. Typological classification of the nineteenth century.

Hoenigswald, H. M., *Language Change and Linguistic Reconstruction,* University of Chicago Press, Chicago, 1960. An attempt to apply structural terminology and methodology to historical linguistics.

Kuryłowicz, J., *L'Accentuation des langues indo-européennes* (2nd ed.), Zaklad Narodowy, Wrocław, 1958.

Kuryłowicz, J., *L'Apophonie en indo-européen* (2nd ed.), Polska Akademia Nauk, Wrocław, 1956.

Meillet, A., *Les Dialectes indo-européens,* Champion, Paris, 1950. Goes in depth into the branches of Indo-European.

Paul, H., *Prinzipien der Sprachgeschichte,* Niemeyer, Tübingen, 1960. Old standard work on the subject, with full presentation of Neogrammarian principles.

Pokorny, J., *Indogermanisches etymologisches Wörterbuch,* Francke, Bern, 1951–   . Standard dictionary on Indo-European etymology.

IV. *a.* WORKS DEALING PREDOMINANTLY WITH GEOLINGUISTICS

Gil'arevsky, R. S., and Grivnin, V. S., *Opreditel' Yazykov Mira po Pis'mennost'am,* Izdatel'stvo Vostochnoi Literatury, Moskva, 1961. Good description of the world's present-day writing systems, with stress on U.S.S.R. languages, and with sample passages.

Meillet, A., and Cohen, M., *Les Langues du monde* (2nd ed.),

Champion, Paris, 1952. Good description of language types and individual families from the geographical and structural standpoints, with excellent maps, but little or no attempt to place the languages in the framework of present-day conditions.

Milewski, T., *Zarys Językoznawstwa Ogólnego*, Polskie Towarzystwo Ludoznawcze, Lublin-Kraków, 1948. Excellent modern survey of the world's languages, with English-language summaries of sections; Volume 2 consists entirely of linguistic maps of all areas of the globe, brought up to date and with English-language descriptions.

Muller, S. H., *The World's Living Languages*, Ungar, New York, 1964. Discussion of over 200 languages from the comparative, social, and anthropological point of view, with criteria for identification, and up-to-date statistics.

Pei, M., *Talking Your Way Around the World*, Harper, New York, 1962. Easy layman's presentation of a dozen major languages. (Crest-Fawcett paperback)

Pei, M., *The World's Chief Languages* (4th ed.; formerly *Languages for War and Peace*), Vanni, New York, 1960. Survey of present-day languages, with brief grammatical description, basic vocabulary, speaking population figures, abundant maps, and evaluation of the languages from a practical standpoint.

Schmidt, P. W., *Sprachfamilien und Sprachenkreise der Erde*, Winter, Heidelberg, 1926. Consists mostly of somewhat antiquated language maps showing distribution of language families.

(NOTE: Good geolinguistic sections appear in the works by Bloomfield, Hughes, and Pei [*Language for Everybody*] cited under I. a.)

IV. *b*. SPECIALIZED WORKS

Greenberg, J., *Studies on African Linguistic Classification*, Yale University Press, New Haven, 1955.

MacDougald, D., Jr., *The Languages and Press of Africa*, University of Pennsylvania Press, Philadelphia, 1944.

IV. c. IN PREPARATION

Hughes, C., *World Languages Series,* Devin-Adair, New York, 1964–65 (?). Presentation of some 50 languages in the form of manuals for practical use. Includes treatment of several African and American Indian languages.

V. WORKS DEALING WITH THE APPLICATION OF LINGUISTICS TO LANGUAGE TEACHING AND LEARNING

Allen, B. (ed.), *Applied English Linguistics,* Appleton-Century-Crofts, New York, 1958. A somewhat heterogeneous collection of articles by G. P. Faust, W. N. Francis, C. C. Fries, A. Hill, S. Ives, J. S. Kenyon, D. J. Lloyd, J. B. MacMillan, P. Roberts, and others. Offers good over-all survey of thinking of modern American descriptive school.

Angiolillo, P., *Armed Forces Foreign Language Teaching,* Vanni, New York, 1947. Description and criticism of "Army Method" used during World War Two.

Brooks, N., *Language and Language Learning,* Harcourt, Brace and World, New York, 1960. A generally sound approach to language teaching for speaking purposes.

Carroll, J. B., *The Study of Language,* Harvard University Press, Cambridge, 1953–55. A good presentation of the application of linguistics to language learning.

Cornelius, E. T., *Language Teaching,* Crowell, New York, 1953. A somewhat disjointed statement of linguistic principles applied to language teaching.

Fotitch, T. (ed.), *Teaching Foreign Languages in the Modern World,* Catholic University Press, Washington, 1962. Articles by various contributors and of varying merit. Gives good cross section of present-day thought on linguistic pedagogy.

Fries, C. C., *Linguistics and Reading,* Holt, Rinehart & Winston, New York, 1963. Description of the application of linguistics to the teaching of reading.

Fries, C. C., *Teaching and Learning English as a Foreign Language,* University of Michigan Press, Ann Arbor, 1945.

Lado, R., *Linguistics Across Cultures,* University of Michigan

Press, Ann Arbor, 1957. Method of comparing descriptively two or more languages and cultures.

Parker, W., *The National Interest and Foreign Languages* (3rd ed.) U. S. Department of State, Washington, 1961. Excellent survey of the place of language and languages in the American educational system, and of the practical uses to which languages may be put.

Politzer, R. L., *Teaching French: an Introduction to Applied Linguistics,* Ginn & Co., New York, 1960.

Politzer, R. L., and Staubach, C. N., *Teaching Spanish: a Linguistic Orientation,* Ginn & Co., New York, 1961.

Smith, H. L., *Linguistic Science and the Teaching of English,* Harvard University Press, Cambridge, 1956. Contains some good examples of the application of linguistics to instruction in the national tongue.

VI. WORKS DEALING WITH THE ENGLISH LANGUAGE

a. PREDOMINANTLY HISTORICAL

Alexander, H., *The Story of Our Language,* Dolphin, Doubleday, New York, 1962. A good historical outline, with main differences between British and American.

Baugh, A., *A History of the English Language* (2nd ed.), Appleton-Century-Crofts, New York, 1957. A standard and excellent work on the subject.

Bloomfield, M. W., and Newmark, L., *A Linguistic Introduction to the History of English,* Alfred A. Knopf, New York, 1963. An ingenious combination of the descriptive and historical approaches.

Jespersen, O., *The Growth and Structure of the English Language* (9th ed.), Doubleday, 1955. A perennially standard work, despite its traditional approach.

Pei, M., *The Story of English,* Lippincott, Philadelphia and New York, 1952. A layman's popularization of the past, present, and future of the language. (Premier-Fawcett, paperback, revised, 1962)

Potter, S., *Our Language,* Pelican, London, 1950. A brief but good presentation of English from the British standpoint.

Robertson, S., *The Development of Modern English* (2nd

ed.), Prentice-Hall, New York, 1954. A standard and excellent work on the subject.

VI. *b*. PREDOMINANTLY DESCRIPTIVE

Bronstein, A., *The Pronunciation of American English*, Appleton-Century-Crofts, New York, 1960. A clear, precise, soundly presented description of American regional pronunciations. Highly recommended.

Fries, C. C., *American English Grammar*, Appleton-Century-Crofts, New York, 1940. A standard modern work in the field, with controversial features.

Jespersen, O., *Essentials of English Grammar*, Allen & Unwin, London, 1933. Presents a traditional viewpoint.

Marckwardt, A., *American English*, Oxford University Press, New York, 1958. A good standard work.

VI. *c*. FOR MORE ADVANCED STUDY

Francis, W. N., *The Structure of American English*, Ronald, New York, 1958.

Fries, C. C., *The Structure of English*, Harcourt, Brace & World, New York, 1961.

Jones, D., *Outline of English Phonetics*, Dutton, New York, 1956.

Kenyon, J. S., *American English Pronunciation*, Wahrn, Ann Arbor, 1951.

Pike, K., *The Intonation of American English*, University of Michigan Press, Ann Arbor, 1956. (University of Michigan Press paperback)

Prator, C. H., *American English Pronunciation*, Rinehart, New York, 1957.

Trager, G., and Smith, H. L., *An Outline of English Structure*, American Council of Learned Societies, Washington, 1962.

Whitehall, H., *Structural Essentials of English*, Harcourt, Brace & World, New York, 1956.

VII. *a.* SEMANTICS AND GENERAL SEMANTICS

Chase, S., *The Tyranny of Words,* Harcourt, Brace, New York, 1938. A popularization of the principles of Korzybski.

Chase, S., *The Power of Words,* Harcourt, Brace, New York, 1954. A further popularization of general semantics, and of the metalinguistic ideas of Whorf.

Hayakawa, S. I., *Language and Thought in Action,* Harcourt, Brace, New York, 1949. Perhaps the clearest statement of the principles of general semantics.

Hayakawa, S. I. (ed.), *The Use and Misuse of Language,* Harper, New York, 1962. Collected articles by several authors, including Hayakawa and Johnson. Gives good cross section of thinking on the subject. (Premier-Fawcett paperback)

Johnson, W., *Your Most Enchanted Listener,* Harper, New York, 1956. A clear, readable exposition.

VII. *b.* FOR ADVANCED STUDY

Korzybski, A., *Science and Sanity* (4th ed.), International non-Aristotelian Library, Lakeville, 1958.

Ogden, C. K., and Richards, I. A., *The Meaning of Meaning,* Harcourt, Brace, New York, 1923.

Ullmann, S., *Language and Style,* Barnes & Noble, New York, 1964.

Ullmann, S., *The Principles of Semantics,* Jackson, Son & Co., Glasgow, 1951.

Ullmann, S., *Words and Their Use,* Muller, London, 1951.

VIII. *a.* THE INTERNATIONAL LANGUAGE PROBLEM

Guérard, A. *A Short History of the International Language Movement,* T. Fisher Unwin, London, 1922. Excellent but limited description of the problem up to the time of writing.

Jespersen, O., *An International Language,* Allen & Unwin, London, 1928. Advocacy of the author's own type of solution.

Pei, M., *One Language for the World,* Devin-Adair, New

York, 1958. History of past attempts, with full description of problem and possible types of solution.

VIII. b. FOR MORE ADVANCED STUDY

Couturat, L., and Léau, L., *Histoire de la langue universelle*, Hachette, Paris, 1903.

Monnerot-Dumaine, M., *Précis d'interlinguistique*, Maloine, Paris, 1960.

Stojan, P. E., *Bibliografio de Internacia Lingvo*, Universala Esperanta Asocio, Genève, 1929.

IX. a. HISTORY OF LINGUISTICS

Hall, R. A., Jr., *Idealism in Romance Linguistics*, Cornell University Press, Ithaca, 1963. Description of Neolinguistic thought, with a decided Neogrammarian bias.

Jordan, J., and Orr, J., *Introduction to Romance Linguistics*, Methuen, London, 1937. Full recorded history of controversy between Neogrammarians and Neolinguists, with a decidedly Neolinguist slant. Good coverage for nineteenth-century linguistic history, but use with previous work to get full picture.

Mohrmann, C., Sommerfelt, A., and Whatmough, J. (eds.), *Trends in European and American Linguistics, 1930–1960*, Spectrum, Utrecht, 1961. Series of articles by different contributors. Gives good coverage for last thirty years. Use in conjunction with following work.

Pedersen, H. (tr. J. Spargo), *Linguistic Science in the 19th Century*, Harvard University Press, Cambridge, 1931. Good coverage up to time of writing. Use in conjunction with previous work.

Robbins, R. H., *Ancient and Medieval Grammatical Theory in Europe*, Bell, London, 1951. Excellent coverage for the development of linguistic thought before the Renaissance.

Waterman, J. T., *Perspectives in Linguistics*, University of Chicago Press, Chicago, 1963. Brief but good factual coverage. Overstresses American structural school.

(NOTE: Brief but useful sections appear in L. H. Gray, *Foun-

dations of Language, Macmillan, New York, 1939; and M. Pei, *Voices of Man*, Harper, New York, 1962.)

IX. *b*. FOR MORE ADVANCED STUDY

Devoto, G., *I Fondamenti della storia linguistica*, Sansoni, Firenze, 1951.

Tagliavini, C., *Panorama di storia della linguistica*, Patron, Bologna, 1963.

X. DICTIONARIES AND GLOSSARIES OF LINGUISTIC TERMINOLOGY

Hamp, E. P., *Glossary of American Technical Linguistic Usage to 1950*, Spectrum, Utrecht, 1958. Brief and unsatisfactory by reason of lack of clear definitions (terms are presented only in their coiners' contexts).

Long, R. B., *The Sentence and Its Parts*, University of Chicago Press, Chicago, 1961.

Marouzeau, J., *Lexicologie de la terminologie linguistique* (2nd ed.), Geuthner, Paris, 1951. Quite antiquated. Almost completely disregards terminology of American structural school.

Pei, M., and Gaynor, F. (with editorial collaboration of E. Dorfman), *Dictionary of Linguistics*, Philosophical Library, New York, 1954. Good coverage, but out of date, particularly for recently coined American structural terminology.

Walsh, D., *What's What*, Modern Language Association, New York, 1963. Extremely brief, and interspersed with terminology from pedagogical and other fields, but very good and up to date as far as it goes.

(NOTE: Excellent partial coverage of modern linguistic terminology appears in the Merriam-Webster Third International Dictionary of 1961. Partial coverage of traditional grammatical terminology appears in M. Pei, *The World's Chief Languages* [Glossary].)

(In Preparation: Pei, M., *A Glossary of Linguistic Terminology*, Doubleday, New York, 1965 [?]. Expected to cover the field adequately up to the time of publication.)

Index

Latin (cont'd)
    117, 127 f, 131, 144, 150 f, 160,
    164 f, 235 ff
Latino Sine Flexione, 131
Latvian, 196
Lautgesetz, 89, 239
Lautverschiebung, 97
Learned development, 103
Learned influence, 90
Lehmann, W., 118, 122
Lesghian, 199
Lettish, 196, 212
Lexeme, 69 f, 81
Lexical change, 99 ff
Lexicography, 9
Lexicology, 68
Lexicostatistics, 118 ff, 241
Liaison, 64
Libyan, 115
Linear B., 114
Linguistic analysis, 227 f
Linguistic atlas, 84 ff, 171
Linguistic distribution, 129
Linguistic geography, 86
Linguistic Institute, 229
Linguistic Reporter, 277 ff
Linguistics, 1
Linguistic Society of America, 229
Linking, 64
Liquid, 47
Liquid l, 47
Literacy, 5, 137, 147, 152 f, 228
Literacy coefficient, 28, 130
Literary language, 26, 28, 31 f
Literary output, 29
Lithuanian, 23, 57, 113, 196, 210, 212
Liturgical coefficient, 28
Liturgical language, 3, 127, 144, 218
Loan translation, 102
Loan word, 102
Logographic writing, 24, 106 f
Loudness, 52 ff
Low vowels, 41
Low pitch, 54
Luanda, 219
Luba, 199, 220

Macassar, 198
Macedonian, 196, 209 ff
Machine translation, 228 f
Madurese, 198, 225
Makua, 199, 221
Malagasy, 115, 198, 221
Malay, 129, 198, 216, 225
Malayalam, 198, 215
Malayo-Polynesian, 115, 198, 225
Maltese, 126
Manchu, 111, 197, 214
Mandarin, 135, 197, 214
Mandingo, 199, 220 ff
Manx, 197
Maori, 30, 115, 198, 226
Marathi, 196, 215
Marr, N., 168, 247
Masai, 221
Maya, 199, 201
Media Analysis Bureau, 174, 243 f
Meillet, A., 168, 241
Melanesian, 198, 224 ff
Melanesian pidgin, 126
Mende, 222
Merovingian script, 202
Metalinguistics, 234, 241, 247

Metaphony, 94 f
Metathesis, 96
Miao-Hakka, 214
Micronesian, 198, 224 ff
Middle vowels, 41
Mid pitch, 54
Mid vowels, 41
Min, 197, 214
Minangkabau, 198
Minimal pairs, 50, 75, 77 ff
Minoan inscriptions, 114
Mixtec, 199
MLA. See Modern Language Association
Moabite, 115
Modern Language Association, 154, 227 ff
Modified languages, 28, 131
Moldavian, 212
Mongol, 111, 197, 214, 216 f
Mon-Khmer, 199, 216, 218
Monogenesis, 89, 168, 172
Monophthong, 43
Monotony test, 78
Mordvinian, 197, 217
Morph, 58 f, 80
Morpheme, 17 f, 58 ff, 68, 80
Morphemic analysis, 73 ff
Morphemics, 57 ff
Morphology, 9, 17, 169
Morphophonemics, 63 ff, 84
Mossi, 199, 221 ff
Muddy transition, 54
Multilingualism, 28, 129, 134, 213
Munda languages, 99, 215
Muong, 218

Nahuatl, 199
Nasalization, 93
Nasals, 46
Nasal sounds, 39
Nationalism coefficient, 28, 130
National language, 28, 31 f, 124
Naturalization language, 28, 127
Nda-Kongo, 223
Neatness of pattern, 78
Neogrammarians, 85, 166, 239, 245, 257
Neolinguists, 85, 166, 239, 257
Nepali, 196, 216
Neutralization, 49
New York dialect, 147
Ngala, 220
Ngola, 219
Nigero-Chad languages, 219
Non-contrastive distribution, 16
Non-immediate situation, 4
Non-Indo-European languages, 112 ff
Normative grammar, 106
North Africa, languages of, 31, 114 f, 129, 137, 224
North Semitic alphabet, 204
Norwegian, 195, 210
Noun, 60 f
Nuba, 220, 223
Nubian, 223
Numidian, 115, 197
Nupe, 222
Nyamwezi, 223
Nyanja, 222 f
Nyoro, 223